MW01253141

Textbook of
FABRIC SCIENCE
Fundamentals to Finishing

Second Edition

SEEMA SEKHRI

Associate Professor
Department of Fabric and Apparel Science
Lady Irwin College
Delhi

PHI Learning Private Limited
Delhi-110092
2017

₹ 275.00

TEXTBOOK OF FABRIC SCIENCE: Fundamentals to Finishing, Second Edition
Seema Sekhri

ISBN-978-81-203-5239-1

The export rights of this book are vested solely with the publisher.

Fifth Printing (Second Edition) . . . . . . **June, 2017**

Published by Asoke K. Ghosh, PHI Learning Private Limited, Rimjhim House, 111, Patparganj Industrial Estate, Delhi-110092 and Printed by Raj Press, New Delhi-110012.

Dedication

In the loving memory of my father

Professor Ram Nath Chopra

(October 12, 1928–October 23, 2007)

Who taught me how to hold a pencil...
And so much more...

Contents

v

PART III: YARNS

PART IV: FABRICS

Preface

Ever since its birth in February 2011, the "Textbook of Fabric Science: Fundamentals to Finishing" has faced many tests. The Delhi University curriculum changed to semester mode from annual, then to FYUP and finally to CBCS from July 2015. What was extremely encouraging as an author was that this textbook was selected as a recommended reading in several papers of each system! Today this book is also followed in the technical universities of Punjab and Uttar Pradesh. The warm welcome and acceptance of this book have encouraged the author to bring out its second edition.

In this edition, a new unit (VI) titled "Consumer Concerns" with a chapter on Choosing an Appropriate Fabric: Guidelines for Consumers is introduced. This is aimed at educating consumers so that they can make informed choices and gain satisfaction from what they purchase.

In addition to this, five university test papers are also added. This will help students check their preparation levels before the examinations.

The author hopes that the second edition will also receive an enthusiastic response from the readers. Their valuable comments and suggestions are welcome!

Seema Sekhri
seemasekhri@gmail.com

Preface to the First Edition

This comprehensive book is aimed for students of Fabric and Apparel Science (formerly textiles and clothing) being offered by home science colleges across the country. It would also serve as a useful reference book for the course of fabric science offered by various fashion designing institutes. With CBSE offering courses in the field of textile, this book will also serve as a comprehensive reference material for both teachers and students. Professionals can also benefit from the sections that explain technical terminology and can gain conceptual clarity.

There are fifteen chapters organised in five units. Part I (*Fundamentals*) has four chapters which explain many behind-the-scene factors that contribute to the aesthetics as well as performance of a textile product. In the first chapter the origin of clothing has been explored. Indian Textile Research Associations have been listed, thus carrying information that no other book on the subject carries. Textile fibre classification, composition and properties set the base for subsequent topics. It may also be mentioned here that the chemistry related topics are dealt with an easy-to-comprehend and student-friendly manner.

Part II deals with *Fibres* and consists of four chapters. Each fibre has been discussed under the heads of history, status in India, production/processing, chemical composition, properties (physical, chemical, biological, others), uses and care. Highlights include Indian organisations associated with the fibre and also an Indian historical perspective which has not been mentioned in any book by foreign authors. Protein fibres, viz., silk and wool are also explained. It would be of interest to note that a statewise production table for silk and breeds of Indian sheep have also been mentioned, contributing once again to culturally specific information. Natural cellulosic fibres with a section devoted to jute fibre, of which India is the leading producer have also found a place in this book. Subsequent chapters deal with manufactured fibres and synthetics, respectively. A comparative table on properties of various synthetic fibres will also serve as a ready reckoner for students.

Part III covers the area of *Yarns*, with a discussion on yarn production and salient yarn properties.

Fabric information is the theme of Part IV. The three chapters in this part discuss weaving, knitting and non-woven felts and miscellaneous methods. The properties of each of these fabrics are explained, along with the procedures involved.

Part V covers finishing and has two chapters that discuss the basic and functional finishes applied to fabrics. Colouration finishes are dealt under the heads of dyeing and printing.

Each chapter carries questions to help students judge their understanding of concepts. There is also a list of suggested readings for more details on topics covered in the chapter.

The author would welcome any constructive criticism which would help shape up the subsequent editions. Needless to add, words of encouragement are also welcome!

Seema Sekhri

Acknowledgements

First of all I would like to thank a wonderful person, Sarla Manchanda, who gave me the confidence to realise this dream! I am indebted to all my teachers for imparting clear concepts, both in life and in fabric science. Notable among these are Rev. Father Ignatius, Late Sanjambir Randhawa, Veena Kapur, Anu Verma, Poornima Kumar and Neerja Sharma. I would like to thank my students at the undergraduate, postgraduate and PhD levels for being the chief inspiration behind this book. I would specially like to thank Surbhi Jain for her help in preliminary typing of the manuscript and Megha Goyal along with Sarita Kataria and Richa Tyagi who helped in the organisation of illustrations. My special thanks to Dr. Anupa Siddhu, Director and to the faculty members of Lady Irwin College, for extending their cooperation throughout this project. My sincere thanks to the laboratory staff, Department of Fabric and Apparel Science, staff at the computer centre and library of Lady Irwin College, for their prompt help. For photographs in this book, I wish to express my gratitude to Parveen Chopra and Rochan for their time and effort. I am grateful to Saraswati and Jaya for the supply of teacups that helped me put in hours of work!

On a more personal front, I would like to thank my wonderful sisters and brothers for being who they are! My heartfelt thanks also to friends like Anjy, Anka and Shubh who made the journey simple and full of fun! I do not have words to express my gratitude to the five fantastic pillars of love and support in my life—Sharda Sekhri, Sudesh Chopra, Tarun, Sukriti and Tejas.

Last but not the least, I would like to thank Pushpita Ghosh, Managing Editor and Marketing Director, K.C. Devasia, Senior Editor and Shivani Garg, Editor at PHI Learning, for thier help and guidance.

Seema Sekhri

PART I
Fundamentals

Many times we see things around us and take them as the complete picture. But think for a moment and you would agree that what meets the eye is only a part of the big picture! Similarly, in the world of fabrics, you may have noticed that some products perform extremely well while others may disappoint you as a consumer. Have you ever wondered why this is so? The reasons for difference in performance can many a times be traced to the foundations of that fabric. Just as the durability and performance of a building is dependent on the quality of the foundation laid, so also, that of a fabric depends on its fibres.

This part comprises four chapters that discuss the history, composition, classification and properties of textile fibres.

CHAPTER

1

Introduction

As per an old adage, the three primary needs of Man are food, clothing and shelter. The fact that clothing precedes shelter goes to prove that it is indeed man's "second skin". Clothing, as used today across the world, is made of a piece of fabric or textile, both the terms are used interchangeably. The word textile is derived from the Latin word *textilis*, 'woven' and root word *textere*, "to weave" (Joseph, 1977).

1.1 EVIDENCE OF EARLY USE: WHEN DID CLOTHING ORIGINATE?

The Old Testament, Bible, written around fifth century BC carries the following lines:

"And the eyes of Adam and Eve were opened
And they saw that they were naked
So they sewed fig leaves together
And made themselves aprons"

Mankind has come a long way from the days of the fig leaf aprons! Let us try to reconstruct the genesis of the cloth. By and large, the origins of cloth are relatively obscure since the early materials used were of natural origin and hence biodegradable. However, some artefacts have been discovered by archaeologists of the world where the climatic conditions were conducive to their natural preservation. Natural dyes and pigments have also been discovered and it is presumed that these were used to paint the body (Gurel, 1979). Some of the first body coverings resembling clothing were in the form of sheep fleece and animal hides. These were thought to have been worn during the Old Stone Age in Northern Russia (Kaiser, 1985). A great advance occurred when the art of spinning and weaving became known in Neolithic times. By the beginning of the Bronze Age, woven fabrics from fibres such as linen, silk and wool were in common use. The Egyptians produced finely woven Linen cloth in the era 2000 BC. Remains of the Swiss lake dwellings, discovered in 1854, provided direct evidence of flax fibres used for weaving (Landi and Hall, 1979).

Beals and Hoijer (1965) have summarised the direct and indirect evidence of emergence of clothing as follows:

3

1. Body paints were used to adorn the self.
2. Animal skins and furs were draped around the body.
3. Garments of animal skins and furs were tailored, probably to provide warmth and physical mobility to the wearer.
4. Emergence of spinning and weaving produced textile fabrics which were draped around the body.
5. Tailored textile garments were produced.

1.2   REASONS FOR EARLY USE: WHY DID CLOTHING ORIGINATE?

Primitive man must have been spurred by an instinct for creative expression. He would have discovered that unlike animals who walked on all fours, his anatomical frame could support many adornments. Headgears could denote his superior status among his peers. Charms and amulets around his neck, arms, waist and legs could ward off the evil spirits and black magic.

Traditionally, clothes have served the following purposes:

1. Adornment which served to exalt the ego and arouse emotions in others;
2. Communication by means of symbols;
3. Modesty or the feeling of shame;
4. Physical protection against extreme climatic conditions, wild animals & insects; and
5. Psychological protection against evil forces and black magic.

These are also referred to as *theories of clothing*. A brief reflection will indicate that even today a mix of these factors is responsible for clothing. The relative importance of these factors varies from culture to culture. Even within one culture, the accepted norms of clothing undergo a change with time. To cite an example, Bollywood heroines of yesteryears had a different style of dressing up as compared to heroines today.

1.3   TEXTILE HISTORY IN INDIA

India can boast of a rich and varied textile heritage. The first literary reference to textiles is seen in Rig Veda, the oldest of the four Vedas. The fact that a host of rich textiles were used is further corroborated by the two eminent Indian epics, viz., Ramayana and Mahabharata. The spinning of cotton in India dates back to 3000 BC. As far as the actual artefacts are concerned, excavations have revealed that elaborate textile construction practices were followed as long back as the Indus Valley civilization. Bone needles and wooden spindles have been found from the Harappan and Mohenjodaro sites. The depiction of richly decorated garments in sculptures of Mauryan and Gupta ages as well as Ajanta caves bear testimony to the fact that India has a diverse textile tradition. There has been a close association between textiles and ritualistic events from ancient times. This association still continues in the form of specific colours and forms of dress during important occasions such as marriage, birth, puberty and death. It is a common practice to wrap religious texts in bright textile pieces. Strips of cloth are hung on trees, poles, gates and bridges as offerings around the shrines (Chattopadhyay, 1985) Many poets and saints of ancient India have composed numerous songs referring to textiles. Salient among these mystics is Kabir, a weaver from Benaras.

In the international commerce of the pre-industrial era, textiles assumed a position of importance. The Indian masterpieces soon became known to the outside world. The earliest evidence has been obtained from excavations of the Egyptian tombs at Fostat, dated as early as second century BC. For centuries thereafter, India reigned supreme for her superior quality of exquisite textiles. Towards the end of the seventeenth century, the British East India Company began exporting Indian cottons and silks to other countries. With time, its strong hold increased and led to a complete capture by the British. For nearly two centuries, India became a British colony till she gained her independence in 1947. Once again textiles figure importantly in the annals of our history book with Mohandas Karamchand Gandhi championing the *Swadeshi* movement. At the central fulcrum of this nationwide stir was *Khadi* i.e., hand-spun, hand-woven fabric. The spinning wheel or *Charkha* became a symbol of self-reliance and independence.

1.4 CURRENT SCENARIO

Today, the textile industry enjoys a special place in our country. As the second largest employment generator after agriculture, this industry contributes to nearly 30% of the total exports. If all segments of this 'elephantine' industry, from growth and production of fibres to processing into yarns, fabrics and finally garments are considered, then it definitely involves more money and people than any other industry. Under the umbrella of this industry, both organized as well as decentralized sectors spanning urban and rural areas coexist. At the helm of this industry is the Ministry of Textiles.

The Ministry of Textiles is responsible for the growth, policy formulation and planning of its various sectors. The primary areas of the ministry cover the following:

- Textile policy and formulation
- Man-made fibre/filament yarn industry
- Cotton textile industry
- Jute industry
- Silk and silk textile industry
- Wool and woollen industry

- Decentralised powerloom sector
- Export promotion
- Planning and economic analysis
- Integrated finance matters
- Information technology

There are two categories of organisations under the Ministry of Textiles.

1. *Public sector undertakings*

   (a) National Textile Corporation Limited, New Delhi
   (b) British India Corporation, Kanpur
   (c) Cotton Corporation of India Limited, Mumbai
   (d) Jute Corporation of India Limited, Kolkata
   (e) Birds, Jute and Exports limited, Kolkata
   (f) National Jute Manufacturers Corporation, Kolkata
   (g) Handicrafts and Handlooms Export Corporation, New Delhi
   (h) Central Cottage Industries Corporation, New Delhi
   (i) North Eastern Handicrafts and Handlooms Development Corporation, Shillong
   (j) National Handloom Development Corporation, Lucknow

2. *Textile research associations*: The main objective of these associations is to carry out research and render consultancy services (quality management series_ ISO 9001) to the industry on various aspects of textile technology. There are eight such associations, spread across India. These are:

   (a) Ahmedabad Textile Research Association, ATIRA, Ahmedabad
   (b) Bombay Textile Research Association, BTRA, Mumbai
   (c) South India Textile Research Association, SITRA, Coimbatore
   (d) Northern India Textile Research Association, NITRA, Ghaziabad
   (e) The Synthetic and Artificial Mills Research Association, SASMIRA, Mumbai
   (f) Man-made Textile Research Association, MANTRA, Surat
   (g) Indian Jute Industry's Research Association, IJIRA, Kolkata
   (h) Wool Research Association, WRA, Thane

These associations work with a view to reducing the cost, improving quality as well as durability, reducing pollution, conserving energy and utilizing water, adopting new technology and improving the techniques in the decentralized sectors.

1.5 APPLICATIONS OF TEXTILES

Broadly speaking, there can be the following uses for textiles:

Apparel

This category can be further subdivided into innerwear and outerwear for infants, children, women and men.

Home textiles

Also referred to as domestics, linens, household textiles or home furnishing textiles. The major categories in this segment are bed, bath, table and kitchen linens, floor coverings, window treatments and outdoor furnishings.

Industrial textiles

These are fabrics designed with specific end uses in mind. Salient among these are filters, conveyor belts, geotextiles, building materials, tyre cords, agriculture, fibre reinforced plastic (FRP), synthetic turf, parachute fabrics, medical textiles and sports.

EXERCISES

1.1 Trace the origin of clothing from prehistoric times.
1.2 Name the sources of reference that point towards India's textile lineage.
1.3 Give the salient areas of textile usage today.
1.4 What do the following acronyms stand for?
   ATIRA, NITRA, MANTRA, SASMIRA

REFERENCES

Beals, R. and Hoijer, H., *The Origins of Clothing:* In Dress, Adornment and the Social Order, Eds. Roach, M.E. and Eicher, J.B., John Wiley & Sons, New York, 1965.

Bible:Old Testament, *The Book of Genesis*, Chapter 3, Verse 7, 5th century, BC.

Chattopadhyay, K., *Handicrafts of India*, 2nd ed., Indian Council of Cultural Relations and Indraprastha Press, New Delhi, 1985.

Gurel, L.M., *Eskimos: Clothing and Culture:* In Dimensions of Dress and Adornment, 3rd ed., Eds. Gurel, L.M. and Beeson, M.S., Dubuque Kendall/Hunt, 1979, pp. 38–43.

Joseph, M., *Introductory Textile Science*, 3rd ed., Holt, Rhinehart and Winston, New York, 1977.

Kaiser, S.B., *The Social Psychology of Clothing and Personal Adornment*, Macmillan, New York, 1985, pp 28–29.

Landi, S. and Hall, R.M., The discovery and conservation of an ancient Egyptian linen tunic, Studies in Conservation, 24, 1979, pp. 41–152.

(Also available in www.ministry of textiles.com)

SUGGESTED READING

Batterberry, M. and A., *Fashion: The Mirror of History*, Greenwich House, Crown Publishers, New York, 1982.

Horn, M.J. and Gurel, L.M., *The Second Skin: An Interdisciplinary Study of Clothing*, 3rd ed., Houghton Miffin, USA, 1981.

Marshall, S.G., Jackson, H.O., Stanley, M.S., Kefgen M. and Specht, *Individuality in Clothing Selection and Personal Appearance*, 6th ed., Pearson Education, NJ, 2004.

CHAPTER

2

Classification of Textile Fibres

Internationally there is no common taxonomy adopted by textile scientists. The classification system used in the United States is dictated by the Textile Fibre Product Identification Act (TFPIA) which came into effect in 1960. Its enforcement is done by the Federal Trade Commission (FTC) which has given generic names to help clear any confusion in the minds of the consumers.

Broadly speaking, textile fibres can be divided into two groups viz., natural and manufactured.

2.1 NATURAL FIBRES

Natural fibres are obtained from nature in fibrous form. All natural fibres (except silk from undamaged cocoons) are short and measured in inches. These are also known as **staple fibres.** These can be further divided into four groups depending on their source and chemical composition. These are animal/protein fibres, plant/cellulose fibres, rubber and mineral fibres.

2.1.1 Animal/Protein Fibres

These can be further divided into hair fibres (named on the basis of the animal from which they are obtained) and extruded fibres. The larvae of silk moth extrude a continuous filament from their mouth to form a cocoon which is processed to recover silk fibres.

2.1.2 Plant/Cellulosic Fibres

These can be subdivided according to the part of the plant that produces the fibre. Thus, there exist the categories of seed hair fibres, bast or stem fibres, leaf fibres and the miscellaneous category.

2.1.3 Natural Rubber

This is processed from the latex of the rubber tree. Slashes are given on the stem and the thick, milky exudate is collected and converted into rubber.

2.1.4   Natural Mineral

Asbestos is a natural mineral fibre which is obtained from a variety of rocks that contain silicates of magnesium and calcium. It is inherently non-flammable but is being replaced because of its carcinogenic properties.

2.2   MANUFACTURED FIBRES

These are created by technologists under controlled conditions. Manufactured fibres are extruded as filaments. **Filament fibres** are long and may be cut into staple lengths if required. They can be broadly divided into three groups depending on their raw material, viz., regenerated fibres, synthetic fibres and inorganic fibres.

2.2.1   Regenerated Fibres

Here, raw materials are dissolved through a series of chemical reactions and then extruded to produce a continuous fibre strand. The starting materials and the fibres produced have the same chemical polymer. Raw materials are obtained from nature and include small cotton fibres (linters), wood, milk protein and other diverse substances which cannot be used for textiles in their original form. Hence the need for reforming or regenerating them. Rayon is the first regenerated fibre produced in 1905. It was followed by Acetate, another cellulosic fibre. Several protein based fibres have also been experimented with. Varied sources have been tried out for these, like proteins obtained from milk, soyabean, cornmeal and peanuts. Only the casein fibre from milk has attained some commercial status.

2.2.2   Synthetic Fibres

These are fibres produced from chemicals to form a polymer not previously existing in a natural state. Nylon was the first synthetic fibre to be invented. It was marketed in 1938 by Du Pont USA.

In general, the era after World War II (mid-twentieth century) witnessed increasing introduction of manufactured fibres. This was to combat the problem of acute shortage of natural textile materials.

2.2.3   Inorganic Fibres

There are some inorganic substances which do not have the conventional long chain molecules. However, it is possible to soften them by heat application and then form into thin, long strands which are pliable and resemble organic fibres. Uses of inorganic fibres normally do not include apparel. But there are numerous industrial uses for them.

Except natural mineral fibres and man-made inorganic fibres such as glass and some metals, all textile fibre polymers are organic compounds. This means that they are predominantly composed of carbon and hydrogen atoms with some oxygen, nitrogen, chlorine and/or fluorine atoms. Table 2.1 gives a classification chart of fibres.

Table 2.1 Classification of Textile Fibres

Textile fibres	
Natural	**Manufactured**
(a) Animal/Protein	**(a) Regenerated**
• Extruded	• Cellulosic
– Silk (silk moth-domesticated and wild)	– Rayon (viscose, cuprammonium, HWM)
• Hair	– Acetate
– Wool (sheep)	– Triacetate
– Speciality (Alpaca, Cashmere, Llama, Mohair Vicuna)	– Lyocell
– Fur (animal pelt)	• Protein
	– Azlon (from soyabean and corn)
(b) Plant/Cellulosic	**(b) Synthetic**
• Seed hair (cotton, kapok, coir)	• Nylon
• Stem or bast (flax, jute)	• Polyester
• Leaf (pina from pineapple leaves, sisal from agave leaves)	• Acrylic
• Miscellaneous (from parts other than above three)	• Modacrylic
	• Olefins (polyethylene, polypropylene)
	• Spandex
	• Aramid (Nomex, Kevlar)
	• Carbon
(c) Rubber	**(c) Inorganic**
(d) Mineral	• Glass
• Asbestos	• Metallic

2.3 FIBRE IDENTIFICATION

Fibres in one category are similar to each other in their chemical composition, physical properties, performance characteristics and care procedures. There are many tests for fibre identification that can be performed.

2.3.1 Visual Examination

This refers to the look and feel of a fibre as observed by the eye and hand. However, with the introduction of finishes, characteristic visual features of one fibre can be imparted to another fibre. Thus, it is possible to produce polyester filaments that closely resemble silk. Hence, the visual test alone fails to be a reliable one for identification of fibres.

2.3.2 Microscopic Evaluation

Each natural fibre and the group of synthetic fibres have certain specific characteristics which help in their identification. The longitudinal section slide can be prepared (detailed in Chapter 4) and examined using a compound microscope.

Chapters 5 to 8 (Part II) carry the longitudinal sections of various fibres.

2.3.3 Burning Test

Burning behaviour comprises behaviour of the fibre when approaching flame, in flame, removed from flame, its odour and residue. This is a simple and reliable means of judging the family (cellulosic, protein or synthetic) of a fibre. Broadly speaking, cellulosics have a similar burning behaviour. They emit the odour of burning paper and have a residue which is grey ash. Cellulosics also exhibit an after glow. Protein fibres on the other hand do not burn readily, are self-extinguishing and have an odour of burning hair or feathers. The residue obtained is a bead which is brittle and can be crushed. Synthetics curl away from flame and melt. This is why you are advised not to wear synthetics while burning crackers on Diwali. The smell is chemical and the residue is a bead which is non-crushable.

2.3.4 Chemical Tests

These are aimed at confirming a given fibre and have to be carried out systematically. Different reagents react with specific compounds present in the fibres and hence the latter can be inferred. Some fibres also solubilise in certain chemicals and hence the term "solubility tests" can also be used for this method of fibre identification.

Table 2.2 gives a list of burning and chemical tests that help to distinguish the commonly used fibres.

Table 2.2 Fibre Identification Tests

(a) Burning test

Fibre class	Approaching flame	In flame	Removed from flame	Odour	Residue
Cellulosic	Do not shrink away, ignite on contact	Burn readily	Continue burning with an after glow	Smell of burning paper	Grey, fluffy ash, easily crushable
Protein	Curl away from flame	Burn slowly	Self extinguishing	Smell of burning hair	Black bead like residue which is easily crushable

(Contd...)

Table 2.2 Fibre Identification Tests (*Contd...*)

(a) Burning test

Fibre class	Approaching flame	In flame	Removed from flame	Odour	Residue
Synthetic	Fuse, melt and shrink away from flame	Burn readily with sputtering, dripping or black sooty flame	Self extinguishing, may continue to melt	Smell of chemicals	Black bead, non-crushable

(b) Chemical test

Fibre class	Experiment	Observation	Inference
Cellulosic	Take the fibre and dip it in 30–50% sulphuric acid. Heat	The fibre chars and dissolves	Cellulosic fibres could be cotton or rayon
	Take the fibre and dip it in 60% sulphuric acid solution in a test tube and leave it for 5–10 minutes at room temperature	Fibre dissolves	Rayon confirmed
		Fibre does not dissolve (it may disintegrate)	Cotton confirmed
Protein	To the fibre, add 5% of sodium hydroxide. Heat	Fibre dissolves	Protein fibre confirmed
	Cool the above solution, add lead acctate	Black precipitate	Wool confirmed
		White precipitate	Silk confirmed
Synthetic	To the fibre, add 85% of formic acid at room temperature	Fibre dissolves	Nylon confirmed
	To the fibre, add dimethyl formamide solution. Heat slightly	Fibre dissolves	Acrylic confirmed
	To the fibre, add metacresol solution. Heat	Fibre dissolves	Polyester confirmed

Note: The correct sequence for addition of chemicals must be followed to avoid errors. The reason is that both nylon and acrylic also get dissolved in metacresol. This can lead to incorrect inferences.

EXERCISES

2.1 Classify natural cellulosic fibres with examples.

2.2 Match the following natural fibres with the country of their origin:

Linen   India

Wool   China

Cotton   Egypt

Silk   Mesopotamia

2.3. Enlist the various aspects that are observed and compared for conducting a burning test on fibres.

2.4. "The microscopic test can serve as a confirmatory test for natural fibres but not for man-made textile fibres". Give reasons to substantiate this statement.

SUGGESTED READING

Collier, B.J., Bide, M.J. and Tortora, P.G., *Understanding Textiles*, 7th ed., Pearson Education, NJ, 2009.

Editors of American Fabric Magazine, *Encyclopedia of Textiles*, Prentice Hall, Englewood Cliffs, New Jersey, USA, 1960.

Hudson, P.B., Clapp, A.C. and Kness, D., *Joseph's Introductory Textile Science*, 6th ed., Harcourt Brace Jovanovich College Publishers, USA, 1993.

Kadolph, S.J. and Langford, A.L., *Textiles*, 10th ed., Pearson Education, NJ, 2007.

CHAPTER 3

Textile Fibre Composition

If you notice the various kinds of structures used for housing, you will see how different a hut in a village looks from an urban apartment. What makes the two so different is that the materials used for their construction are mud and bricks respectively. Similarly, the properties of textile fibres result from their chemical building blocks or monomers. These can also be seen as the basic unit of construction of any textile.

3.1 THE FOUNDATIONS OF FABRIC

Let us look at an analogy (Table 3.1). If a textile fabric is compared with a chapter in a book, then the paragraphs can be likened to yarns. The sentences can be compared with fibres; the words in a sentence can be likened to polymers or macromolecules. Each word is made of many letters and so also, each polymer is made of many monomers or molecules. Prior to an alphabet is the phonetic (sound) and similarly, it is atoms that precede the molecules. Once again coming to the chapter, you would agree that it needs to be bound in a book: a fabric too needs 'finishing' before it is made available to the consumers. The analogy will have to end here but not before noting that a well-written chapter is satisfying to the writer and reader just as a well-made fabric is to the manufacturer and consumer!

Table 3.1 Similarities Between a Book and a Fabric

Book	Fabric
Phonetics	Atoms
Letters	Monomers
Words	Polymers
Sentences	Fibres
Paragraphs	Yarns
Chapters	Fabric
Book	Finishing

3.2 MONOMERS AND POLYMERS

In Latin, *mono* means 'one' and *mer* means 'unit'. Thus, monomers are very small but chemically reactive units. Numerous monomers have to be combined to form polymers (many units). Polymers are very long, linear and chemically unreactive. This process or chemical reaction, in which monomers join in an end-to-end manner to form a polymer, is called **polymerisation**. The number of monomers (or repeating units) which join to form one polymer is referred to as the *degree of polymerisation (dp)*.

Table 3.2 gives the details of monomers, polymers and degree of polymerisation for common fibres. It may be noted that while nearly exact figures of dp are known for the man-made fibres, there is a lack of data for some natural fibres (e.g., silk and wool). Thus, nature still reigns as the supreme mysterious creator!

Table 3.2 Basic Building Blocks and Degree of Polymerisation for Common Fibres

Fibre	Basic unit (monomer)	Degree of polymerisation
Cotton	Cellobiose which is composed of two glucose units	5,000

Flax	Cellobiose	18,000
Silk	Fibroin polymer which is composed of 16 different amino acids	Not known

$$H_2N - \underset{\underset{H}{|}}{\overset{\overset{R}{|}}{C}} - COOH$$

(R is a radical which varies in each amino acid)

Wool	Keratin polymer, composed of 20 different amino acids	Not known
Viscose, Rayon	Cellobiose	175 (approx)
Cuprammonium,	Cellobiose	250 (approx)

(Contd...)

Table 3.2 Basic Building Blocks and Degree of Polymerisation for Common Fibres (*Contd*....)

Fibre	Basic unit (monomer)	Degree of polymerisation
Polynosic	Cellobiose	300 (approx)
Acetate or secondary acetate or diacetate	About 2 hydroxyl groups per glucose unit (i.e., four per cellobiose) are acetylated	130

Triacetate or primary acetate	About 3 hydroxyl groups per glucose unit (i.e., 6 per cellobiose) are acetylated	225

In the above two diagrams, the underlined sites indicate replacement of hydroxyl (–OH) group with acetyl (–OOCCH$_3$) group.

Nylon 6	Caprolactam monomers combine to form polycaprolactam (repeating unit)	200

Caprolactam (monomer)

Polymer: Polycaprolactam

$\cdot$ [—(CH$_2$)$_5$CONH—]$_n$

(*Contd...*)

Table 3.2 Basic Building Blocks and Degree of Polymerisation for Common Fibres (*Contd....*)

Fibre	Basic unit (monomer)	Degree of polymerisation
Nylon 6, 6	2 monomers with 6 carbon atoms each (hence the name) Monomers: Adipic acid $HOOC(CH_2)_4COOH$ Hexamethylene diamine $H_2N(CH_2)_6NH_2$ Polymer: Polyhexamethylene diamino adipate $\cdot[—OC(CH_2)_4\ CONH(CH_2)_6\ NH—]_n$	50–80
Polyester	Monomers: Ethylene glycol $HO\cdot CH_2CH_2OH$ and Terephthalic acid $HOOC$ —⬡— $COOH$ Polymer: Polyethylene terephthalate $\cdot[— OOC$ —⬡— $COO — (CH_2)_2 —]_n$	115–140

| Acrylic | Acrylic is made of Acrylonitrile monomer (At least 85%) and copolymer (at most 35%)
Acrylonitile monomer | 2000 |

$$\begin{array}{cc} H & H \\ | & | \\ C = & C \\ | & | \\ H & CN \end{array}$$

Copolymer

$$\begin{array}{cc} H & H \\ | & | \\ C = & C \\ | & | \\ H & A \end{array}$$

where A is usually an anionic radical like
$— CONH_2, — Cl_2$ or $— OOCCH_3$

| Modacrylic | Modacrylic is made of Acrylonitrile (at least 35%) with copolymer (at most 65%) | 2000 |

$$-\left[\begin{array}{cc} H & H \\ | & | \\ C & - C & - \\ | & | \\ H & CN \end{array}\right]_x \quad \left[\begin{array}{cc} H & H \\ | & | \\ C & - C & - \\ | & | \\ H & A \end{array}\right]_y - H$$

In acrylic, x is atleast 85%.
In modacrylic, x is atleast 35% but not more than 85%

3.3 TYPES OF POLYMERISATION

Textile technologists have inadequate information about the precise nature of polymerisation in natural fibres such as cotton, flax, wool and silk. However, for man-made fibres, it can be stated that polymerisation is of two types—addition and condensation.

Addition polymerisation

Two, usually identical monomers combine in an end-to-end fashion. There is no formation of any by-product.

Examples of addition polymerisation are acrylic, modacrylic, polypropylene, polyethylene and polyvinyl chloride.

Monomer   Polymer

Condensation polymerisation

Two, usually different, chemically reactive monomers combine to produce a polymer with the elimination of a small by-product (generally water). Examples include polyester, nylon and elastomers.

Monomer   Copolymer

By-product

3.4 TYPES OF POLYMERS

The given discussion explains the processes of polymerisation as seen in man-made fibres. There are also different outcomes of polymerisation, or kinds of polymers that can form from the addition and condensation polymerisation. These are described by terms like *homopolymers* and *copolymers* with the latter further divided into alternating, block, graft and random types of polymers. Let us understand these terms with examples.

When the reactive monomers are identical, the resultant polymer is called a **homopolymer**. Examples of homopolymers are nylon 6, polypropylene, polyethylene and polyvinyl chloride.

If the polymerising monomers are different from each other, the polymer then formed is a **copolymer**. There are four sub-categories of copolymers (Gohl and Vilensky, 1987).

(i) Alternating copolymers in which the constituent monomers are arranged in an alternate manner. Examples, polyester, nylon 6, 6.
$$A^n + B^n = (ABABAB)_n$$
A; first monomer   B; second monomer

(ii) Block copolymers have blocks or slabs of the constituent monomers. Example,

$$A^n + B^n = (AAAABBBBBAAAA)_n$$
A; first monomer   B; second monomer

(iii) Graft polymers have a backbone of alternating or random arrangement. Grafted (attached) onto this is a side chain formed of one or more of the reacting monomers. Example, an acrylic graft copolymer fibre.

C

C

C

ABABAB A

A; first monomer   B; second monomer C; reacting monomer

(iv) Random copolymer has an unplanned or random arrangement of monomers (generally of two types). Examples include acrylic and modacrylic.

3.5   BONDING IN FIBRES

Bonding is important for textile materials. There are bonds which exist between molecules in a polymer (intra-polymer bonds) and then there are forces which bind polymers, thus forming fibres (inter-polymer bonds). The terms can be remembered by recalling the example of cultural activities in any educational institution. Thus, an intra-class match would mean that all sections of a class would compete (e.g., XA, XB and XC). On the other hand, an inter-class match would be held between classes X, XI and XII. A brief description of various inter- and intra-polymer bonds seen in textiles is given below.

3.5.1   Intra-polymer Bonding

These are the bonds which hold the atoms together to make up the fibre polymers.

1. *Single covalent bonds:*   Chemically very stable and unreactive, these form the backbone of many fibres.

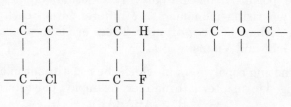

2. *The amide or peptide group:* When present in protein fibres, this group is called the **peptide group**; in nylon fibres, it is referred to as **amide group**.

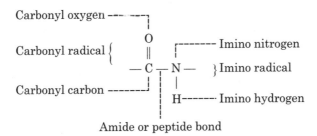

Amide or peptide bond

3. *Benzene ring* (aromatic radical): It imparts chemical stability and is present in polyester.

4. *Ether linkage:* Found in such polymers as cellulose, elastomers, ester cellulose and polyesters. It exists between carbon and oxygen atoms. Generally unreactive and quite stable with the exception of the ether linkage in cellulosics.

$$-\overset{|}{\underset{|}{C}} - O - \overset{|}{\underset{|}{C}} -$$

In cellulose, ether linkage is known as **glucoside link**. It links all the glucose units.

It can lead to hydrolysis and rupture of the two glucose units in acidic conditions.

5. *Ester groups or organic salts:* These are formed during reaction of a Carboxyl group —COOH with a Hydroxyl group —OH. Ester group is not resistant to alkalis.

$$
\begin{array}{c}
\overset{\displaystyle H}{\underset{\displaystyle H}{|}} \overset{\displaystyle O}{\underset{}{\|}} \\
- C - C - OH \\
\end{array}
$$

H   O   H   H   O   H
| ‖ | | ‖ |
— C — C — OH   +   HO — C —   ⟶   — C — C — O — C —
| | | |
H   H   H   H

         Carboxyl group   Hydroxyl group   Ester group

6. *Hydroxyl group:* Its polarity (slight positive charge) leads to the formation of hydrogen bonds which impart strength to a polymer. This group also contributes to the hygroscopic nature of a fibre.

—OH

7. *Nitrile group:* It is resistant to acids but undergoes alkaline hydrolysis or saponification.

—CN

3.5.2   Inter-polymer Bonds

These are bonds between polymers in a fibre. There are four such forces of attraction.

1. Cross links
2. Salt linkages
3. Hydrogen bonds
4. Van der Waal's Forces

Table 3.3 gives the prevalence and chief characteristics of the inter-polymer bonds.

Table 3.3   Characteristics and Prevalence of Inter-polymer Bonds in Textile Fibres

Inter-polymer bond	Characteristics	Fibres present
Cross links/covalent bonds	Strongest in nature, excessive cross links can in fact make the material stiff and inelastic.	Elastomerics, protein fibres except silk
Salt linkages/ electrovalent/ ionic bonds	Strong bonds, attract water molecules, offer good absorption sites for acid dyes, increase tenacity	Nylon, protein fibres
Hydrogen bonds	Weak electrostatic bonds, attract water, enahance tenacity, improve durability, impart heat setting properties	Cellulose, protein, nylon, PVA
Van der Waal's Forces	Weakest in nature	All fibres (predominant in acrylic and polyester)

3.6 POLYMER ARRANGEMENT

Once you have understood how the intra- and inter-polymer forces of attraction work to produce coherent structures, let us now see how polymers arrange themselves in a fibre.

1. Polymers have the option of lying around without any order or in a random manner. This is called the **amorphous arrangement** or **structure**. Figure 3.1 depicts the amorphous arrangement.

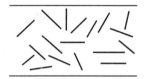

Figure 3.1   Amorphous.

2. Polymers may be arranged in parallel bundles giving more ordered appearance than the amorphous arrangement. This is called the **crystalline arrangement** (see Figure 3.2). A variation of this is the **oriented arrangement** in which the bundles of fibres are not only parallel to each other but also to the longitudinal axis of the fibre. Figure 3.3 depicts the oriented arrangement of textile fibres.

   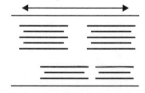

Figure 3.2   Crystalline.   **Figure 3.3**   Oriented.

The arrangement of molecules also affects a host of properties in fibres. Table 3.4 draws the comparisons between the two arrangements.

Table 3.4   Characteristics of Amorphous and Crystalline Regions

Amorphous	Crystalline
Lower inter-polymer forces of attraction	Strong internal bonds
Better water absorption and dye uptake (more absorbent)	Do not permit easy entry to water and dyes
Lower chemical resistance	Chemically strong
Plastic, more easily distorted	Inflexible
Soft handle	Stiff handle

Textile scientists have observed that both the amorphous and crystalline regions exist in varying proportions in fibres. Thus, instead of being a completely crystalline or amorphous fibre, it is more apt to describe them as being predominantly crystalline or amorphous. Table 3.5 presents the distribution of the two polymer arrangements in salient fibres.

Table 3.5 Polymer System of Some Common Fibres

Fibre	Amorphous	Crystalline
Cotton	35–30%	65–70%
Flax	35–30%	65–70%
Viscose	65–60%	35–40%
Acetate	60%	40%
Wool	75–70%	25–30%
Silk	35–30%	65–70%
Acrylic	30–20%	70–80%
Nylon 6, 6	35–15%	65–85%
Nylon 6	35–15%	65–85%
Polyester	35–15%	65–85%
Elastomeric	Extremely amorphous (when not stretched)	Extremely crystalline (when fully stretched)

3.7 REQUIREMENTS OF FIBRE-FORMING POLYMERS

There are certain properties that a polymer must possess in order to be a useful fibre-forming substance. Salient among these are listed below. It must be noted that not all the listed requirements are met by all textile polymers in use. This explains why certain fibres have restricted applications in apparel.

1. *Non-toxicity*: The polymer must not be hazardous for human use. The use of asbestos (a natural inorganic fibre) has declined considerably over the past few years owing to research which proved its carcinogenic properties. The same concern also holds good for textile auxilliaries and dyes. The ban on use of azo dyes is one example of man's concern for safety. While other requirements may be met in varying degrees, all textile polymers must possess this first requirement.
2. *High molecular weight*: This is achieved by high degree of polymerisation. There is a range of molecular weights which are suitable for fibre-forming processes. If polymers have lower molecular weights, they will result in fibres which are brittle and extremely weak. On the other hand, excessively high molecular weights of polymers will make them difficult to melt or dissolve in solvents, thus making their spinning difficult.
3. *High degree of orientation*: The polymer bundles must be parallel to each other as well as to the longitudinal axis. The manufactured filaments are subjected to a process of stretching, termed *drawing*,

in which the extruded strands are stretched to nearly five times their original length. With increase in the length, the diameter decreases, molecules come much nearer to each other and align along the longitudinal axis. On the other hand, natural polymers have an inherent high orientation which qualifies them for use as textile fibres.

4. *Linearity*: Fibre forming polymers should be linear in structure with as few crosslinks and branches as possible. They may possess side groups but should not be branched. This is important for strong inter-polymer bonding.

5. *Hydrophilicity or readiness to absorb water*: This property makes textile products comfortable to wear, owing to ready absorption of perspiration. This also helps to curb the problem of static charge build-up, since water molecule carries the electric charges to surrounding atmosphere.

6. *Chemical resistance to agents and conditions:* It is important to have high resistance to washing, drycleaning and bleaching agents, acids, alkalies, sunlight and ageing. Generally speaking, strong intra-polymer bonding results in chemically resistant polymers. Synthetics have greater chemical resistance than natural fibres. Among synthetics, olefin fibres have the highest chemical resistance.

7. *High melting point*: Melting point is in turn directly proportional to molecular orientation and bonding in polymers. It is also important that in case the polymer is heated for melt spinning, then the product is stable and does not decompose. High melting points are relevant for manufactured fibres. It may be noted that not all polymers in use melt on heating. For example, cotton or wool do not melt but decompose when subjected to very high temperatures.

8. *Fair elongation at break and elasticity*: Both of these are essential for subsequent processing of textile fibres.

9. *Economic considerations*: These also play an important role in deciding the suitability of a polymer for usage in textile fields. Thus, a polymer might possess all the above requirements but may be exorbitantly priced, thus discouraging its use.

EXERCISES

3.1 Differentiate between the following:
   (a) Intra- and inter-polymer bonds
   (b) Homopolymers and copolymers
   (c) Amorphous and crystalline arrangements
   (d) Block and graft copolymers
   (e) Addition and condensation polymerisation

3.2 Name and draw the structures for the basic building blocks of cellulosic and protein fibres.

3.3 Fill in the blanks:

(a) .... is the strongest inter-polymer bond.

(b) The weakest inter-polymer bond is ....

(c) The dp of flax is ...., while that of viscose is ....

(d) Cotton has .... % of crystalline regions, while Polyester has .... %.

3.4 Give the names and formulae for monomers of:

(a) Cotton

(b) Nylon 6

(c) Nylon 6, 6

(d) Polyester

SUGGESTED READING

Gohl, E.P.G. and Vilensky, L.D., *Textile Science*, CBS Publishers and Distributors, Delhi, 1987.

Jacob, T., *A Textbook of Applied Chemistry for Home Science and Allied Sciences*, Macmillan, Delhi, 1979.

CHAPTER

4

Fibre Properties

If we look around, we can notice many substances in nature which have a fibrous form. However, it is not practical to use all of these as textile fibres. The reason is that they do not meet the requisite properties. Conversely it can be said that all fabrics available in the market for various end uses are made of fibres which 'qualify' on the basis of certain parameters. These parameters are the fibre properties. Broadly speaking, fibre properties can be classified into two categories, viz., **primary** and **secondary.**

4.1 DIFFERENCE BETWEEN PRIMARY AND SECONDARY PROPERTIES

Primary properties are absolutely essential for any substance to qualify as a textile starting material. Only those fibres possessing these can be converted into yarns and subsequently into fabrics. For example, admission to a women's graduate programme has certain eligibility criteria. The candidate has to be a female and has to have a particular set of subjects and marks to qualify for admission. These could be likened to the "primary properties". Having met with the pre-requisites, there are some other qualifications that a candidate might possess. Active participation and training in extra-curricular activities would brighten a candidate's chances of securing a seat in competitions.

Similarly, in the field of fibres, in addition to primary properties, there are other properties which are desirable but not essential. They affect the processing suitability for various end uses and level of consumer satisfaction. Such properties are called **secondary properties**. These influence the selection, use, comfort, appearance, durability and maintenance of a textile product. It may also be noted that manufacturers can introduce, modify or even eliminate these properties by applying functional finishes, blending fibres or selecting a specific yarn and fabric construction techniques.

4.2 PRIMARY PROPERTIES

These include:

- High fibre length to width ratio

- Tenacity (adequate strength)
- Flexibility or pliability
- Cohesiveness or spinning quality
- Uniformity

4.2.1   High Length to Width Ratio

A pre-requisite for processing of fibres into yarns and fabrics is that their lengths must be more than their widths. The minimum length to breadth ratio is 100 : 1. Generally, all fibres exceed this minimum by a very large amount.

Length of fibres is also a basis for classifying them into two groups: staple and filament. **Staple fibres** are of relatively short lengths and measured in centimetres; **filament fibres** are long and measured in metres. Generally speaking, filaments form smooth and lustrous yarns, while staple fibres make duller yarns.

All natural fibres except silk are staple fibres. Man-made fibres can be extruded in filament form but can also be cut into staple lengths if required.

The fineness of a natural fibre is a major factor in ascertaining quality and is measured in microns (1 micron = 1/1000 millimetre). Natural fibres have a range of diameters e.g., Cotton ranges from 12 to 20 microns. In general, finer fibres are softer, more pliable and have better drapability. They are, thus, considered superior and form better yarns and fabrics. Fineness of man-made fibres is controlled by the size of the spinneret holes. It is measured in denier. Denier is the weight in grams of 9000 metres of yarns.

Microfibres are defined as all fibres with an individual filament fineness of less than 1 dtex (1 dtex or decitex is the weight in grams of 10,000 metres of yarn). Table 4.1 gives the classification of fibres on the basis of their diameter. Fibres such as polyester, nylon, acrylic, propylene and viscose are processed into microfilaments by using any of the following three methods:

Direct spinning method

The microfibres are made directly by melt, wet or dry spinning. Careful selection of polymers and conditions for polymerisation, spinning and drawing needs to be done.

Split and separation method

First, a thick component filament is prepared and it is then subjected to physical or chemical splitting to obtain the two different components, each with a diameter of less than 1 dtex.

Dissolution and removing method

Here again a bicomponent filament is produced by spinning. This is converted into fabric which is subjected to controlled chemical treatment.

The choice of reagent and conditions is such that one of the component gets dissolved and is removed, leaving the remaining component which is very fine.

Table 4.1   Categories of Fibres on the Basis of Fineness

Filament fineness	Category
Below 0.3 dtex	Super microfibres
0.3–1.0 dtex	Microfibres
1.0–2.4 dtex	Extremely fine fibres
2.4–7.0 dtex	Fine fibres
Above 7.0 dtex	Coarse fibres

Uses

A fabric made from microfibres has an excellent softness and drapability. This makes it popular in fashion apparel, belts, bags and furnishings. The fabrics produced are light weight, wind proof but breathable and waterproof but water vapour permeable, thus ranking them high on comfort. They have better wicking properties which lead to quick evaporation of perspiration. They are used in high performance fabrics for sportswear, trekking and weather protection. Fabrics made with very small pores prevent the transfer of bacteria, thus making them useful in clear room garments and hospitals. Industrial applications include filters, microelectronic industry and wiping cloths. These can also be finished to produce suede, imitation leather and peach skin surfaces.

Limitations

These include low single filament strength, abrasion resistance and poor resistance to slippage. With greater surface area, microfilaments require larger quantities of reagents for sizing, desizing and dyeing.

It is, thus, common to use blend fabrics e.g., cotton warp and microfilament polyester weft to balance the properties.

4.2.2   Tenacity

The strength of textile fibres is referred to as their tenacity. It is determined by measuring the force required to rupture or break the fibre. Sufficient tenacity is required to withstand the mechanical and chemical processing as well as make textile products which are durable.

Tenacity is, in general, directly related to the length of the polymers, degree of polymer orientation, strength and types of inter-polymer forces of attraction formed between the polymers.

Units of tenacity are grams per denier (g/d) or grams per tex (g/t). In other words, tenacity is the number of grams of weight required to break a fibre of one denier (or tex).

Denier is a unit of yarn fineness such that 1 denier is the wt. in grams of 9000 m of yarn while tex is the wt in grams of 1000 m (1 km) of yarn.

Table 4.2 gives the tenacity of commonly used fibres under dry conditions.

Table 4.2   Tenacity of Various Textile Fibres Under Dry Conditions

Fibre	Tenacity (gpd)
Cotton	3 – 5
Flax	6.5
Wool	1 – 1.7
Silk	2.5 – 5
Rayon	1.5 – 5
Acetate and Triacetate	1.2 – 1.4
Polyester	2.5 – 9.5
Nylon	4.6 – 8.8
Acrylic	2 – 4.2
Modacrylic	2 – 3.1
Olefin	1 – 5-8
Aramid	5.3 – 22.0
Spandex	0.5 – 1.03
Glass	– 6.9

When viewing the tenacity of a fibre, it helps to know its strength under dry as well as wet conditions. Accordingly, the handling technique of the fabric during washing is decided. Cotton is stronger when wet, as against wool which weakens on wetting. You must have observed that cotton can be subjected to harsh action like brush friction and even thrashing (by *Dhobis*). Woollen fabrics on the other hand have to be handled gently using techniques such as kneading and squeezing.

Tensile strength measures textile strength in terms of the pounds of weight required per square inch to break a yarn or fabric. This is more applicable to woven fabrics than to fibres.

4.2.3   Flexibility

Fibres must be flexible or pliable in order to be made into yarns and thereafter into fabrics that permit freedom of movement. Certain end uses require greater flexibility, e.g., automobile seat belts. Wood is composed of fibres but these lack flexibility and, thus, cannot be spun into textiles. Glass is another material which has low elasticity and is, thus, unfit for apparel usage. It serves useful as an industrial textile.

4.2.4   Spinning Quality or Cohesiveness

It is the ability of the fibre to stick together properly during yarn manufacturing processes.

Natural fibres have inherent irregularities in their longitudinal or cross sections which permit them to adhere to each other during fibre arranging. Wool, for instance, has an inherent crimp that imparts a high degree of cohesiveness. In everyday life you must have noticed that a girl with smooth, soft hair finds it difficult to plait them. On the other hand, a girl with rough or curly hair can make a braid that does not lose its shape easily. The same principle holds true when combining fibres to form a yarn. In case of synthetics, filament lengths aid in yarn formation. Texturing introduces coils, crimps, curls or loops in the structure of an otherwise smooth filament. It is used to impart cohesiveness.

4.2.5 Uniformity

It is important that fibres have uniformity in all the given primary properties. This will ensure production of even yarns which can then form fabrics of uniform appearance and consistent performance.

4.3 SECONDARY PROPERTIES

There can be many ways of listing these properties. Authors have used different heads: Collier *et al.* (2009) describe these as physical, chemical and environmental properties. Joseph (1993) relates secondary properties to four performance parameters and describes them as properties affecting appearance, durability, comfort and maintenance.

In this chapter, we will use the following heads for secondary properties.

- Morphology [physical shape, longitudinal section (L.S.) and cross section (C.S.), colour, lustre]
- Specific gravity
- Elongation and elastic recovery
- Resiliency
- Moisture regain
- Flammability and other thermal reactions
- Electrical conductivity
- Abrasion resistance
- Chemical reactivity and resistance
- Biological resistance
- Sensitivity to environmental conditions

Some of these are measured quantitatively while others are described qualitatively. A comparative picture is also given for the various fibres.

In subsequent units, the same heads will be used for describing the properties of various fibres in detail. Before starting a discussion on the definitions and description of secondary properties, let us dwell briefly on two aspects, viz., cost and inter-relatedness of fibre characteristics.

A textile fibre must be commercially available. It must have a constant supply and be available in large quantities at a price which will permit it to be handled at a reasonable profit. Continuous efforts are being made in the direction of adding names to the family of fibres worldover. However, the research is considered successful only if it is commercially viable.

One also needs to understand that it is difficult to isolate any one property of a textile fibre. There exists a link between the various properties. To cite an example, a hygroscopic (water absorbing) fibre will not pose the problem of static charge build-up since water is a good conductor of electricity. Such a fibre will accept dyes and special finishes readily. It will also be comfortable to wear in hot conditions but might take a little longer to dry up after washing.

4.3.1 Morphology

It is the study of physical shape and form of a substance. It includes microscopic structures like longitudinal and cross sections (studied by a microscope) as well as macroscopic or those assessed with the naked eye. These include fibre length, fineness, crimp, colour and lustre.

Physical shape

Shape of a fibre includes its longitudinal section, cross section, surface contour, irregularities and average length. These in turn affect the macroscopic (low magnification) and microscopic (high magnification) characteristics.

Longitudinal Section (L.S.) and Cross Section (C.S.)

Pick a cucumber and view it along its length. What you see is the L.S. Next, slice the cucumber and view the inner part. You can observe the C.S. now which is nearly circular with seeds that were not visible earlier. So is the case with fibres. The L.S. of a fibre can be easily checked using a compound microscope. For this, a few fibre strands are placed on a glass slide. A drop of glycerine is put and the coverslip is then placed carefully, ensuring that no air bubble is entrapped.

The L.S. is a good guide for identification of cotton, wool and silk fibres. The reason is that each of these natural fibres has some characteristic features. Thus the flat, twisted ribbon-like L.S. of cotton cannot be confused with the overlapping scales in the L.S. of wool. The L.S. also serves as an indicator for man-made fibres. However, identification for specific fibres (nylon, polyester, acrylic) is not possible. The reason is that, features like regularity of structure and particles of delustrant seen in the L.S. are common to all of these.

It is not possible to prepare the slides for C.S. of fibres with the optical microscope. These have been studied by the textile scientists using advanced equipment and shared in literature. This book carries the L.S. and C.S. diagrams of all the major fibres in the respective chapters.

Colour

There is a wide range of colours in natural fibres. Fibres obtained from plants vary in this property on the basis of the crop variety as also processing techniques. Animal fibres like wool have a colour based on the breed from which they come. The colour of manufactured fibres is generally off-white or yellowish and becomes white on use of bleach.

Lustre

Lustre refers to the sheen or gloss that a fibre possesses. It is directly proportional to the amount of light reflected by a fibre. This in turn is affected by their cross section shape. Table 4.3 gives a list of various possible cross sectional shapes and their impact on lustre. This property is described qualitatively.

Table 4.3   Effect of Cross Section on Lustre

Description of cross section	Degree of lustre
Round	High
Irregular	Low
Kidney shaped	Low
Oval	High
Trilobal	High
Octagonal	Low

Among the natural fibres, silk or the 'queen' of fibres has a high lustre while unmercerised cotton has a low lustre.

The lustre of man-made fibres (like their lengths and diameters) can be controlled by the manufacturers. This is done by regulating the quantity of delusterant used.

A **delusterant** is a substance that is added to the dope before spinning of manufactured fibres. Finely powdered metallic salts like titanium dioxide (TiO_2) and geranium dioxide (GeO_2) are used. These act as discontinuities in an otherwise regular, uniform reflection of light. The amount of delusterant added could vary and thus result in semi-lustered or delustered fibres.

It is also believed that addition of a delusterant makes a fibre more sensitive to actinic degradation.

4.3.2   Specific Gravity (SG)

The specific gravity of a fibre is the density relative to that of water (at 4°C).

The density of water at that temperature is 1. Fibre density will affect their performance and laundering. If the specific gravity of a fibre is less than 1, it will float in water, making its washing and dyeing very difficult. Olefins are examples of such a fibre.

A related proprety is density which is defined as the mass per unit volume and measured in g/cubic cm.

4.3.3 Elongation and Elastic Recovery

The amount of extension or stretch that a fibre accepts is referred to as *elongation*. Elongation at break is the amount of stretch a fibre can take before it breaks.

Elastic recovery indicates the ability of fibres to return to their original length after being stretched. A fibre with 100% elastic recovery will come back to its original length after being stretched to a specific degree for specified period of time. After removing the stretch, the fibre is allowed to recover for a short period of time and re-measured.

The properties of elongation and elastic recovery must be considered together in fabric evaluation. They govern comfort and appearance through shape retention. The present-day popularity of lycra blends proves this point. A fabric made from fibres with low elastic recovery will pose a problem of bagginess.

4.3.4 Resiliency

Resiliency refers to the ability of a fibre to come back to its original position after being creased or folded. Resilient fibres recover quickly from wrinkling or creasing. Good elastic recovery usually indicates good resiliency. This property is described qualitatively and ranges from excellent to poor. Excellent resiliency is exhibited by polyester, wool and nylon fibres. Flax, rayon and cotton, on the other hand, have a low resiliency.

Table 4.4. enlists the qualitative rating of selected secondary properties in ascending order.

Table 4.4　Qualitative Rating of Selected Secondary Properties in Ascending Order (i.e., low to high)

Resiliency	Abrasion resistance	Resistance to sunlight
Flax	Glass	Silk
Rayon	Acetate	Wool
Cotton	Rayon	Nylon
Acetate	Wool	Olefin
Silk	Silk	Acetate
Triacetate	Cotton	Rayon
Olefin	Acrylic	Cotton
Acrylic	Flax	Flax
Modacrylic	Spanic	Polyester
Nylon	Polyester	Modacrylic
Wool	Olefin	Acrylic
Polyester	Nylon	Glass

4.3.5   Moisture Regain

The ability of a bone dry fibre to absorb moisture is called **moisture regain**. Measurements are done under standard testing conditions (70° ± 2 F and 65% ± 2% relative humidity). Saturation regain is the moisture regain of a material at 95–100% relative humidity. Both regain and content are expressed as a percentage.

$$\text{Moisture regain} = \frac{\text{Weight of water in a material}}{\text{Oven dry weight}} \times 100$$

$$\text{Moisture content} = \frac{\text{Weight of water in a material}}{\text{Total weight}} \times 100$$

Thus, if oven dry weight of a material is 5 gms and it has absorbed 1 gm of moisture, the moisture regain will be 1/5 × 100 while moisture content will be 1/6 × 100.

Moisture may be absorbed by some fibres, while others may adsorb it.

Adsorption refers to the travelling of moisture along the surface of the fibre. Most synthetics have low absorbency but still give satisfaction to the consumers owing to this wicking property.

Many aspects of a textile product are affected by its absorbency behaviour. High moisture regain (hydrophilicity) will mean good acceptance of dye and special finishes, easy laundering and greater comfort value in hot conditions. However, the other side of the coin is that such fabrics will dry slowly and be easily stained by water-borne soil. The reverse is true for fibres with low moisture regain (hydrophobic).

Strength of some fibres is affected by the moisture they contain. Cotton becomes stronger when wet, while rayon is weaker when wet. This means greater care must be taken in laundering and processing. There are some fibres in the synthetic category whose strength is not adversely affected on wetting, example polyester.

4.3.6   Flammability and Other Thermal Reactions

Burning characteristics of fibre groups vary from each other and can, thus, be used as an authentic identification method. Reaction to flame can be further broken down into: behaviour when approaching flame, when in flame, after being removed from flame, odour and residue. Flammability of textile products is an important criterion for consumer's safety. These norms are much more rigid in developed countries like United States and United Kingdom but not so in a developing country such as India.

Thermal characteristics of fibres are important in their use and care. You would have observed that temperatures for washing, drying and ironing are selected on the basis of a fibre's ability to withstand heat.

Thermoplastic materials are sensitive to heat. At temperatures known as **Glass transition temperature** (Tg), they soften and melt. Their inter-polymer forces of attraction break and the polymers can then move freely. This property of heat setting is present in most synthetic fibres and proves useful for permanent incorporation of features such as pleats, darts and crease lines in garments as well as texturing yarns. It should however, be remembered that temperatures for care and maintenance of such garments should not exceed the temperatures used for heat setting.

Melting temperature (Tm) is that at which a material begins to liquefy and, thus, get permanently damaged. Both Tg and Tm are important in processing of thermoplastic man-made fibres.

Safe ironing temperatures are a major concern for use of any textile product. The care label carries specific information about the fibre content as well as ironing instructions and these should be followed. When in doubt, it is always good to first check the ironing temperature on the inside seams of the garment.

4.3.7 Electrical Conductivity

It is the ability of a fibre to transfer or carry electrical charges. Poor or low conductivity results in building up of static charges. This leads to the clinging of clothing and in extreme cases can produce electrical shocks. You might have noticed a crackling sound or even a tiny spark when removing an acrylic pullover. Acrylic is a poor conductor of electricity.

Water is an excellent conductor of electricity and fibres with high moisture regains will never face the problem of static build-up. Synthetics are poor conductors of water and also face the problem of static charge build-up.

There are certain finishes which can be imparted to combat this problem.

4.3.8 Abrasion Resistance

The wearing away of a material by rubbing against another surface is called **abrasion**. Three kinds of abrasions have been identified by textile scientists. These are:

(i) Flex abrasion: when a fabric bends/folds and rubs against another surface e.g., on elbow or knee areas.
(ii) Flat or plane abrasion: when a flat surface rubs against another surface, e.g., on thigh area of a pair of jeans.
(iii) Edge abrasion: which occurs on the curved edges e.g., collars, cuffs and trouser hems.

Fibres with poor abrasion resistance break and produce worn out areas in fabrics. Sometimes these effects are in fashion and carried out on brand new garments like jeans and jackets to give them a worn out look.

Pilling is the formation of a small bundle of fibres which cling to the fabric surface. Due to abrasion, the surface fibre ends break and curl up into tiny balls. You must have noticed this in acrylic sweaters and nylon socks. In weaker fibres, these tiny structures break and fall off the surface, while in strong fibres they continue to cling. Now do you now why pilling is a more serious problem for synthetics?

Abrasion resistance is described qualitatively: Synthetics (nylon, polyester) have excellent, acrylic has good, viscose has fair, while silk has poor abrasion resistance (see Table 4.4).

4.3.9 Chemical Reactivity and Resistance

This secondary property plays a key role in manufacture, application of finishes and care of fabrics.

Resistance to acids, alkalies and organic solvents is similar for fibres of one chemical composition. Thus, cellulosics are fairly resistant to alkalies but get harmed by acids and the reverse is true for protein fibres.

4.3.10 Biological Resistance

This includes the capacity of a fibre to withstand microbes and insects. It is a key factor in deciding the end uses and maintenance. Cotton was earlier used as boat sails but it is susceptible to damage by mildew which is even more pronounced in humid conditions. Now, this slot is filled by synthetics which have excellent biological resistance. Wool is susceptible to damage by carpet beetles and it is for this reason that its storage takes so much effort. This is one reason why acrylics are replacing wool for winterwear, apart from the cost factor which is much low for acrylics.

4.3.11 Sensitivity to Environmental Conditions

Behaviour of a fibre on exposure to sunlight and air pollution are also important in their use and care. Many textile fibres are known to weaken on exposure to sunlight (actinic degradation). Protein fibres have low resistance to sunlight. Glass, acrylic and polyester fibres can withstand sunlight (Table 4.4). Acetate fibres get discoloured by air pollution and this makes them a less popular fabric for interiors in areas that have high levels of air pollution.

EXERCISES

4.1 Differentiate between the following:
  (a) Primary and Secondary properties
  (b) Denier and Tex
  (c) Absorption and Adsorption
  (d) Qualitative and Quantitative tests

    (e) Bright and Dull fibres

    (f) Tg and Tm

    (g) Edge and Flat abrasion

    (h) Staple and Filament

    (i) Hydrophilicity and Oleophilicity

    (j) L.S and C.S. of fibres

4.2 Write down a list of secondary properties that you would consider important while selecting fabrics for the following end uses:

    (a) School uniform

    (b) Curtains

    (c) Table napkins

4.3 Match the following properties with the correct unit:

    (a) Staple fibre length   excellent to poor

    (b) Filament length   grams per denier

    (c) Fibre diameter   centimetre

    (d) Resiliency   metre

    (e) Tenacity   microns

4.4 "Textile fibre properties are interlinked with one another". Using examples from the chapter, substantiate this statement.

REFERENCES

Collier, B.J., Bide, M.J. and Tortora, P.G., *Understanding Textiles,* 7th ed., Pearson Education, NJ, 2009.

Kness. D., Hudson P.B., and Clapp, A.C., *Joseph's Introductory Textile Science*, 6th ed., Harcourt Brace Jovanovich College Publishers, USA, 1993.

SUGGESTED READING

Gohl, E.P.G. and Vilensky, L.D., *Textile Science*, 2nd ed., CBS Publishers and Distributors, Delhi, 1979.

Kadolph, S.J. and Langford, A.L., *Textiles,* 10th ed., Pearson Education, NJ, 2007.

Morton, W.E. and Hearle, J.W.S., *Physical Properties of Textile Fibres*, 3rd ed., The Textile Institute, Manchester, UK, 1993.

Skinkle, J.H., *Textile Testing Physical, Chemical and Microscopical*, 2nd ed., Taraporevala Sons and Co., Mumbai, 1979.

PART II
Fibres

In this part, you will learn about the various textile fibres that you use. Just as persons belonging to one zodiac sign have certain traits that are typical and can be spotted easily so also the fibre families such as natural and synthetics have easily distinguishable properties. Extending the analogy further, just as each individual is unique so also each member of the natural fibre family has certain specific properties. At the end of this part, perhaps you would be able to assign zodiac signs of fibres too—much to the amusement of Linda Goodman!

This part covers four chapters. Chapters 5 and 6 deal with natural animal and cellulosic fibres. The next two chapters discuss manufactured fibres. Chapter 7 gives the details of regenerated fibres while Chapter 8 deals with synthetic and inorganic fibres.

CHAPTER

5

Natural Protein Fibres

As discussed in Chapter 2, natural protein fibres can be broadly divided into two categories, viz., animal extrusion and animal hair. Animal hair can be further categorised as sheep hair (wool), speciality fibres and fur. On the other hand, animal extruded fibres include cultivated and wild silks.

SILK

5.1 HISTORY OF SILK

Silk, also known as **"the queen of fibres"**, owes its discovery to China. Although its exact origin is shrouded under the shadows of many tales, but it is generally believed that Princess Si Ling Shi (2600 BC) accidentally discovered the silk filament. While having tea in the garden, a cocoon fell into the hot liquid. As the princess attempted to pull it out, she caught hold of one end of the strand and this led to the use of silk filaments for weaving. For nearly 3000 years, the Chinese kept the art of silk cultivation and processing a well guarded secret. Many stories abound regarding the leak of this secret to other places. Silk was considered as a precious commodity in the ancient civilizations of Greece and Rome. It is believed that during the Roman empire, silk was sold for its weight in gold.

Silk also paved the way for the man-made industry which started with an attempt to produce inexpensive silk fabrics. This is substantiated by the fact that both rayon and acetate were referred to as *art (artificial) silk* before separate names were coined for them.

5.2 SILK IN INDIA

Today, China, India and Japan are the major silk producers in the world. India has the distinction of cultivating all the four commercially known varieties of silk, namely, mulberry, tussar, eri and muga. Of these, the first two are most popular among the consumers. In the year 2005–2006, India's raw silk production has been 17,305 metric tonnes. Of these, 89.25% is mulberry while the remaining 10.75% is

42 Textbook of Fabric Science: Fundamentals to Finishing

wild silk, also referred to as *vanya* silk. The states of Karnataka, Andhra Pradesh, West Bengal and Tamil Nadu lead in the production of mulberry silk. Table 5.1 lists the statewise production of silk in the year 2005–2006.

Table 5.1 Statewise Production of all Four Varieties of Raw Silk (2005–2006)
Unit: Metric tonne

State	Mulberry	Tussar	Eri	Muga	Total
Andhra Pradesh	5375	20	27	—	5422
Assam	8	—	745	104	857
Arunachal Pradesh	1	Neg.	10	0.24	11.24
Bihar	3	14	2.8	—	19.8
Chhatisgarh	3	90	2	—	95
Himachal Pradesh	16	—	—	—	16
Jammu & Kashmir	95	—	—	—	95
Jharkhand	1	96	Neg.	—	97
Karnataka	7471	—	—	—	7471
Kerala	12	—	—	—	12
Madhya Pradesh	23	16	—	—	39
Maharashtra	44	6	—	—	50
Manipur	48	3	23.5	0.06	74.56
Mizoram	6	Neg.	3.2	0.07	9.27
Meghalaya	3	—	280	5.4	288.4
Nagaland	1	Neg.	1.3	0.18	13
Orissa	2	21	2	—	25
Punjab	4	—	—	—	4
Tamil Nadu	739	—	Neg.	—	739
Tripura	4	—	—	—	–4
Uttar Pradesh	19	3	0.5	—	24
Uttaranchal	14	5	Neg.	Neg.	19
West Bengal	1552	34	4	0.2	1591

[Neg: less than 50 kg. No silk is produced in Haryana, Rajasthan and Sikkim.]

In the year 2005–2006, the Indian states of Karnataka and Andhra Pradesh, with production of 7471 and 5375 metric tonnes respectively, accounted for 83% of the total mulberry silk production. Tussar silk, also called **wild silk**, is obtained from the wild moth *Antheraea millita* which feeds on oak leaves. There are two sub-varieties of tussar. The tropical tussar is more abundant and mainly found in the states of Jharkhand and Chhatisgarh. Data from 2005–2006 shows a production of 96 and 90 metric tonnes respectively for these two states. West Bengal is the third largest producer, with a figure of 34 metric tonnes. The temperate variety is found in the sub-Himalayan belt of India, covering the states of Manipur, Himachal Pradesh, Uttar Pradesh, Assam and Meghalaya. Eri silk (also known as **endi** or **errandi**), is mainly found in Assam and the Northeastern states. These worms feed mainly on castor and kasseru leaves. During the same time span Assam led in eri silk production with 745 metric tonnes. Meghalaya followed with 280 metric tonnes. Muga silk is known for its golden colour and smooth feel. The muga silkworms feed on *som* and *sualu* leaves. The variety is primarily found in Assam which showed a production of 104 metric tonnes in the same period (2005–2006).

5.3 PRODUCTION AND PROCESSING OF SILK

Sericulture plays an important role in the rural economy of India. *Sericulture* means production of cultivated silk. It is an extremely labour intensive job. The adult female moth lays about 500 eggs. These are tiny, pin head sized with a soft spot on one end from where the larvae will hatch.

On hatching, the larvae are fed mulberry leaves in abundance. For the next month, the larvae eat and moult 4 times. After the fourth moulting, the eating continues for 10 more days. There is a stupendous increase in weight as the larvae weigh 10,000 times more than their birth weight. Their length and diameter increase to nearly 8 cm and 1 cm, respectively. The larvae stop eating and are shifted to a straw frame. From the two orifices or spinneretes on its head, the larva extrudes two strands of fibroin with a coating of sericin (water soluble protective gum). On contact with air, these strands harden. Figure 5.1 shows a caterpillar that has begun to spin. As can be observed in the picture, the outer cocoon gets formed first, followed by the inner part. The caterpillar moves its head in the shape of the digit 8 to form a cocoon that encases it. In 2–3 days, the cocoon is complete. Figure 5.2 shows a freshly formed cocoon.

Figure 5.1 A silkworm beginning to spin.   **Figure 5.2** Fresly formed cocoon.

Some of the silkworms are allowed to reach the moth stage for breeding purposes.

A majority are stifled, that is put in hot water to kill them and soften the case which is then brushed to pick the filament end. Figure 5.3 gives a schematic of silk yarn production.

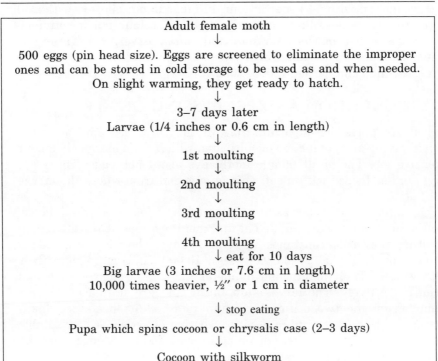

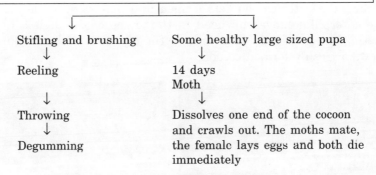

Figure 5.3 Schematic of silk production.

On an average, 5000 silk worms produce about 1000 kg of cocoons. These are processed to obtain nearly 120 kg of raw silk.

Processing steps for silk are unique and include:

- Reeling
- Throwing
- Degumming

After stifling and brushing, the ends of filaments are combined and passed through a guide before winding them onto a circular frame (reel). This process is named **reeling** and is carried out in a manufacturing plant called **filature**. This is a hand operation and expert reelers know how many cocoons to combine in order to get a uniform yarn.

During this step, a slight twist can be imparted to the strands in order to hold them together. This is called **throwing** and produces a thrown yarn.

Variations in the number of filaments used and the amount of twist imparted can result in interesting aesthetic effects.

Staple silk/silk waste or noils are broken or damaged cocoons that yield shorter lengths of yarns which are less expensive and of inferior quality.

Dupion silk is when two silkworms spin their cocoons together (i.e., 4 strands instead of two). The yarn is irregular and produces an interesting texture which resembles linen.

Degumming is a step in which soap and boiling water are used to remove the gum from a yarn or fabric.

5.4 CHEMICAL COMPOSITION OF SILK

Silk protein is **fibroin**. It is a less complex protein than keratin that is present in wool. Fibroin is made up of at least 17 amino acids of which glycine, alanine, tyrosine and serine account for 90%. There are no cystine or sulphur linkages. The gummy substance that holds the filaments together is **sericin**. It is this component which is partially removed in the processing step of degumming.

Silk has reactive carboxyl (COOH) and amino (NH_2) groups. The molecular chains are almost fully extended and packed closely together to give a high orientation. There are very few cross links between fibroin protein chains, but presence of hydrogen bonds gives a high degree of crystallinity and resultant strength to silk.

5.5 PROPERTIES OF SILK

5.5.1 Microscopic Properties

Longitudinal section (L.S.): As shown in Figure 5.4, degummed mulberry silk has a smooth, transparent, rod-like longitudinal section. Raw silk (with gum) has an irregular and rough surface. In the case of Tussar silk, the L.S. reveals an even but darker structure with longitudinal striations.

Figure 5.4 Longitudinal section of silk.

Cross Section (C.S.): Silk has a triangular cross section in which the two brins (strands) are visible, i.e., placed face to face. (see Figure 5.5)

Figure 5.5 Cross section of silk.

5.5.2 Physical Properties

Length: Silk is the only natural filament where each filament measures about 900–1200 metres though sometimes even upto 2750 m.

Diameter: Silk is very fine with a diameter of 9–11 microns.

Colour: Raw mulberry silk is off-white to cream in colour. Degumming lightens the colour to some extent. Tussar silk is tan to light brown in colour due to the tannin present in oak leaves on which the larvae feed. Muga silk is golden yellow in colour.

Lustre: Silk has a soft lustre with an occasional sparkle. The triangular cross section and smooth surface are responsible for this. Wild silks have a duller lustre due to the irregular surface.

Tenacity: Silk is one of the strongest natural fibre. It has a dry strength of 2.5 to 5 g/d and a wet strength of 2 to 3 g/d which is 80 to 85% of the dry strength.

Elongation and elastic recovery: Silk has a moderate elongation of 10–25% (33–35%). At 2% elongation, it has a good elastic recovery of 92%.

Resiliency: Silk has a medium resiliency which is less than wool due to the absence of cystine linkages. However, its resiliency is better than cotton.

Density: Silk has a density that ranges between 1.25–1.34 g/cm^3.

Moisture regain: 11% moisture regain makes silk quite absorbent, comfortable to wear and an easy to dye fabric. It can readily take up finishes and absorb metal salts which are used in weighting of silk (Chapter 14).

Thermal properties: Safe ironing temperature ranges from 120–135°C. At temperature greater than 150°C, silk will scorch, while if the temperature exceeds 175°C, there will be a rapid degradation. Silk has a lower thermal conductivity than cotton, making it warmer and, thus, a preferred choice in winter clothing.

The burning behaviour of silk conforms to that of a protein fibre. Silk burns with sputtering, is self-extinguishing, emits an odour of burnt hair (though not as pungent as wool) and leaves a residue of brittle black bead.

5.5.3 Chemical Properties

Acids: Fibroin protein in silk is decomposed by strong mineral acids used in finishing. Fibroin is more susceptible to damage than keratin present in wool. It can withstand weak acids. Organic acids also do not damage silk. Thus, acetic acid can be safely used to impart scroop or a rustling sound to silk after washing.

Alkalies: Alkalies have an adverse effect on fibroin and should thus be avoided. It is for this reason that detergents such as Rin, Surf and Ariel are never used for silk washing. Instead, neutral pH cleaning reagents such as Genteel and Ezee are employed.

Organic solvents: These are used in dry cleaning and do not harm the silk fibres.

5.5.4 Biological Properties

Silk is damaged by carpet beetles, although it is fairly resistant to attacks by clothes moths, mildew, bacteria and fungi. This necessitates careful storage of silk products when not in use.

5.5.5 Other Properties

Dimensional stability: Silk exhibits good resistance to stretch or shrinkage when laundered or dry cleaned.

Static charge: Silk being a poor conductor of electricity can pose the problem of static charge build up.

Sunlight: The UV rays in sunlight can damage silk.

5.6 USES OF SILK

Silk has reigned supreme in the family of fibres since its discovery. It continues to enjoy this position of supremacy as the 'queen' of textile fibres. It is expensive and has a luxurious look. Its chief uses can be summed up as follows:

Apparel: Silk is commonly used in sarees, suits, formal dresses and sophisticated lingerie.

Accessories: It is common to use silk in ties, scarves, stoles and handbags.

Home textiles: Conveying a luxurious look, silk is also used for making cushion covers, bedspreads, handmade oriental rugs, carpets, fine drapes and upholstery fabrics.

Industrial textiles: In this sector, silk is used for medical sutures, embroidery threads, sewing threads, typewriter ribbons and racing bicycle tyres.

Tussar silk, being less shiny and rough as compared to mulberry silk, has lesser usage in apparel fabrics. It is widely used in furnishings and interiors. Eri silk is mainly used for making *chhadars.* Muga, also called *the pride of Assam*, is commonly used in sarees and sheets.

5.7 CARE OF SILK

Being an expensive fabric, silk needs special care. Many users feel that silk has to be dry cleaned only. Contrary to this belief, silk can also be hand washed at home. However, some precautions need to be taken. Detergents which are safe include Genteel and Ezee since these are free from strong alkalies. During the washing and rinsing, the water temperature should be lukewarm. Brush friction, which is a common method of washing cotton, is obviously too harsh for this delicate fibre. Gentle kneading and squeezing should be adopted. In the last rinse, a few drops of acetic acid may be added to impart scroop (rustling sound) to silk. Stiffening, if required, is done using Gum Arabic. Wet silk fabrics are pressed between the palms of the hand, then wrapped in a towel and pressed to squeeze out excess moisture. Drying in the sun is avoided. Ironing is done using a steam iron or a damp muslin. Spraying of water directly on the silk fabric can lead to water marks and should hence be avoided.

5.8 SILK ORGANISATIONS IN INDIA

- Central Silk Board, CSB, Ministry of Textiles, Government of India
- Indian Silk Export Promotion Council, ISEPC
- Silk Mark Organization of India, SMOI

In the recent years, the Central Silk Board has worked on a certification mark, the **Silk Mark,** to authenticate the quality of silk.

WOOL

The Federal Trade Commission (1986) defines wool as "the fibre from the fleece of the sheep or lamb or hair of the Angora or Cashmere goat (and may include so called specialty fibres from the hair of the camel,

Alpaca, Llama and Vicuna). Over the years, the word 'wool' has become synonymous with sheep hair.

5.9 HISTORY OF WOOL

Wool is believed to be one of the earliest known fibres which was used before the recorded history. Perhaps man would have noticed the natural coat of hair on animals that gave them warmth. The earliest actual remains of wool fibres come from Egypt and date back to the fourth millennium (Collier *et al.*, 2009). It is believed that the first sheep were probably domesticated in Mesopotamia. Pile rugs were probably woven from the fibres before 500 BC. The early Greeks wore wool and the Roman soldiers were supplied with wool garments during their occupation of England.

In India, sheep rearing, spinning and weaving were a part of life since pre-historic times. There is a prayer in *Rigveda* for God *Pasham*, the God of Shepherds, entreating him to make wool white and helping in its knitting. It has been a common practice to use rugs of wool as prayer mats for ceremonies since wool is considered as a pure fibre. There is a mention in the Indian epic *Mahabharata* that while performing the *Rajsuya Yagna*, King *Yudhisthir* was presented woollen clothes with gold embroidery. The ancient civilization of the Indus Valley has also revealed that our ancestors were well-versed in the art of wool felting, spinning and weaving.

During the Muslim period, India became popular for its fine woollen fabrics. The early British days also witnessed acceleration in demand for Indian Pashmina shawls and carpets produced in Kashmir and Punjab.

Traditionally, Merino sheep, which was bred in the fourteenth century in Spain, has been considered to be very special. It is noted for its long, thick, high quality white fleece. Today, there are hundreds of breeds and cross breeds of sheep. Initially major wool-producing countries were Australia, Soviet Union and New Zealand. In recent years, China has gained the second position, after Australia. It is closely followed by New Zealand. In India, hair from the Cashmere goat yields superior fibres and fabrics. The Indian government has issued a ban on the manufacture and use of "tus/asli tus" shawls in an effort to protect the endangered species.

5.10 WOOL PRODUCTION IN INDIA

After independence, development programmes have been formulated under successive five year plans for sheep and wool development. Salient among these have been the Integrated Wool Improvement Programme (IWIP) and the Sheep and Wool Improvement Scheme (SWIS). The woollen industry in the country is small in size and widely scattered. It is basically located in the states of Punjab, Haryana, Rajasthan,

Uttar Pradesh, Maharashtra and Gujarat. 40% of the woollen units are located in Punjab, 27% in Haryana, 10% in Rajasthan, while the rest of the states account for the remaining 23% of the units. The Indian states could be ranked in the following order based on their raw wool production:

Rajasthan > Jammu & Kashmir > Karnataka > Andhra Pradesh > Gujarat > Haryana.

Of the indigenous wool production, 50% is used for blankets, 30% for mills, 10% for carpets and the remaining 10% for manufacturing of shawls and sweaters.

Since indigenous production of fine quality wool required by the organised mill and the decentralised hosiery sector is very limited, India depends upon imports. These have been mainly from Australia and New Zealand.

India has a wide variety of sheep breeds that contribute to its wool production. The country is divided into four zones namely North Western arid and semi-arid regions, Southern peninsular regions, Eastern regions and Northern temperate regions. Each of these areas has its own sheep breeds. Table 5.2 lists the names of sheep breeds found in India. This list includes the pure breeds as well as cross-breeds.

Table 5.2 Sheep Bread in India

Eastern region	North temperate region	North western arid and semi-arid	Southern peninsular region
Balangir	Bhakarwal	Chokla	Bellary
Bonpala	Bushar	Hissardale	Coimbatore
Chottanagpur	Changathangi	Jaisalmeri	Deccani
Ganjam	Gaddi	Jalauni	Hassan
Shahabadi	Gurez	Magru	Kenguri
Tibetan	Kashmir Merino	Malpura	Kilakarsal
	Poonchi	Malwari	Macheri
	Rampur	Muzzafarnagri	Madras red
		Nagi	Mandya
		Pattanwadi	Nellore
		Pungal	Nilgiri
		Sonadi	Ramnad white
			Tiruchy black
			Vembur

Source: Adapted from CSWRI, Avikanagar.

5.11 STEPS IN WOOL PRODUCTION

Just as the quality of hair in human beings depends on a multitude of factors, so also sheep hair are dependent on their breed, diet, health and surroundings. Good breeding practices in developed countries include inoculation of the animals against diseases, feeding good diet and preventing insect infestations by dipping the animals in chemicals. Sheep should be vaccinated for important diseases like sheep-fox and entero-toxaemia.

Shearing

Shearing refers to the removal of hair. It is done by one of the following methods:

(a) Hand shearing using a huge pair of scissors. This labour intensive method is common in developing countries.
(b) Machine shearing using electric shears. This is faster than hand shearing.
(c) Chemical shearing where the animals are fed a chemical, which leads to hair loss in about two weeks time. Growth resumes after that.
(d) Use of depilatory cream in the case of pulled wool.
(e) EGF Biological Wool Harvesting was first used by Ryder, an Australian researcher who injected a chemical called **epidermal growth factor** (EGF). This stops hair growth for one day and then it resumes. When this weak point reaches the surface of the skin, the hair then can be removed by hand (Collier *et al.*, 2009).

In India, shearing is done manually either with clippers, a pair of scissors or by power-operated machines depending on the size of operations. Figure 5.6 shows the mechanical shearing. Most flocks are usually shorn twice a year, i.e., March–April after the winter and September–October after the rains. In some states like Jammu & Kashmir and Rajasthan, sheep are shorn thrice a year.

Figure 5.6 Mechanical shearing.

Grading and sorting

Various criteria used for this step are length, fineness, colour, age of the animal, part of the body, crimp and impurities present. In other words, evaluation criteria include physical attributes, mechano-chemical properties and end use suitability.

Generally speaking, there is a variation in hair sheared from a single sheep. Under belly and lower legs have contaminated fibres since a lot of vegetable matter gets entangled during grazing. The hair get matted and torn too. The best fibres are found in the shoulders, sides and back of the sheep. Grades vary from 1 (best) to 4 (worst) and the use is accordingly decided. Figure 5.7 shows a woman carrying out grading and sorting of the shorn fleece. There are five grades of wool produced in India. These are as follows:

- Thin and fine wool
- Medium wool
- Long wool
- Cross-bred wool and
- Carpet wool

Figure 5.7 Grading of fleece.

An unscoured fleece weighs between 1 and 6 kgs. Raw or grease wool is sent for the next step, i.e. Scouring.

Scouring

The fleece is treated with a warm, alkaline, soapy solution to remove the grease, perspiration (suint) and impurities (see Figure 5.8). The natural oil, lanolin, is recovered and used in the cosmetic industry (e.g., creams such as Nivea), ointments and soaps. The weight of the cleansed and scoured fleece becomes nearly half.

Figure 5.8   Scouring of fleece

Carbonizing

The alkaline solution used in scouring does not harm the vegetable matter (leaves, twigs, burrs) entangled in the fleece. These are collected during the grazing done by sheep and the rough surface of hair helps to keep them entrapped. As already discussed, cellulosics can be destroyed by the action of acids. Thus, a dilute solution of sulphuric acid (H_2SO_4) is used to carbonize (char) and remove the vegetable matter.

Carding

This is done using fine wire-teethed cylinders. It helps in the removal of impurities and straightening of fibres to some extent. Using the woollen spinning system, bulky and coarse yarns are produced. Fabrics produced from such yarns are called **woollen fabrics**. These are not very smooth and will not hold a crease.

Combing

This is an optional process. If combing is carried out, the yarns produced are fine and smooth (worsted). Carpet wools are made from long, coarse fibres that are only carded. However, fine fabrics for men's suits are made from worsted yarns. Worsted fabrics are smoother, lighter, more lustrous and can hold a crease easily as compared to woollens. They are also more expensive.

5.12   SOME TYPES OF WOOLS

Depending on the source

Sheared wool/clip/fleece: These terms denote that the wool has been removed from live domesticated animals bred for wool.

Pulled wool: This is hair fibre obtained from the skin of dead animals. It is inferior in quality, less elastic and lustrous than the sheared wool.

Lamb's wool: As the term suggests, lamb's wool is collected from lambs less than 7 months of age. It is soft, fine, extremely warm and has a natural tip.

Depending on past use of the fibre

Virgin wool: This term is used for fresh, unused wool.

Recycled wool: This term is used for wool that has been used previously. It is further demarcated into reused i.e., from worn clothing and reprocessed i.e., from unused cutter's scrap. These fabrics are converted back to the fibre form, then re-spun into yarns and fabrics. These are inferior in quality to virgin wool and are also cheaper.

Ideally, the label should carry all information pertaining to the quality of wool fibre that it is made of. However, in India, strict regulations are missing and hence consumers are often cheated. It would, thus, be safe to buy a reputed brand while shopping for woollens.

5.13 CHEMICAL COMPOSITION AND MOLECULAR STRUCTURE OF WOOL

The wool fibre is composed of keratin (protein molecule). These molecules have 18 different amino acids of which the major ones are glutamic acid, serine, cystine, leucine and proline. The molecules combine to form long chain macro molecules which club together in the form of fibrils and then into fibrillar bundles. These form the bulk of the cortex. Wool is a natural bicomponent fibre. The cortex has ortho and para cortical cells on the two sides (bilateral structure) which react differently to heat and moisture. This results in a natural crimp which is unique to wool.

Protein fibres including wool and speciality hair fibres are made up of peptide chains or amino acid residues joined together by amide linkages. Major elements present include C, H, O, N, S. Three types of bonds are present. These are cystine bonds (sulphur linkages), ionic bonds (salt linkages) and hydrogen bonds. Most important among these are the cystine bonds.

Within the wool fibre, the polypeptide molecules are not straight and extended. In their relaxed state, they are arranged in a spring or helix form (α keratin). Figure 5.9 depicts the structural formula for wool molecule.

When the fibre is stretched, the polypeptide chain straightens out (β keratin), only to spring back to the α position on releasing the strain. This property gives wool its high elongation, elastic recovery and resiliency.

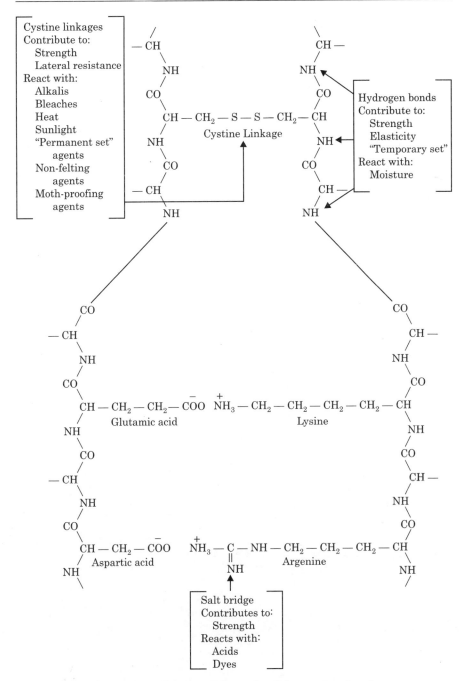

Figure 5.9 Structural formula of the wool molecule.

Source: KADOLPH, SARA J.; LANGFORD, ANNA L., TEXTILES, 10th Edition,© 2007, p.68, Reprinted by permission Pearson Education, Upper Saddle River, NJ.

5.14 PROPERTIES OF WOOL

5.14.1 Microscopic Appearance

Longitudinal Section: The L.S. (Figure 5.10) shows the overlapping scales pointing towards the tip. These scales are epithelial cells present on the surface. Their number varies from 700 per inch in coarse wool to 300 per inch in fine wool.

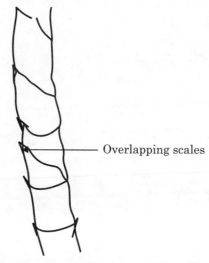

Overlapping scales

Figure 5.10   Longitudinal section of wool.

Cross Section: Wool fibre is oval or elliptical. Figure 5.11 depicts the cross section of wool. The structure resembles a sheath—core

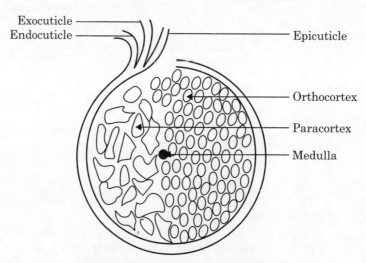

Exocuticle
Endocuticle
Epicuticle
Orthocortex
Paracortex
Medulla

Figure 5.11   Cross section of wool.

arrangement in which the bulk is constituted of cortex. This is sheathed all around by the cuticle. At the macro level, there are three parts in a wool (see Table 5.3). The inner most part is the medulla. It is an air space which helps nutrients travel. It also has the colour pigment, melanin. In most fine wools, the medulla is not visible.

Table 5.3 Macrostructure of Wool

Cuticle	Cortex	Medulla
Epicuticle	Orthocortex (regular, small cells)	
Exocuticle	Paracortex (irregular cells)	
Endocuticle		

The **cortex** occupies 90% of the area. As already mentioned, it is composed of ortho and para cortical cells. The differential behaviour of these imparts crimp to wool. Fine wool has about 30 crimps in an inch while inferior quality wool has 1–5 crimps per inch.

The outer layer is called the **cuticle** and contains scales. This layer is in turn constituted of three parts:

Epicuticle: It is the outermost section of the cuticle. It is a thin, non-protein membrane with numerous pores that cover the scales. It is water-repellent and gets damaged by mechanical action encountered in normal wear.

Exocuticle: It is the scaly layer. These are non-fibrous, horny and can even cause skin irritation. Scales impart felting property to wool by interlocking and shrinking.

Endocuticle: It acts as a cementing layer that helps the next layer (exocuticle) to stay bound with the cortex.

5.14.2 Physical Properties

Length: Being a natural fibre, the length of wool fibre varies from 1.5 to 15″. Wool is categorised as short (1.5 to 5″), medium (2.5–6″) and long wool (5 to 15″). Length varies between breeds and is also dependent on the time between two shearings. Usually fine wool is shorter than coarse wool.

Fineness: Very coarse wool has a diameter of 40 microns, while very fine wool (Merino) has a diameter of 18 micrometres. The average diameter ranges from 24 to 34 microns.

Colour: Colour is decided by the breed of the sheep. Unscoured wool ranges from off white, grey, tan, brown to black; scoured wool is mostly yellowish white in colour.

Lustre: Scales present in wool reduce lustre. Generally, the lustre of poor quality wool is greater than the lustre of better grade of wool.

Crimp: Wool has a natural 3D crimp or waviness which aids in yarn manufacture.

Specific Gravity: Density is 1.32 g/cm^3. Wool is heavier than degummed silk.

Strength: 1.0 to 1.7 g/d. Water breaks the hydrogen bonds in wool. Hence, wet strength decreases (0.7–1.5 g/d). Wool is one of the weaker natural fibres.

Elasticity and resiliency: This becomes excellent because of natural crimp which also helps wool recover from wrinkling.

Moisture regain: Wool has some initial hydrophobic behaviour due to its scaly structure. However, on continued exposure, it absorbs a good amount due to a high moisture regain of 13.6 to 16%. This water is held inside the fibre and not on the surface. Reasons for high absorbency include amorphous structure (70%) and presence of many chemical groups that attract water.

Wool is an ideal choice for cold and damp climate. When wool absorbs moisture, it provides heat (heat of absorption), which keeps the wearer comfortable.

Heat and electrical conductivity: Wool has low heat and electrical conductivity. This means that wool fabrics are insulating and help provide warmth to the wearer without being bulky. Inspite of a low electrical conductivity, wool fabrics do not pose much problem of static when the atmosphere is very dry.

Heat and combustibility: Wool burns slowly with slight sputtering, is self-extinguishing, gives the odour of burning hair and a residue which is a black crushable bead. At temperatures greater than 130°C, wool turns yellow and above 300°C, it chars. Wool has an inherent flame resistance which makes it ideal for blankets.

5.14.3 Chemical Properties

Acids: Wool can withstand the action of acids (except very strong concentrated mineral acids). For this reason, carbonization with dilute sulphuric acid is a safe step for removal of vegetable impurities without damaging the wool protein.

Alkalies: Keratin (wool protein) is very sensitive to alkalies—even relatively weak ones. Thus, detergents such as Surf, Ariel and Rin which have a high alkaline content cannot be used for laundering wool. Special mild detergents (Genteel, Ezee) are thus used.

Most organic solvents used in cleansing and stain removal do not damage wool.

Chlorine bleaches harm wool and hence wool can be bleached with H_2O_2 or the use of stoving (reduction) process. Here, damp wool is kept in an atmosphere with SO_2 fumes which bleach it.

5.14.4 Biological Properties

Wool protein is food for insects like carpet beetles and larvae of clothes moths. It is important to remove stains before storing wool to prevent attack by bacteria. There are moth proof finishes (Chapter 14) but careful storage can also go a long way in protecting wool fibres. Mildew can also appear in damp conditions. Thus storage should be in air tight, dry conditions.

5.14.5 Other Properties

Dimensional stability: Woven wool fabrics face relaxation shrinkage, which is progressive, and also felting shrinkage. When fabrics are subjected to heat, moisture and agitation, the scales tend to pull together and move towards the fibre tip [directional friction effect (DFE)].

Thus, wool requires careful, minimal handling when being laundered. Finishes can combat the problem of felting (Chapter 14).

Sunlight: UV rays of the sun lead to the breakage of disulphide bonds in cystine, thus causing photochemical degradation and deterioration.

5.15 USES OF WOOL

Apparel

Properties like warmth, resiliency and absorbency make wool popular in the apparel sector. The other side of the coin is that wool is generally expensive, requires care in laundry and storage, is prone to shrinkage and moth damage, and can also cause allergic reactions on skin contact.

In home textiles, wool finds usage as rugs and carpets, blankets, upholstery fabrics and even draperies.

Industrial uses: these include felts which are popular for filtration, medical and geotextile applications.

5.16 CARE OF WOOL

It is a misconception that woollen garments cannot be home laundered and have to be dry cleaned each time. As already mentioned, wool can be washed using lukewarm water and detergents such as ezee or genteel.

The method of washing is kneading and squeezing. The water temperature has to be lukewarm throughout. No wringing of the garment is done which is gently pressed between the palms to remove excess moisture. The garment is spread out flat on the ground on newspaper sheets and dried in shade. Steam ironing can be done at temperatures not exceeding 200°F.

Storage of wool is a time-consuming job as most of you would have noticed in your homes. However, if properly taken care, wool has a very long life.

5.17 ORGANISATIONS AND CERTIFICATION MARKS DEALING WITH WOOL

International level
- International Wool Secretariat (IWS)
- International Wool Textile Organisation (IWTO)

National level
- Central Wool Development Board (CWDB), Jodhpur, Rajasthan.
- Central Sheep and Wool Research Institute (CSWRI), Avikanagar, Rajasthan.
- Indian Woollen Mills Federation, Mumbai
- Wool and Woollen Export Promotion Council (WWEPC), New Delhi.
- Wool Research Association (WRA), Thane.
- Woollen Textile Export Promotion Council (WOOLTEXPRO).

International Wool Mark

(see Figure 5.12a) This mark of certification is used worldover to convey that products are made of 100% wool fibres. This mark guarantees a certain product quality level, strength, dimensional stability and colour fastness.

Wool blend symbol

(Figure 5.12b) This mark helps to communicate that at least 60% of virgin wool fibres have been blended with only one other fibre. Both these marks are strictly regulated and controlled. However, consumers in India still face the problem of imitation certification marks.

WOOLMARK

WOOL BLEND

Figure 5.12(a) Wool mark.   **Figure 5.12(b)** Wool blend symbol.

Source: The Woolmark & Wool Blend logo is reproduced with the permission of Australian Wool Innovation Limited, owner of The Woolmark Company.

5.18 SPECIALITY HAIR FIBRES

This term is used for hairs that are derived from animals other than sheep. In most cases, such hair fibres are produced in limited quantities and also have some special features hence the term 'speciality'. These are classified on the basis of the animal from which the fibre is obtained. A brief description of such fibres is given hereinafter.

Alpaca

The Alpaca is a relative of the camel and thus bears some resemblance (Figure 5.13). It is native to South America where it was domesticated by the Incas in the upper reaches of the Andes mountains. Today, Alpaca is found in Peru, Chile and Bolivia. Its natural colours range from off white, gray to light and dark browns. The animal has long, soft and silky hair. There are two varieties of Alpaca—huacaya and suri. The former is a stronger variety with spongier, short hair. The suri, on the other hand, is delicate with extremely long hair which are thinner and have more natural grease than the huacaya.

Figure 5.13 Alpaca.

Angora

The fibre is obtained from the Angora rabbit. These are extremely soft and fine with lengths ranging from 3 to 5 inches. There are four main breeds of the Angora rabbit: English, French, German and Satin. The first two are the original breeds while the last two were bred in the 1980s. Britain and USA are the main breeding regions of the Angora rabbit today. The harvesting is done annually by brushing, plucking or clipping. It is a common practice to blend the angora with wool or cotton. Common applications include baby clothes, sweaters and mittens.

Camel

During springtime camels shed hairs from their bodies which are collected and processed into fibres. The best grade is obtained from the downy undercoat although many a times guard hair is also blended. There are two types of camels—one humped camels found in the Arabic desert (Dromedary) and two humped camels found in Asia (Bactrian Camel). Camel hair has a unique property of being extremely light and at the same time possessing incredible insulation capacity. The extremely soft, fine camel hairs are used alone or blended with wool.

Cashmere

This fibre derives its name from Kashmir in India. It is obtained from the downy undercoat of the wild Alpine goat (Capra hircus) or cashmere goat which is native to the high plateaus of India, Afghanistan, China, Mongolia and the mountainous regions of Iran (Figure 5.14). The fibre is unarguably one of the world's most desirable woollens. The average length ranges from 1 to 3 inches while the diameter ranges from 12 to 18 micronaires. Renowned for its extraordinary fineness and strength, the fibre comes in natural shades of brown, grey, black and rarely white. This goat is bred at altitudes of 12000 to 15000 feet. The produce from the goats of the highest and coldest regions is of the best quality and referred to as Pashmina. Being expensive, it is a common practice to blend cashmere fibres with wool, silk or cotton.

Figure 5.14 Cashmere goat.

Llama (pronounced 'yama')

This animal is native to South American Andes region which includes Peru, Argentina, Columbia. Bolivia and Ecuador (Figure 5.15). The llama was first domesticated by the Incas of Peru who also held them as icons in fertility and spiritual rites. The fibre obtained is durable and soft.

Figure 5.15   Llama.

Mohair

This fibre is obtained from the Angora goat which is a native of the mountains of Tibet. The animal has long, fluffy and shiny hair, the lustre deciding its value. The average lengths range from 4 to 12 inches and extremely resilient and durable yarns are made. Mohair is used in garments as well as home decorating fabrics.

Quiviot

Sheared from the downy undercoat of the musk ox, these fibres are very warm and soft. Being expensive, they are often blended with cashmere or silk fibres.

Vicuna

This is a wild member of the South American camel family and a close relative of the Llama and Alpaca (Figure 5.16). The fibres have a natural cinnamon brown colour and possess extraordinary qualities of softness and fineness, making vicuna the most expensive and rarest of speciality hairs in the world.

Figure 5.16   Vicuna.

Yak

This is a hairy animal commonly found in the Himalayan regions of India. It is also referred to as the domesticated Tibetan ox. The hair collected are coarse and generally black in colour.

It is of interest to note that while many speciality hair fibres enjoyed a coveted position some decades back, the present global trend towards environment-consciousness has made consumers more aware about issues such as animal rights.

5.19   FUR

Furs are animal pelts. The pelt comprises the skin, which needs to be tanned and the hair. The first clothing of primitive Man was made of fur. Many gods are also depicted sporting furs as clothes or as *asanas* (seats). Fur fibres are produced from a wide range of animals both wild as well as specially bred and farmed animals. Examples include beaver, chinchilla, fox, mink, muskrat, nutria, rabbit and raccoon. The process of converting pelt to fur clothing is long and tedious; needless to say that such articles are expensive. They have also carried a prestige value for years.

In recent decades, strict regulations have been imposed on international fur trade. These steps have been taken in the wake of growing concerns for endangered animal species. Another fallout of this concern has been that manufacturers have come up with good synthetic imitations.

EXERCISES

5.1 Define 'sericulture'. Give an outline of steps carried out for processing of silk.

5.2. Give reasons for the pleasant lustre of silk.

5.3 'Home laundering of silk and wool requires care'. Elaborate this statement with a list of dos and donts.

5.4 Differentiate between

(a) Mulberry and tussar silk
(b) Fibroin and sericin
(c) Pulled wool and clipped wool
(d) Woollen and worsted fabric
(e) Scouring and carbonising

5.5 Explain the reasons for the inherent crimp found in wool.

5.6 Name three speciality fibres found in India. Give their salient features.

REFERENCE

Collier, B.J., Bide, M.J. and Tortora, P.G., *Understanding Textiles,* 7th ed., Pearson Education, NJ, 2009.

SUGGESTED READING

Corbman, B.P., *Textiles Fiber to Fabric,* 6th ed., McGraw-Hill, 1983.

Dantyagi, S., *Fundamentals of Textiles and Their Care,* 5th ed., Orient Longman, 1996.

Labarthe, J., *Textiles: Origins to Usage,* Macmillan, USA, 1964.

Morton, W.E. and Hearle, J.W.S., *Physical Properties of Textile Fibres,* The Textile Institute, Manchester, 1993.

Trotman, E.R., *Dyeing and Chemical Technology of Textile Fibres,* 6th ed., Griffin, 1984.

CHAPTER 6

Natural Cellulosics

COTTON: THE UNIVERSAL FIBRE

Natural cellulosic or plant fibres are obtained from various parts of plants. Four common categories include seed hair (cotton, kapok), bast or stem (flax, jute), leaf (pina, abaca) and miscellaneous (from parts other than these three).

6.1 HISTORY

The origin of cotton is lost in legend for it is older than the recorded history. Probably it originated in India for it is mentioned in "Rig Veda", written nearly 3,500 years ago. Evidence points to its production in India, China, Egypt and Peru. Spinning and weaving as an industry also began in India with good quality fabric being produced around 1500 BC Indian cotton fabrics were sold in the Mediterranean area from the time of Alexander (around fourth century BC). These were known for their outstanding fineness and quality. The actual woven cotton fabric was found in an excavation of Mohenjodaro, which is dated back to third century BC. The 'Charkha' or roller gin was imported by other countries from India. Many years later this humble spinning device became a potent symbol of Indian freedom movement under the leadership of Mahatma Gandhi.

The word cotton is derived from 'quton' which means a plant found in a conquered land. Perhaps cotton was being used in areas which were invaded by the Arabs.

6.2 COTTON IN INDIA

India ranks second in global cotton production after China. Today, India accounts for nearly 25% of the world's total cotton area and 20% of global cotton production. Using 8–9 million hectares of land, India produces nearly 3 million tonnes of cotton per year. This includes cotton of all staple lengths and varieties. Figure 6.1 depicts the cotton growing states of India. These include Andhra Pradesh, Gujarat, Haryana, Karnataka, Madhya Pradesh, Maharashtra, Meghalaya, Orissa, Punjab, Rajasthan, Sikkim and West Bengal. Indian trade officials estimate that the country's cotton production will go upto 27 million bales in the cotton year ending September 2007, which will be 4% higher than the last year. The Indian cotton industry has 1,543 spinning units, more than 281 composite mills, 1.72 million registered looms and an installed capacity of 36.37 million spindles. Since the new textile policy in 1985 and liberalization of the raw cotton imports, the industry has modernized itself significantly. Today, about 40% of India's spindleage is less than 10 years old, giving the industry an important edge over other international rivals.

Figure 6.1   Cotton growing states of India.

The cotton industry contributes in a big way to industrial output, employment and balance of payments, making it one of the most important industries in the country. Out of India's agricultural gross domestic products, cotton contributes 30%. It contributes 27% to export earnings, 14% to industrial production and 4% to GDP. As the second largest employer after agriculture, this sector employs 30 million people directly. If indirect employment is included by way of agriculture and processing, this figure doubles up to 60 million.

Cotton is also called the **white gold**. There are four cultivated and a little over forty wild species and some semi-wild forms of cotton in India.

6.3 GROWTH AND PRODUCTION

Cotton belongs to the family **Malvacae** and genus **Gossypium**. The world's cotton belt is located mainly in the tropics and sub-tropics having warm and humid climates. Over the years, cotton production has increased as a result of improvement in agricultural techniques (irrigation facilities) and cotton varieties. It grows in almost hundred countries of the world with soil and climate bringing about variations. The level of development of a place will decide the manner in which cotton is grown and harvested. Important producers are USA, China, India, Pakistan and Uzbekistan. During the active growing period, the plant requires about 4 inches of water, followed by a dry period for maturing.

Each fibre is a single plant cell called a **seed hair** or **lint**. After 100 days of being planted, the cotton blossom appears. It is creamy white or pale yellow on the first day and changes to pink/red/lavender on the second day (Figure 6.2). After two days, petals fall off and the seed pod (cotton boll) is visible. In a span of 50–80 days, the pod bursts open, exposing the fleecy cotton fibres which cover the seeds (Figure 6.3). In each boll there are about 30 seeds. The number of hair on each seed ranges from fewer than 1000 to more than 10,000, depending on the variety of cotton. When the seed boll opens, the seed hairs are exposed to air, dry up and collapse.

Figure 6.2 Cotton blossoms.   **Figure 6.3** Cotton boll.

These are now ready for *harvesting or picking*.

A warm dry weather is required at this stage. *Hand picking* allows the removal of mature fibres only, thus leading to better quality (Figure 6.4). This may be an easy option for the developing countries such as India but high costs of this labour intensive method (in developed countries) have led to other options. In *mechanical picking*, a machine pulls the fibres from open bolls after plants are sprayed with defoliant to make them shed leaves. Sometimes devices called **strippers** are employed which pull the entire boll from the plant (Figure 6.5). Needless to say, this affects the quality of the raw material. Cotton is dried in warm air after harvesting.

Figure 6.4 Hand picking.   **Figure 6.5** Mechanical picking.

The harvested cotton is quite dirty owing to the presence of foreign matter (Figure 6.6).

Figure 6.6 Cotton boll with impurities.

The next step is *ginning* (Figure 6.7). This helps to separate the fibres from the seed. Eli Whitney is reported to be the inventor of the ginning machine, which was earlier done by hand at a much slower pace (Figure 6.8). Now with the help of the gin, it takes about 12–15 minutes to gin 1500 lbs. of seed cotton (Figure 6.9). 100 kgs of clean seed cotton yields about 35 kgs fibre, 62 kg of seeds and 3 kg of waste. Cotton seed is used for production of oil, cattle feed and fertilizers. Modern gins also remove foreign matter like parts of seed boll, leaves, twigs and dirt.

The ginned cotton fibres are then compressed into bales (Figure 6.10). A bale is a large package of compressed fibres weighing about 500 lbs/ 250 kg. In India, nearly 27 million bales are produced with each bale weighing 170 kilograms. A fibre sample from each bale is sent for classification on the basis of their lengths, fineness, colour and foreign matter present. This helps establish its price.

Seed cotton

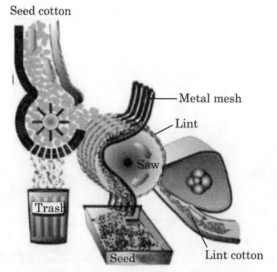

Metal mesh

Lint

Saw

Trash

Seed

Lint cotton

Figure 6.7 Schematic diagram of a cotton gin.

Figure 6.8 Hand ginning.

Figure 6.9 Ginning machine.

Bales are then sent to the manufacturers of yarn and fabrics.

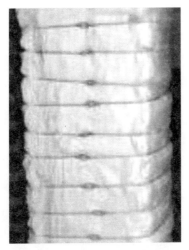

Figure 6.10 Cotton bale.

6.4 CHEMICAL COMPOSITION OF COTTON

The basic unit of the cellulose molecule is cellubiose which is a pair of glucose monomer (Figure 6.11). A cotton fibre with 10,000 glucose units will have 5,000 cellubiose building blocks and thus a dp of 5,000.

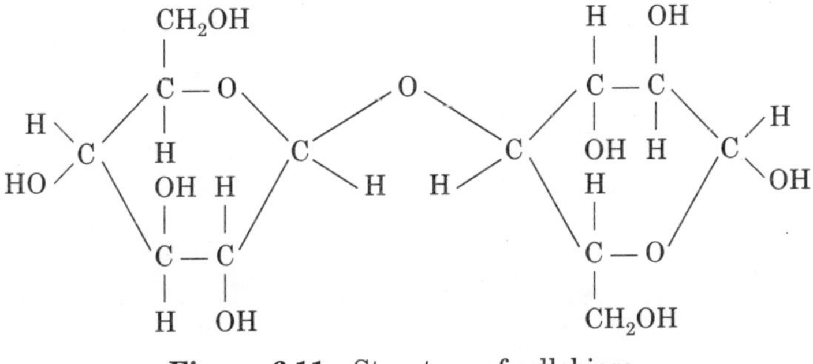

Figure 6.11 Structure of cellobiose.

6.5 COTTON PROPERTIES

6.5.1 Microscopic Appearance

Longitudinal section or L.S.: Ribbon-like structures which twist with convolutions at irregular intervals. The fibre has a hollow lumen inside. There is a protective waxy coat around the fibre which helps in its spinning (Figure 6.12).

Figure 6.12   Longitudinal section of cotton fibres.

Cross section: The cross section reveals kidney shaped structures with a hollow lumen inside (Figure 6.13). The process of mercerization, cotton is treated with a dilute alkali solution. The alkali is absorbed by cotton and pushes out the convolutions just as water gushes in to make a flat rubber pipe swell up. This would naturally impact the cross section which would become more regular and circular. Needless to say, the light reflected by such mercerised cotton is much more, and hence it possesses a greater lustre. Details of this finishing process are given in Chapter 9 under yarn manufacture.

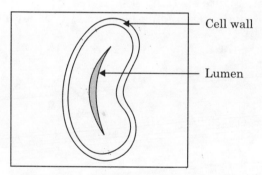

Figure 6.13   Cross section of cotton fibres.

6.5.2   Physical Properties

Length: 3\8–21\2″

Fineness: 12–20 micrometres. Thus, the length of the cotton fibre is 1–3 thousand times its diameter.

Colour and lustre: The colour of raw cotton varies from white to yellow and gray. The fibres are fairly dull inherently. On being mercerised (treated with dil. NaOH), the cross section becomes more regular, thus increasing their lustre.

Tenacity: Cotton has moderate strength ranging between 3.0 and 5.0 g/d. When wet, its strength increases by about 20%.

Elongation and resiliency: 3–7% elongation at break. Elastic recovery is poor and resiliency is low, thus making the fabric prone to wrinkling.

Density: 1.54 g/cm^3.

Moisture regain: 8.5% mercerised cotton has a moisture regain of 10.3%.

6.5.3 Thermal Properties

Cotton is flammable i.e., it ignites quickly, burns freely and has an afterglow. Its odour while burning is similar to burning paper. The residue obtained is a fluffy grey ash. Safe ironing temperature for cotton is 200°C, at temperature greater than 250°C rapid deterioration can occur. Scorching is a problem faced by the use of very hot iron and becomes more pronounced in case of starched cotton fabrics.

6.5.4 Chemical Properties

Acids: Cotton is not resistant to acids. Hot dilute and strong acids cause fibre disintegration. In general, harm is caused by mineral acids, though not much by organic acids.

On the other hand, cotton has high resistance to alkalies. Detergents with high alkali content (e.g., Nirma, Rin) can be safely used for laundering cottons.

Chlorine bleaches can remove stains on cotton using the recommended conditions.

Cotton is highly resistant to organic solvents and thus can be easily dry cleaned.

6.5.5 Biological Properties

Silver fish attacks starched cotton fabric. It is, thus, recommended that cotton sarees be stored without starch. Moths and carpets beetle which eat up protein fibres do not attack cotton (cellulosic) fibres.

Mildew fungus can grow on cotton especially in damp, dark and warm surroundings. This leads to colour loss and eventual strength loss through rot and decay.

Bacteria in soil can also degrade cotton.

6.5.6 Other Properties

Sunlight: Prolonged sunlight exposure can cause degradation in cotton.

Static build-up: Cotton does not face any static problem.

Dimensional stability: Cotton fibres are relatively stable and do not stretch or shrink. Fabrics made of cotton may exhibit some shrinkage.

6.6   USES OF COTTON

Cotton has high value due to aesthetics, its pleasant texture and matte look. Because of its high capacity to absorb, hold and dry moisture, cotton offers maximum comfort under extreme heat and humidity.

It is a fibre that 'breathes'. Consumers prefer cotton for its comfort, good heat and electrical conductivity, laundrability, absorbency, ease of finishing and dyeing, strength and cost. It can be made into loosely woven, light weight, soft, smooth material on one hand and tightly woven, almost air resistant fabric on the other. It is a preferred fabric for children and for anyone who has a sensitive skin and is allergic to other fibres, since cotton is non-allergenic. It would not be an exaggeration to say that cotton is the principal clothing fibre of the world.

Cotton is considered quite versatile. It can be converted into fluffy as well as firm yarns. A wide range of fabric construction methods can be employed including weaving, knitting as well as non-woven techniques. Blending of cotton fibres can be done at the fibre, yarn or fabric stage. Cotton is used universally for a variety of *apparel* (both inner and outerwear). It finds extensive usage in *home textiles*. The products include towels, sheets, pillowslips, bedspreads, upholstery and table linen. The fibre also has innumerable *industrial applications* including medical, surgical and sanitary supplies.

6.7   CARE OF COTTON

Cotton is strong when wet and can thus face harsh washing conditions as well as high temperatures in washing and ironing. It can be safely boiled and sterilized, thus making it valuable in the hygiene sector. However, sometimes the dyes on cotton may not be very fast, thus necessitating use of cold water and gentle washing. It is a good idea to wash dyed fabrics carefully at least for the first time.

6.8   SOME OTHER COTTONS

Naturally coloured cottons

These have a botanically formed pigmentation lodged in the lumen of the fibre. The result is fibres which have inherent green or brown colour. Archaeological evidences indicate that the oldest cottons in use were brown and not white (Figure 6.14). Colour development of lint in naturally coloured cottons is controlled by the soil type, water hardness and exposure to sunlight. Salient advantages include saving of cost (since bleaching and dyeing are omitted) and medical benefits. Drawbacks include lower yield, fibre strength and length as compared to conventional white cotton fibres. However, these can be overcome by blending at the yarn or fabric stage.

Figure 6.14   Naturally coloured cotton.

The Cotton Council of India (CCI) has decided to develop naturally coloured cottons for commercial cultivation to meet the domestic as well as export demands. This would also increase the income of the tribals who also grow the coloured cotton.

Organic cotton

This term is used for cotton produced in a field where organic practices have been followed for three years. If the organic cotton fibre certification standards have been in practice for a period less than three years, the produce is referred to as *transition cotton*. There is a phenomenal spurt in demand for organic cotton with increasing environment awareness and strict eco-legislations pushing industries to use less polluting practices. Green cotton textile products include fabrics made of cotton that have not been subjected to chemical treatments, with the exception of mild natural based soaps and natural dyes. The term 'green' refers to the processing and not to the growing practices.

Bacillus thuringiensis (or Bt) cotton

This refers to genetically modified cotton which has a superior yield and is guarded against boll worms. Based on the technology from seed giant Monsanto Co., Bt cotton covers about one third of the total cotton area. The technology has, however, come in for criticism from environmentalists who claim that such products deplete bio-diversity.

6.9   INDIAN ORGANISATIONS FOR COTTON

- Cotton Corporation of India Limited (CCI). This is the Indian governmental marketing organisation for local cotton industry.
- Cotton Export Promotion Council (TEXPROCIL)
- Cotton Textile Research Association (CTRA)
- Central Institute for Cotton Research, Nagpur
- Indian Council for Agricultural Research (ICAR)
- Central Institute for Research on Cotton Technology (CIRCOT), Mumbai.

- The Indian Cotton Mills Federation (ICMF) is a central organisation representing the mill industry and enjoys consultative status with the national Government and international agencies. The ICMF. came into being on 18th March, 1958.
- Cotton Development and Research Association (ICMF CDRA), a subsidiary body in the name and style of ICMF. It has been carrying out cotton extension and seed development work since 1964.

LINEN

6.10 HISTORY

Flax fibres (botanical name: *Linum usitatissimum*) are among the oldest fibre crops in the world. Pictures on tombs and temple walls at Thebes depict the flowering flax plants. Fragments of linen cloth pre-date the earliest pre-historic ages. Flax was being cultivated by ancient Egyptians, Phoenicians, Babylonians and other civilisations between 5000–4000 BC. Archaeologists have discovered woven linen cloths in tombs as wrappings of Egyptians mummies, dating from 4000 BC. The dry and hot climate of Egypt helped preserve these materials. The use of flax fibres in the manufacturing of cloth in northern Europe dates back to Neolithic times.

Linen was especially popular in the Middle Ages and is even today regarded as a valued 'prestige' fibre. Terms like "table linen" and "bed linen" prove the widespread use of linen in home textiles. Interestingly, the terms still continue being used even though modern home textiles employ fibres other than linen.

The Latin word *usitaissimum* means 'most useful', proving the popularity of this fibre in ancient times.

6.11 GROWTH AND PRODUCTION

Linen is a bast fibre which is obtained from the stalk of the plant. The fibres are long, hairlike and covered by the woody stem. They are held together by pectin (a gummy substance).

The major fibre flax- or linen-producing countries are the former USSR, Poland, France, Belgium, Ireland and the Czech Republic.

Flax is an erect annual plant with slender stems, which thrives in temperate climates. The soils most suitable for flax, besides the alluvial kind, are deep friable loams and containing a large proportion of organic matter. Heavy clays are unsuitable, as also soils of a gravely or dry sandy nature. *Planting* is done in March–April; delicate pure pale blue flowers appear in June and harvesting is done in July–August. After 90–120 days of sowing, the plants attain a height of 2–4 feet, the lower two-thirds of the stem defoliates and stalks begin to turn yellow at the back. If the stalks are green, it implies that the fibre is underdeveloped and on the other hand, once the stalks turn brown, the fibres begin to degrade.

Harvesting can be done manually or with machines. In developing countries, labour is cheap and easily available while developed countries adopt mechanical harvesting. In either of the methods, the plant is pulled up completely with the roots from the ground and not cut. This ensures maximum fibre length that is possible.

Drying and thrashing follow to remove the flax seeds that have appeared at the top part of the stem. This step is also called **rippling** and can be done with hands or machines. The flax seeds are used for making linseed oil, cattle feed and sowing for the next season.

The next step is *retting* (rotting) which loosens the outer woody stalk and the intercellular gummy substance holding the fibres together, thus permitting the removal of the flax fibres.

Stalks are tied in bundles for *retting* which can be carried by any of the following methods, which have self-explanatory names:

- *Dew or field retting:*   It is the most primitive and time-consuming method which employs the use of dew, sunlight and rain. The process takes 4–6 weeks and results may not be uniform. The other side of the coin is that the fibres thus obtained are the strongest and most durable as compared to other methods. The process also produces the least pollution.
- *Stream retting:*   Bundles are anchored in the running stream water to allow rotting to take place. This method is not much in use these days.
- *Pool or pond retting:*   Bundles are placed in clean stagnant water, weighed down by stones after covering with straw. It takes around 2–4 weeks for the bacteria in water to hydrolyse the gummy substance. This darkens the flax giving it a bluish grey colour. Some drawbacks of this process are that the product can become dirty owing to the stagnant water. There are chances of over retting which can damage the fibre. A strong odour is also produced.
- *Vat retting:*   Wooden containers called **vats** are filled with warm water at 25–30°C. The process is less time consuming and is completed in a few days. Any other type of container made of plastic, concrete or earthenware can also be used. Metal containers cannot be used since retting produces an acid which corrodes metals.
- *Chemical retting:*   Stalks are boiled in dilute sulphuric acid, sodium hydroxide or sodium carbonate and then steamed. Least time is required but use of chemicals affects the fibre strength.

When retting is complete, the bundles of flax feel soft and slimy, with quite a few fibres standing out from the stalks. After retting, the stalks are thoroughly rinsed and dried by placing in the fields.

Dressing the flax: This is the term used for the next three steps in processing of linen, namely, breaking, scutching and hackling (Wikipedia, 2007).

Breaking: This is a step in which the retted woody stalk is broken into short pieces. It is done by using wooden blades.

Scutching: The fibres are cleaned or scutched free from the woody fragments by a machine which has fluted iron rollers. These crush the brittle wooden stalks.

Hackling or combing: Scutched fibres are pulled through a series of iron combs of increasing fineness. A good progression is from 4 pins per square inch, to 12, to 25, to 40 and to 80 pins. The first three will remove the straw while the last two will separate the linen fibres. The shorter fibres called **tow** are separated from the long, even fibres called **line**.

Next, the fibres are packed into bales weighing 200–224 pounds and sent to yarn manufacturers. Spinning of the flax fibres can be done in dry or wet conditions. In the latter, the roving is passed through water at 50°C.

6.12 CHEMICAL COMPOSITION

As already discussed, the basic unit of any cellulosic fibre is cellubiose which is a pair of glucose monomer (Figure 6.11). The degree of polymerisation in flax is 18,000. It will thus have 36,000 glucose units.

6.13 PROPERTIES OF LINEN

6.13.1 Microscopic Characterisation

Longitudinal section: (see Figure 6.15) the fibre has an irregular width and somewhat resembles a bamboo shoot. There are no convolutions as in cotton but cross wise marks corresponding to nodes are visible along the length of the fibre.

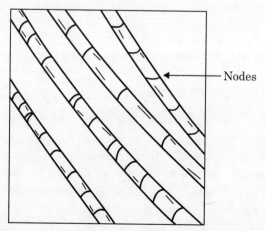

Figure 6.15 Longitudinal section of linen fibres.

Cross section: (see Figure 6.16) flax fibres are polygonal with rounded edges. The central canal (lumen) is visible inside a thick outer wall.

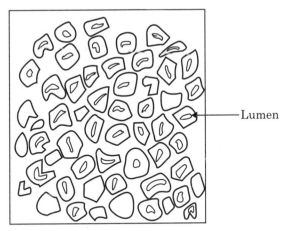

—Lumen

Figure 6.16 Cross section of linen fibres.

6.13.2 Physical Properties

Length: Flax fibres are much longer than cotton and the length varies from ¼–2 1/2″ (from 5 to 12 inches).

Diameter: Not as fine as cotton, the diameter ranges from 12 to 16 micrometres.

Colour: It varies from ivory to grey.

Lustre: Flax has a high natural lustre.

Tenacity: 5.5–6.5 gpd; it is 20% stronger when wet, thus making fabrics which are durable and easy to care for.

Elongation, elasticity and resiliency: These are low thus leading to the problem of wrinkling. However, this same property is used as a characteristic "crushed look" which is quite in vogue.

Density: 1.5 g/cm^3

Moisture regain: 12%. A high regain value makes linen a comfortable fabric to wear.

6.13.3 Thermal Properties

Burning characteristics are similar to those of cotton. Ironing temperatures are higher than those of cotton (260°C). You could observe this on the temperature dial of your electric iron which designates a higher setting for linen than that for cotton.

6.13.4   Chemical Properties

Acids: Flax is not resistant to concentrated acids which cause fibre disinte-gration. It can, however, withstand the action of dilute acids.

On the other hand, flax has high resistance to **alkalies**. Detergents with high alkali content (e.g., Nirma, Rin) can be safely used for laundering flax.

Chlorine bleaches can remove stains on flax using the recommended conditions.

Flax is highly resistant to organic solvents and thus can be easily dry cleaned.

6.13.5   Biological Properties

Silver fish attacks starched flax fabric. Insects do not attack flax (cellulosic) fibres.

Dry linen has excellent resistance to mildew but damage may be caused in humid atmosphere.

6.13.6   Other Properties

Sunlight: Prolonged sunlight exposure can cause gradual loss of strength. However, the degradation in flax due to UV rays of the sun is lesser than that in cotton. Hence, it can be used for curtains.

Static charge build-up: Flax does not face any static problem and ages well.

Dimensional stability: Fibres of flax do not stretch or shrink but woven fabrics can exhibit relaxation shrinkage.

6.14   USES OF LINEN

Linen is known for its high natural lustre and good moisture absorbance. Linen is used in apparel, especially women's wear. Other varied uses include painting canvas, awnings, car seat covers, draperies, table linen, handkerchiefs and covers for field guns. Defence forces use linen fabric to make water bottles (*chaggal*) and water storage tanks that can be folded up and carried to remote locations like deserts and hill areas.

One of the leading fashion fabrics, linen is being used by almost every designer in India. Linen has thick and thin fibre bundles which give texture to fabric. The fact that it is cool in summers, extremely durable and becomes better with age are some of the other desirable characteristics.

6.15   CARE OF LINEN

One drawback is its lack of resiliency, leading to wrinkling. This can be overcome by application of wrinkle resistant finishes.

6.16 OTHER CELLULOSIC FIBRES

Apart from cotton and linen, there are many other fibres in the natural cellulosic family. Table 6.1 summarises their source, salient characteristics and uses. It may be noted that the developments in the field of processing have expanded the use of many of these fibres in areas like apparel, home textiles and industrial uses.

Table 6.1   Other Cellulosic Fibres

Fibre	Source	Salient properties	Uses
Bamboo, also called **Green gold**	Stem of Bamboo plant, (made into a pulp and extruded)	• Antimicrobial • Absorbent • Breathable, soft hand • Anti UV nature	• Innerwear • Medical textiles • Food packing bags
Coir* (seed hair)	Outer husk of coconut (see Figure 6.17)	• Very stiff • Abrasion resistant • Water and weather resistant	• Rugs and floor textiles • Brushes, ropes, cordage
Kapok* (seed hair)	Seed of Java Kapok tree (silk cotton tree) (see Figure 6.18)	• Exceptional buoyancy due to hollow structure • Resistant to wetting • Not very durable	• In flotation devices as fibre fill • Stuffing of pillows
Jute* (bast fibre)	Stem of the jute plant. Creamy white to brown in colour.	• Soft, flexible and lustrous but turns brittle on exposure to air • Resistant to microbial deterioration • One of the cheapest textile fibres • One of the weakest cellulosic fibres	• Sacking • Carpet backing • Ropes and cordage • Food grade jute products (FGJP) • Jute geotextiles (JGT) • Home furnishings • Handicrafts • Gifts and novelty items • Yarn
Kenaf (bast fibre)	Kenaf plant	• Longer and harder than jute	• Ropes and cordage • Paper making • Recently in woven and

(Contd...)

Table 6.1 Other Cellulosic Fibres (*Contd...*)

Fibre	Source	Salient properties	Uses
			non-woven textiles
Ramie (bast fibre)	Stalk of ramie plant (China grass/rhea plant) natural white in colour	• Strongest natural fibre • Excellent absorbency • Fine, long and lustrous • Resistant to insects and microbes • Lacks resiliency	• Used alone or in blends for apparel and home textiles • Ropes • Geotextiles • Non-wovens
Hemp (bast fibre)	Stalk of the hemp plant	• Resembles flax • Very strong • Not very flexible • Does not rot on exposure to water	• Ropes and twines of great strength • Thread • Industrial fabrics
Abaca (Manila Hemp) leaf fibre	Member of the banana family	• Coarse, very long, • Strong, durable and flexible	• Floor mats • Ropes • Clothing • Table linen
Pina (leaf fibre)	Leaves of pineapple plant	• Soft, lustrous • Produces sheer, light weight but stiff fabrics	• Table linen • Bags • Clothing

*Grown and used extensively in India.

Figure 6.17 Coconut husk.

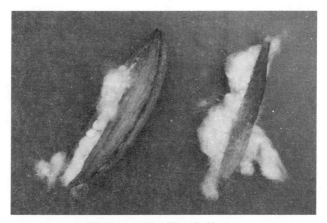

Figure 6.18 Kapok fibres.

6.17 JUTE: PRESENT STATUS AND USES

Jute sector occupies an important position in India's economy in general and the eastern region in particular. The Indian jute sector can boast of a number of strengths. The export history of raw jute and jute products dates back to over a hundred years. The 78 jute mills in the country give direct employment to 2.61 lac workers; livelihood to 40 lac farm families and another 1.4 lac are involved in tertiary trades of this sector. West Bengal has a predominant number of 61 mills. There are 7 mills in Andhra Pradesh, 3 mills each in Bihar and Uttar Pradesh and 1 each in Assam, Orissa, Tripura and Madhya Pradesh. India is the largest producer of raw jute as well as jute goods in the world. There is a wide gamut of applications tailored to customer's requirements. The latest are the food grade jute products or FGJP which are in the form of bags or cloth. These are being used extensively for packaging of cocoa, coffee and shelled nuts. Jute bags were earlier manufactured using mineral oil which led to retention of hydrocarbons and, thus, threatening contamination of food products. However, with the research and development inputs of Indian Jute Industries Research Association (IJIRA), an alternative oil was found out. Rice bran oil is now being used as a hydrocarbon free fibre lubricant. The food grade jute bags and cloth manufactured in India are a boon in the context of global environmental and ecological concerns.

6.18 LIST OF ORGANISATIONS IN THE JUTE SECTOR

- Birds Jute Exports Limited (BJEL)
- Indian Jute Industries Research Association (IJIRA)
- Jute Corporation of India Limited (JCI)
- Jute Manufacturers Development Council (JMDC)
- National Council for Jute Development (NCJD)
- National Jute Manufacturers Corporation (NJMC)

EXERCISES

6.1 Draw a schematic diagram outlining the growth of cotton from sowing of seed to harvesting.

6.2 "Cotton is considered apt for hot, humid weather". Which properties of cotton substantiate this statement?

6.3 Name two Indian agencies associated with the country's cotton and jute production respectively.

6.4 Define 'Retting'. Enumerate the methods employed for this processing step.

6.5 Define and differentiate between organic and naturally coloured cotton.

6.6 Enumerate the salient uses of linen and jute fibres.

SUGGESTED READING

Cook, J.G., *Handbook of Textile Fibres*, Vol. I, Rednook books, Great Britain, 1993.

Hudson, P.B., Clapp, A.C. and Kness, D., *Joseph's Introductory Textile Science*, 6th ed., Harcourt Brace Jovanovich College Publishers, 1993.

Kadolph, S.J., Langford, A.L., Hollen, N. and Saddler, J., *Textiles,* Macmillan, New York, 1993.

Sayed, U. and Marwaha, S., Novel Natural Fibres, *Asian Textile Journal*, pp. 80–85, January 2006.

Sekhri, S., Sardana, C., Parmar, M.S., Enhancing Consumer Appeal of Naturally Coloured Cottons Through Blending and Mordanting, Colourage, June 2008.

Sekhri, S., Naturally Coloured Cottons: Valuable Gift for the Future, *Asian Textile Journal*, pp. 70–73, April 2006.

Tortora, P.G. and Collier, B.J., *Understanding Textiles,* Prentice Hall, USA, 1997.

CHAPTER

7

Regenerated Fibres

Since the early twentieth century, chemists in the West began studying processes which could combine monomers and polymers, just as they do in natural fibres. Observation of the silk worm and the spider inspired scientists to explore methods by which they could extrude a suitable liquid through tiny holes and then solidify the same to yield man-made fibres. After a century of laboratory research and inventing hundreds of fibres, only a handful can be termed as successful creations. These have good properties and are competitively priced to gain mass acceptance. Salient among these are rayon, acetate, nylon, polyester and acrylic.

The first category of manufactured fibres are the regenerated fibres. These are made by using natural raw materials. Chemically, these may be cellulosic in nature or resemble protein fibres. Among the cellulosic regenerated fibres, rayon and acetate are important from commercial point of view. *Azlon* is an example of protein based regenerated fibre. In India, both rayon and acetate are manufactured and also have widespread applications. The present chapter will focus on their production, properties, uses and care.

7.1 HISTORY

The manufactured fibres are made by chemical spinning methods. The polymer is converted into a solution which is then extruded through an orifice and solidified to give filaments. Hence, it would not be an exaggeration to say that all manufactured fibres owe their existence to the invention of the spinning jet (spinnerete). This credit goes to Ozanam who invented the spinnerete in 1862. The first manufactured fibre, viscose rayon was invented in 1892 by Cross and Bevan. Commercial production started in 1904. It may also be noted that many years of tedious research in various countries of the world was responsible for paving the way for the birth of the first manufactured fibre.

The manufacture of cuprammonium rayon is based on E. Schweitzer's research that cellulose is dissolved in a solution of copper hydroxide in ammonia. Early attempts to spin the yarn did not prove quite successful. In 1919, Bemberg finally succeeded in producing cuprammonium rayon (Trotman, 1984).

Acetate owes its birth to the experiments done by Miles in 1905. Commercial production, however, began much later, around the 1920s.

Initially, the term *artificial silk* was used to refer to regenerated fibres. In 1924, the term 'rayon' was coined to refer to these fibres. It was finally, in 1953, that separate categories were established for rayon, acetate and triacetate.

7.2 WORLD PRODUCTION

In 2006, 2.5 million metric tonnes of regenerated cellulose fibres were produced globally. Of these, 97% was rayon (staple and filaments) and 3% was acetate (filaments). A very large chunk (80%) was produced in Asia. 17% was produced in Western Europe, while the remaining 3% was produced by Central and Eastern Europe and Central and Southern America. Among the Asian countries, China reigns supreme, followed closely by India. The Aditya Birla Group's company—Grasim is the world's second largest producer of rayon.

7.3 MANUFACTURING PROCESS

7.3.1 Rayon

The term 'rayon' is used for regenerated cellulosic fibres. This family of fibres has many members. Salient among these are viscose rayon, cuprammonium rayon, high tenacity rayon, high wet modulus rayon and tencel.

Viscose rayon

Cotton linters and chipped wood pulp are first treated with calcium bisulphite. This is followed by boiling with steam for about 14 hours under pressure. Such process helps to soften the lignin without damaging the cellulose in any way. The pulp thus obtained may now be bleached with sodium hypochlorite. After this, the water is pressed out to obtain thin sheets measuring about 2 × 2′. These sheets which have a pure cellulose content of 90 to 94% are steeped in a cold alkaline solution (17.5% NaOH) which converts the cellulose into alkali or soda cellulose. The alkalised sheets are shredded into a crumb form by passing through a shredding machine. These are now stored in a non-reacting container and aged for a fixed time (3 to 4 days), under controlled temperature (22°C) and humidity. After ageing, the crumbs are shifted to a xanthating churn in which 10% on weight of carbon disulphide (CS_2) is added and allowed to react for about 2 hours. This churn has a water cover that prevents increase in temperature. The colour of the crumbs changes from white to bright orange. Chemically, sodium cellulose xanthate is formed. The excess CS_2 is evaporated and the crumbs are dissolved in dilute NaOH (5–8%). The colour changes to that of honey, Titanium dioxide (TiO_2) is added and the liquid is filtered 2–3 times and aged till it gets the right viscosity. Ripening is done for about 4 days. The viscosity initially decreases, then increases. A simple test is done to judge if the correct viscosity has been achieved. The solution is added to 40% acetic acid. If it dissolves, it is not yet ready. But if it coagulates, then it can be taken to a storage tank for filtration and removal of air bubbles.

Wet spinning is done into a dilute acid bath (see Chapter 9 for details on wet spinning). The coagulating bath is made of sheet lead and could be kept at room temperature or at elevated temperature (40–55°C). The composition and temperature of the spin bath influences the rates of coagulation of the cellulose xanthate.

The acid bath interacts with the viscous solution and causes coagulation of the cellulose xanthate into filaments.

Filaments are withdrawn continuously from the acid bath and further treated with hot dilute acid to force the regeneration of the cellulose xanthate back to pure cellulose with the release of CS_2.

The above manufacturing process can be summarised in the form of a simple schematic diagram (Figure 7.1).

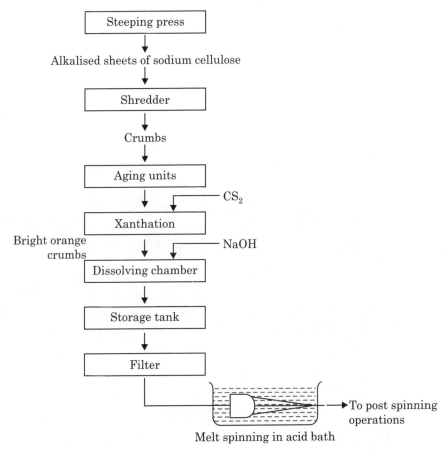

Figure 7.1 Schematic diagram of viscose rayon production.

Contents of the acid bath are as follows:

55–59% water which is the basic ingredient

17–20% Na_2SO_4 which slows the process of coagulation

9–10% H_2SO_4 to neutralise NaOH in the dope

4–10% of corn syrup to give a certain amount of viscosity and 1.1% $ZnSO_4$ to slow down the process of coagulation. This helps to impart greater strength and lesser serration in the cross section.

Figure 7.2 depicts the chemical reactions involved in the manufacture of viscose rayon.

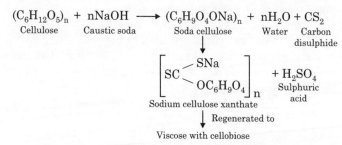

Figure 7.2 Chemical reactions of viscose manufacture.

Cuprammonium rayon

Cotton linters and wood pulp are purified and bleached. The raw material is then dissolved in a solution of aqueous ammonia (NH_3) and copper sulphate ($CuSO_4$). It is put in a mixer along with caustic soda (NaOH). The resulting solution is clear and blue in colour. The step of ripening or ageing, which was so important in viscose manufacture, is not required for cuprammonium production. The solution is filtered to remove any undissolved particles. It is then wet spun (see Chapter 9 for details). The spinneret is dipped in pure, soft water.

Movement of water stretches the new formed filaments and introduces a small amount of molecular orientation. Filaments are neutralised in sulphuric acid, followed by washing, lubrication, drying, twisting into yarn and winding. Figure 7.3 gives a flowchart for this process.

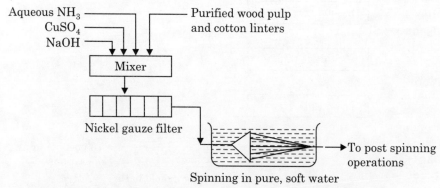

Figure 7.3 Schematic diagram for cuprammonium rayon manufacture.

High tenacity (HT) rayon

As the name suggests, this member of the rayon family possesses superior tensile strength as compared to regular viscose. HT rayon has a greater percentage of crystalline regions which translate to greater strength. To achieve this, certain modifications are made in the composition of the acid bath like increasing the quantities of H_2SO_4 and $ZnSO_4$. These help to retard the coagulation of viscose. A greater stretch ratio is also imparted to improve the orientation.

High wet modulus (HWM) rayon

Such fibres do not exhibit drastic reduction in strength when wet. Once again certain alterations are made in the spinning conditions and bath concentrations. These include longer immersion time, lower bath temperature, shorter ageing time and greater amounts of CS_2 as well as $ZnSO_4$. Apart from these, higher draw ratios are also employed to achieve much higher tenacities in dry as well as wet conditions. The HWM rayon is more like cotton in its physical, mechanical and chemical properties.

Tencel

This is a high tenacity rayon fibre introduced in 1989 by Courtalds. Wood pulp is dissolved in hot amine oxide and the resulting clear viscous solution is filtered. Gel spinning is done in a bath that contains dilute amine oxide. Fibres are washed and dried while the solvent is recovered and recycled. Over the years, use of Tencel fibre is on the increase, even in India.

7.3.2 Acetate

Secondary acetate

Cotton linters and wood pulp are purified by boiling with alkali and bleached with hypochlorite bleach. The prepared raw material is then mixed with glacial acetic acid and acetic anhydride. A small quantity of sulphuric acid is also added and the mixture is stored in pre-treatment tanks for a specified time period. The mixture is then transferred to kneading machines (acetylators) that help to thoroughly blend acetic anhydride solution that is added to the mass. At this stage, triacetate gets formed by a substitution of three hydroxyl groups per glucose molecule with acetyl groups. Ripening or ageing is the next step for which storage tanks are used. Water is added so that some acetyl groups are replaced with hydroxyl groups. Chemically, it can be said that secondary acetate gets formed at the end of the ripening stage. Water is mixed with the aim of precipitating acetate in the form of small flakes. These are thoroughly washed with water and dried.

For spinning into filaments, these flakes are dissolved in acetone, filtered and dry spun in a warm air chamber (see dry chemical spinning,

Chapter 9). A schematic chart for production of acetate is given in Figure 7.4.

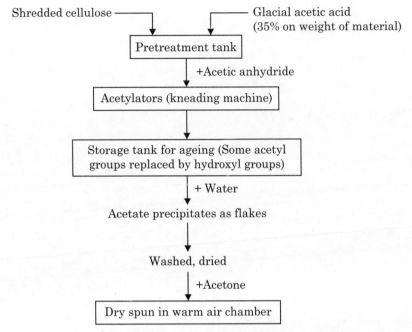

Figure 7.4 Schematic chart for acetate manufacture.

Primary acetate

This is also referred to as *triacetate*. Production steps are like those of secondary acetate with two differences—there is no ageing step employed and the volatile solvent used in this case is methylene chloride.

7.4 CHEMICAL COMPOSITION

Although both rayon and acetate have the same raw material, yet the term 'regenerated' cellulosics can be used aptly only for rayon. The chemical composition of acetate and triacetate is not cellulose but a chemical variation of cellulose known as an **ester** (Collier *et al.*, 2009). The use of the term 'modified' cellulosic would fit these fibres better. This explains why some of the properties of acetate and triacetate do not match with those of other cellulosic fibres.

Chemically, viscose can be termed as a sodium salt of cellulose xanthic acid (Trotman,1984). Just like natural cellulosic fibres, the basic unit of the rayon molecule is cellobiose which is a pair of glucose monomers (Figure 7.5).

One might wonder that if the basic building block for natural and regenerated fibres is the same, then what causes the phenomenal difference in their strength? Well, the answer lies in the number of

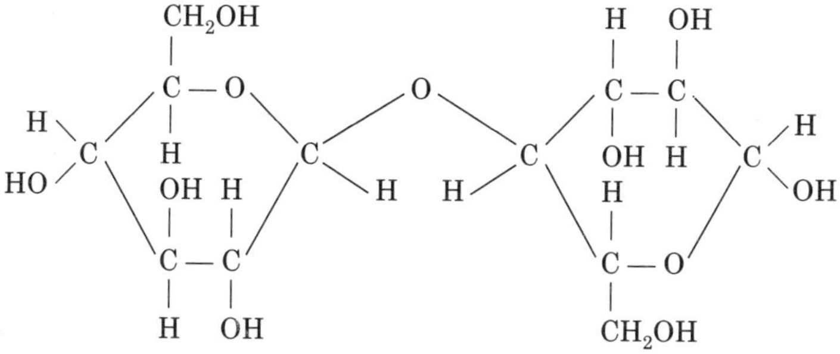

Figure 7.5 Structure of cellobiose.

monomers or the degree of polymerisation of these fibres. There is a major difference, as exhibited in Table 7.1

Table 7.1 Degree of Polymerisation

Natural cellulosic fibres	Regenerated cellulosic fibres
Cotton 5000	Viscose 175
Flax 18000	HWM 300
	Cuprammonium rayon 250
	Acetate 130
	Triacetate 225

Both acetate and triacetate are cellulose polymers, whose —OH groups have been acetylated to form the ester of acetic acid or acetate. In the manufacturing process, triacetate is produced first. Thus, it is also referred to as *primary cellulose acetate fibre*. The prefix 'tri' denotes that three hydroxyl (—OH) groups per glucose molecule are substituted by the acetyl radical (—$OOCCH_3$) during 'acetylation'. Figure 7.6 depicts the repeating unit of triacetate. To obtain the secondary cellulose acetate fibre, triacetate is reacted with water (hydrolysed). This leads to reconversion of about one acetyl group to the hydroxyl group (encircled in the figure). Thus, each glucose unit will have two acetyl groups (underlined in the figure) (Figure 7.7).

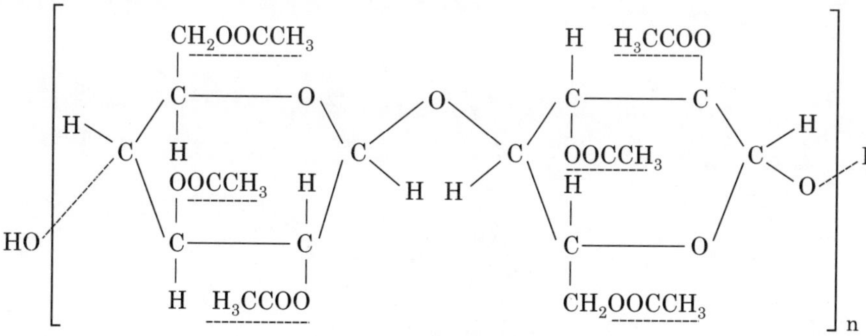

Triacetate polymer

Figure 7.6

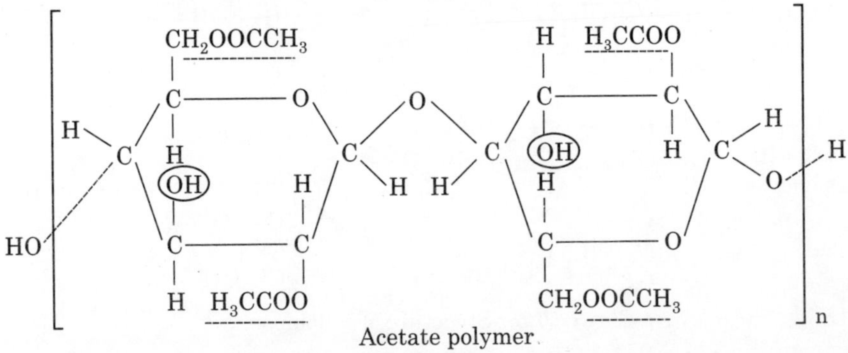

Acetate polymer.

Figure 7.7

7.5 PROPERTIES

Before beginning the discussion on properties of the two regenerated fibres, it must be clearly understood that while these two fibres viz., rayon and acetate have similar raw materials they differ drastically in one respect. Thus, while properties of rayon follow the general trend of natural cellulosic fibres, acetate is thermoplastic in nature like the synthetic fibres.

7.5.1 Microscopic Characterisation

Longitudinal Section (L.S.): Rayon as well as acetate fibres show an irregular L.S. with striations along the length. These lines appear due to uneven light reflection in the convoluted structures. Cuprammonium rayon, tencel and other variants have a more regular structure and hence do not show these striations. Figure 7.8 shows the longitudinal sections of the various regenerated fibres.

Figure 7.8 Longitudinal section of regenerated fibres.

Addition of the delusterant is indicated by specks that are visible in the cross as well as longitudinal sections of the regenerated fibre.

Cross section: Regular viscose has an extremely irregular cross section. The coagulation and precipitation of the filaments in wet spinning involves a two way transfer and it becomes difficult to control the final cross section. High tenacity rayon has a somewhat smoother shape while cuprammonium rayon exhibits a more or less rounded cross section. Tencel, which is solvent spun, has a smooth, cylindrical shaped C.S.

As for acetate and triacetate, the C.S. is somewhat regular since the method of spinning is dry spinning. Figure 7.9 shows the cross sections of various regenerated cellulosic fibres.

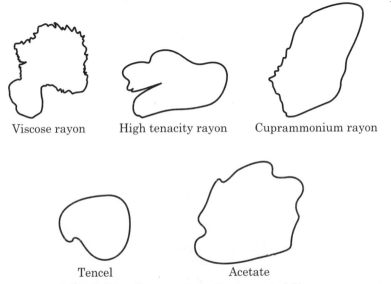

Viscose rayon   High tenacity rayon   Cuprammonium rayon

Tencel   Acetate

Figure 7.9   Cross section of regenerated fibres.

7.5.2   Physical Properties

Length, Fineness, Colour and Lustre: Being manufactured fibres, each of these properties of rayon as well as acetate is variable and can be altered as per requirement. It must also be remembered that wet spinning process used in the case of rayons leads to an irregular cross section and a serrated structure producing high shine in fibres. It was this sheen that made people refer to rayons as "artificial silk" or "art silk" when they first appeared in the market.

Tenacity: In general, it can be stated that regenerated cellulosic fibres are weaker than natural cellulosics. Table 7.2 lists the tenacity of these fibres. As can be observed, these fibres lose strength when wet. It is, thus, important that a careful handling is done while washing or any other wet treatment of fabrics made from these fibres.

Table 7.2 Dry and Wet Tenacities (g/d) of Regenerated Cellulosic Fibres

Fibre	Dry	Wet
Viscose rayon	1.0–5.0	0.5–1.5
HT rayon	3.5–5.3	2.0–3.0
HWM rayon	4.0–5.0	2.0–3.0
Cupra rayon	1.9–2.0	1.0–1.7
Acetate	1.0–1.5	2.5–3.5

Elongation and resiliency: In the case of regenerated cellulosic fibres elastic recovery is poor and resiliency is low, thus making the fabrics prone to wrinkling, creasing and crushing. In the category of rayons, HWM rayon and tencel have better resiliency than regular viscose rayon. Triacetate is more resilient than acetate.

Density: Rayon has a density of 1.5 g/cm^3, while that for acetate and triacetate is 1.3 g/cm^3. Thus, fabrics made from acetate and triacetate are lighter in weight as compared to cotton, linen and rayon.

Moisture regain: At 70°F and 65% rh, (standard conditions), the moisture regain of viscose rayon is 13%, tencel 11.5%, acetate 6.5% and triacetate 3.2%. It may be recalled here that viscose has a high percentage of hydroxyl groups present in amorphous regions that contribute to hygroscopic behaviour. Fibres with high moisture regain will take up dyes and finishes readily and be comfortable to wear.

Inspite of nearly 60% amorphous regions, acetate exhibits lower regain. The reason can be attributed to the relatively low polarity of the acetate polymer. The difference between the moisture regains of acetate and triacetate can be explained on the basis of number of hydroxyl groups. Acetate, with a greater number of these, exhibits more polarity which enhances its hygroscopic behaviour. It may also be noted that heat setting, when carried out for acetate and triacetate fibre, reduces the moisture uptake drastically.

Thermal properties: Rayon is flammable i.e., it ignites quickly, burns freely and has an afterglow. Being cellulosic in composition, the odour is similar to burning paper. After burning, the residue obtained is fluffy grey ash.

Safe ironing temperature falls in the same range as cotton viz., 180–200°C. The ignition temperature for rayon is, however, greater than that of cotton. At 420°C rapid decomposition and charring occurs.

The difference in the chemical composition of regenerated and modified fibres becomes quite obvious when their thermal properties are compared. Acetate and triacetate are thermoplastic in nature. This implies that they can be softened and heat set at their glass transition temperatures (175°C for acetate and 212°C for triacetate). Safe ironing temperatures are around 130°C for acetate and 150°C for heat set triacetate. Both fibres burn in flame with melting and residue is a hard bead.

7.5.3 Chemical Properties

Acids: Rayon is carbonized by hot acids. Cold concentrated acids cause gradual fibre tendering and disintegration. Brief exposure to dilute acids at cold temperatures does not cause any damage.

Acetate is damaged by acids. The fibre gets weakened even by cold, dilute acids if the exposure time is long,

Alkalies: Rayon is not damaged by alkaline solutions.

Acetate can withstand dilute alkalies but gets saponified by concentrated alkaline solutions. At pH values more than 9.5, an irreversible change in hand occurs.

Organic solvents: Rayon is highly resistant to organic solvents and, thus, can be easily dry cleaned. Acetate, on the other hand, is susceptible to damage by many organic solvents. Thus, acetone cannot be used for cleaning of acetate fabric as it will soften and dissolve the fibre. Caution is also needed in using chloroform, trichloroethylene and methyl ethyl ketone. These dry cleaning reagents can swell and soften acetate.

7.5.4 Biological Properties

Silver fish attacks the starch on rayon and acetate fabric. Moths do not attack rayon or acetate fibres but their blends with wool can be chewn up by moths.

Mildew and bacteria can eventually destroy rayon, making it biodegradable and hence an ideal fibre for disposable non-wovens. Mildew leads to discolouration and eventual strength loss in acetate.

7.5.5 Other Properties

Dimensional stability: Both viscose and acetate have a tendency to exhibit relaxation shrinkage during laundering. Shrinkage control finishes can help combat this problem to a great extent. Acetate and triacetate, which have been heat set, shows good dimensional stability. Triacetate retains its shape better than acetate.

Static electricity: Rayon does not develop any static charges but acetate is a poor conductor, thus leading to static charge build-up. The limited hygroscopic behaviour in dry conditions further aggravate the problem in triacetate fibres.

Sunlight: Prolonged exposure to UV radiation can cause tendering in rayon and acetate. On comparison, it can be stated that sunlight resistance is less than natural cellulosics but better than that of silk.

7.6 USES

Rayon is widely used in apparel as well as home textiles. Industrial uses include medical textiles, surgical pads and operating drapes.

The fibre is commonly blended with one or more other fibres from cellulosic, protein or synthetic family. Over the years, Rayon has carved a niche for itself as a substitute for cotton. It is, thus, common to find blends of polyester–viscose flooding the market and people's wardrobes and homes. Compared with cotton, rayon scores in two aspects, viz., lower price and higher moisture absorbency.

Acetate is popular in the area of womens apparel due to its soft hand and drape. It is also a common choice for garment linings. In the sphere of home textiles, acetate is used as upholstery. The fact that it is thermoplastic and can, thus, be imparted interesting surface design features goes in its favour. However, the other side of the coin is that acetate drapery linings can split on exposure to sunlight and its colours (imparted by disperse dyes) can fade or change hue in presence of air pollutants. The fabric also exhibits low abrasion resistance. Among industrial applications, the most predominant usage of acetate is seen in the cigarette industry where it is used as filters.

7.7   CARE

Rayon can be laundered and dry cleaned much in the same way as cotton. It does face the problem of excessive wrinkle formation but use of finishes can tackle this to a large extent. When blended with wool, extra care is needed during the storage to protect the fabric from moths.

Acetate and triacetate are more delicate and hence require greater care. Only recommended solvents can be used for stain removal and cleaning. Being thermoplastic, care is needed to ensure that only safe temperatures are used for laundry and ironing.

7.8   ORGANISATIONS IN THIS SECTOR

- Association of Man-made Fibre Industry of India, Mumbai
- Man-made Textile Research Association (MANTRA), Surat
- Synthetic and Art Silk Mills Research Association (SASMIRA), Mumbai
- Synthetic and Rayon Textile Export Promotion Council.(SRTEPC)

EXERCISES

7.1 Describe the manufacture of regular viscose rayon.

7.2 Give two properties that distinguish 'regenerated' cellulosics from 'modified' cellulosic fibres. What are the reasons for this difference?

7.3 Enumerate the various members of the rayon family. Which are the oldest and youngest of these?

7.4 Enlist the modifications needed to produce HWM rayon.

7.5 Write a note on the uses of acetate.

7.6 Make a schematic diagram for the manufacture of triacetate. Why is it also called **primary acetate**?

REFERENCES

Collier, B.J., Bide, M.J. and Tortora, P.G., *Understanding Textiles,* 7th ed., Pearson Education, NJ, 2009.

Trotman, E.R., *Dyeing and Chemical Technology of Textile Fibres*, 6th ed., Griffin, 1984.

SUGGESTED READING

Corbman, B.P., *Textiles Fibre to Fabric*, 6th ed., McGraw-Hill, 1983.

Joseph, M.J., *Essentials of Textiles*, 4th ed., The Dryden Press Saunders College Publishers, 1988.

Kadolph, S.J. and Langford, A.L., *Textiles,* 10th ed., Pearson Education, NJ, 2007.

Wingate, I.B., *Fairchild's Dictionary of Textiles*, 6th ed., Universal Publishing Corporation, Mumbai, 1988.

CHAPTER

8

Synthetic and Inorganic Fibres

The second category of manufactured fibres are the synthetics. These are made from chemicals as the starting material. These may be further classified as condensation polymers (nylon, polyester), addition polymers (acrylic, olefin) and block copolymers (spandex). This chapter deals with each of these fibres.

In the third and last category of manufactured fibres are the inorganic fibres. These include glass and metallic fibres, which are also discussed in brief.

NYLON

TFPIA defines nylon as "a manufactured fibre in which the fibre forming substance is a long chain synthetic polymer in which less than 85% of the amide linkages attach directly to two aromatic rings".

Although there are many types of nylons, the two commercially popular varieties are nylon 6 and nylon 6, 6. The nomenclature is based on the number of carbon atoms present in the raw material.

8.1 HISTORY AND WORLD PRODUCTION

Nylon and polyester owe their births to the basic research done by Dr. Wallace H. Carothers. The word *nylon* was derived from 'no-run', the name originally considered by its inventors to emphasize the durability of ladies' hosiery manufactured from it (Gohl and Vilensky, 1987). Nylon was first developed in 1938 by Du Pont in USA. Commercial production commenced a year later, in 1939. Today, the global nylon production is 5130 thousand tonnes. As for the world share, 43% comes from Asia, 30% from North America, 13% from West Europe and 3% from Middle East. The remaining is produced in other countries in small proportions. USA as a single country dominates the nylon producer's list.

8.2 CHEMISTRY AND MANUFACTURING STEPS

The reaction of a dibasic acid with a diamine, forms a long chain polyamide, called **nylon**. The nylon polymer has two chemical groups that help in the formation of hydrogen bonds. The polar amide group (—CO—NH—), is the most important chemical group present in nylon. The hydrogen atom (imino hydrogen) has a slight positive charge, while the oxygen atom (carbonyl oxygen) has a slight negative charge. This contributes to the polarity of the amide group. The second chemical group is the amino (—NH_2) group, present at the ends of the nylon polymer. Nylon has 65–85% crystalline and 35–15% amorphous regions.

Raw material for nylon 6 is caprolactam $(CH_2)_5CONH$; the nomenclature is indicative of the fact that there are six carbon atoms. Nylon 6, 6 is made from adipic acid $HOOC(CH_2)_4COOH$ and hexamethylene diamine $H_2N(CH_2)_6NH_2$. As you can observe, each of the two raw materials has six carbon atoms.

The manufacturing steps are given below:

1. *Polymerisation:* Caprolactam is polymerised by any one of the following two methods:

   (a) liquefied, treated and filtered under high pressure;
   (b) water (10% o.w.) is added to caprolactam after which the two are heated to a high temperatures; steam escapes and polymerisation takes place. The unchanged monomer is extracted.

   For nylon 6, 6 the two raw materials are mixed in a reaction chamber. Condensation polymerisation takes place in an air free atmosphere. The degree of polymerisation is 200 for nylon 6 and 50–80 for nylon 6, 6. Water (by-product) is allowed to escape from the reacting tank. Delustrant is added to the polymer in order to reduce its shine.

   The molten polymer formed is extruded from the tank as a ribbon, several inches wide. This is quenched in cold water, dried and made into nylon chips which can be stored and used when needed. The polymer in the case of nylon 6 is linear caprolactam $(—HN(CH_2)_5\ CO—)_n$ while, for nylon 6, 6, it is hexamethylene diaminoadipate $(—HN(CH_2)_6NHOC(CH_2)_4\ CO—)_n$.

2. *Spinning:* Melt spinning is carried out (refer to Chapter 9 for details). An electrically heated grid is used for this purpose such that its gaps are too small to allow unmelted chips. A molten pool is formed which is filtered to remove any impurities. Next, it is pumped through a spinneret. Nylon 6 has a lower melting point than nylon 6, 6.

3. *Drawing:* Cold air is blown when the filaments move out of the spinning jet. This helps to parallelise or orient the molecules, making the fibre somewhat stronger. Lubrication and crimping follows. If required, they are cut or pulled and broken into staple fibres.

8.3   PROPERTIES OF NYLON

8.3.1   Microscopic Properties

The nylon filament is melt spun. This implies that its shape and appearance can be engineered very accurately. Further, the shape of spinneret holes through which the molten polymer is pushed out, will decide the kind of cross section.

Longitudinal section (L.S.):   As shown in Figure 8.1, nylon has a smooth, uniform and rod like longitudinal section. Dark specks are visible all along the L.S. These appear due to use of delustering agent.

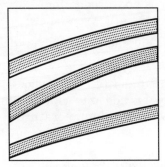

Figure 8.1   Longitudinal section of nylon.

Cross section (C.S.):   Nylon has a regular cross section in which the spots of delustering agent are visible (see Figure 8.2). A circular shape is depicted in the diagram, although variations are possible.

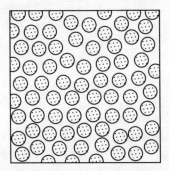

Figure 8.2   Cross section of nylon.

8.3.2   Physical Properties

Length, diameter, colour and lustre: These are controlled by the manufacturer.

Tenacity: Nylon is a strong fibre, with dry tenacity ranging from 4.6–8.8 gpd. There is a slight decline of 10–20% in strength in wet conditions.

Elongation and elastic recovery: Under standard conditions, nylon 6 has an elongation of 16–50%; values for nylon 6, 6 range from 19–40%. Both nylons have an excellent elastic recovery of 100% (at 2% elongation). The reason for such a good elastic nature is the regular grid of strong hydrogen bonds present in the nylon polymer.

Resiliency: Nylon is endowed with very good resiliency, which is further enhanced by heat setting. Thus, apparel made from nylon does not face the problem of wrinkle or crease formation.

Density: A density of 1.14 g/cm^3, makes nylon one of the lightest fibres in use (olefin being the lightest).

Moisture regain: Nylon 6 has a moisture regain of 2.5–5.0%, while that for nylon 6, 6 is 4.0–4.5%. On comparison, it can be stated that nylon has a higher regain than other synthetic fibres.

Thermal properties: Nylon, being thermoplastic, can be heat set. When heat is applied under controlled conditions, some of the hydrogen bonds break. On cooling, they re-form in the desired places and remain thus, provided the heat setting temperature is not crossed in the care procedures. Table 8.1 compares the thermal properties of the two kinds of nylons.

Table 8.1 Salient Thermal Properties of Nylon 6 and Nylon 6, 6

Thermal property	Nylon 6	Nylon 6, 6
Safe ironing temperature	150°C	170°C
Softening temperature	175°C	180°C
Melting temperature	215°C	255°C

It can, thus, be summed that nylon 6 fibres are more sensitive to heat than nylon 6, 6. Burning behaviour shows that nylon curls and shrinks away from flame. It catches fire and begins to melt and drip. An acrid odour and residue of hard black bead are also typical of nylon.

8.3.3 Chemical Properties

Acids: Nylon has a good resistance to mild acids but is harmed by strong acids. It dissolves in formic acid and this fact is used for its identification.

Alkalies, chlorine bleaches and organic solvents: These are used in dry cleaning and do not damage nylon fibres.

8.3.4 Biological and Other Properties

Nylon has excellent resistance to carpet beetles, clothes moths, mildew, bacteria and fungi.

Dimensional stability: Nylon exhibits good dimensional stability when laundered or dry cleaned.

Static charge: Nylon faces the problem of static charge build-up. The problem gets more pronounced under dry conditions.

Sunlight: Nylon does not have very good resistance to sunlight.

8.4   USES OF NYLON

Well-known for its strength and superior chemical as well as biological resistance, nylon finds extensive usage in industrial applications. Parachute and tent fabrics, automobile upholstery, ropes, tyre cords, conveyor belts, mosquito nets and bristles for hair and tooth brushes are common objects made using nylon. Carpets are another popular application area. Being fine and soft, nylon is used in apparel for its pleasant next-to-skin feel. Although the fibre does not have a high moisture absorbance, it can give a sense of comfort to the wearer due to its capillary action. Perspiration from the skin can travel to the outer surface by wicking. Nylon is thus, used extensively for construction of active sportswear. In the West, nylons are synonymous with stockings. Extremely sheer stockings can be made as also lingerie for women. In fact, nylon had a widespread usage only in the field of hosiery before World War II. Today, there are many variants of nylon. These have special properties and hence find applications in specific end uses. Examples are high bulk, high lustre and antistatic nylons.

8.5   CARE OF NYLON

Nylon brought with it the concept of "no fuss" garments for the first time. It can be washed by hand or machine and takes very little time to dry. One precaution that needs to be taken is that use of very hot water should be avoided as this can cause formation of wrinkles. Normal detergents can be used for laundry. It can be dry cleaned and bleached with chlorine bleaches as well. Nylon is hydrophobic to some extent and this makes it oleophilic. Thus, it has a greater tendency to pick up oil based stains. Ironing may be needed for some articles but only the recommended temperature settings should be followed. Storage of nylon does not need any special conditions since it has an excellent biological resistance.

POLYESTER

8.6   HISTORY AND WORLD PRODUCTION

Polyester was first launched in 1946. It is commonly referred to as *dacron* in USA and as *terylene* in England. This fibre accounts for over

75% of all manufactured fibres produced in the world. Today, global polyester production capacities touch 21 million tonnes of filament yarns and 15 million tonnes of staple fibres. Asia prides itself with an impressive lions share of 89% of filament and 83% world's polyester staple fibre capacities. Among the Asian countries, China reigns supreme, contributing to 57% of filament and 53% of staple fibre production. Other major polyester producing countries of Asia include India, Indonesia, South Korea and Taiwan. Outside Asia, the major polyester producers are USA and Turkey.

8.7   CHEMICAL COMPOSITION AND MANUFACTURE

Polyester means *many esters*. An ester, in turn, is formed when an alcohol reacts with an organic acid. It is represented by the formula —CO—O. Although many esters can be formed by use of different alcohols and acids, not all of them are suitable for conversion into filaments. The most commercially viable polyester is polyethylene terephthalate or PET. Other members of the polyester family include polybutylene terephthalate (PBT) and polyethylene oxy benzoate (PEB).

Over the years, PET has become synonymous with polyester. This section will deal with the production, properties, use and care of PET, which will be referred to as *polyester*.

The reaction involved in the synthesis of polyester is given in Figure 8.3.

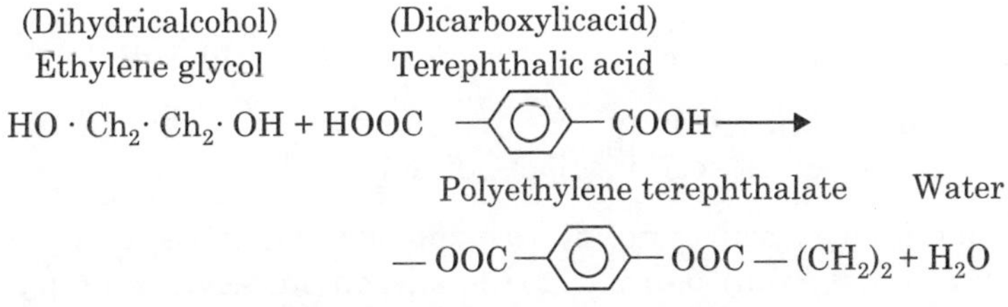

(Dihydricalcohol)   (Dicarboxylicacid)
Ethylene glycol   Terephthalic acid

$$HO \cdot Ch_2 \cdot Ch_2 \cdot OH + HOOC \text{—} \langle O \rangle \text{—} COOH \longrightarrow$$

Polyethylene terephthalate   Water

$$\text{—} OOC \text{—} \langle O \rangle \text{—} OOC \text{—} (CH_2)_2 + H_2O$$

Figure 8.3   Formation of polyester.

There are three important chemical groups present in polyester. These are ester groups (—OCO—), carbonyl groups (—OCO—) and methylene groups (—OCO$_2$—). The polyester polymer is slightly polar and contains two kinds of bonds. Van der Waal's forces predominate and play a significant role. Very weak hydrogen bonds are also present.

Polyester can be termed as a predominantly crystalline fibre with 65–85% crystalline regions and only 35–15% amorphous regions.

The manufacturing steps are as follows:

1. *Polymerisation:* The two raw materials—ethylene glycol HO · CH$_2$· CH$_2$· OH and terephthalic acid HOOC —$\langle O \rangle$— COOH are mixed in a reaction chamber at high temperature and under

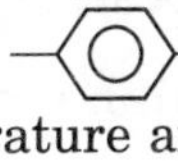

vacuum. Various catalysts may be used. Condensation polymerisation proceeds to form polyethylene terephthalate (PET). Water is the by-product in this case. The degree of polymerisation is 115–140.

The molten polymer that forms is pumped out, dried and cut into chips.

2. *Spinning:* Melt spinning is carried out (refer to Chapter 9 for details). The melting point of polyester is 280°C.

3. *Drawing:* This step of stretching the extruded filaments helps to orient and enhance the strength of the polyester filaments. The manufacturer may utilise 100% of the natural draw ratio present and produce fully oriented yarns (FOY). Alternatively, only some drawing may be done, leaving scope for further processing. Such yarns will be referred to as partially oriented yarns (POY). The remaining orientation occurs during texturing. After drawing, oiling is done. For staple fibres, the filaments prepared are cut or pulled and broken.

8.8 PROPERTIES OF POLYESTER

8.8.1 Microscopic Properties

The polyester filament is melt spun. Hence, its diameter and cross section can be accurately controlled.

Longitudinal Section (L.S.): Polyester has a smooth, uniform and rod like longitudinal section. Delustering treatment leads to dark specks (see Figure 8.4).

Cross Section (C.S.): Many cross sections are possible. Figure 8.5 depicts a circular cross section. Spots of delustering agent are visible.

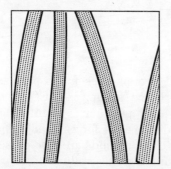
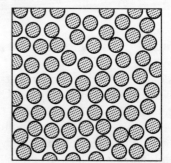

Figure 8.4 Longitudinal section of polyester.

Figure 8.5 Cross section of polyester.

8.8.2 Physical Properties

Length, diameter, colour and lustre: These are controlled by the manufacturer.

Tenacity: Dry tenacity ranges from 2.5–9.5 gpd. There is no deterioration in strength under wet conditions.

Elongation and elastic recovery: Under standard conditions, polyester has an elongation of 10–50%, depending on the type of fibre. Polyester has a very good elastic recovery of 90–100% (at 2% elongation).

Resiliency: Polyester has an excellent resiliency, which helps the fibre to get back to its shape after crushing.

Density: A density of 1.4 g/cm³, makes polyester heavier than nylon.

Moisture regain: A moisture regain of 0.4% makes polyester extremely hydrophobic. However, due to the wicking action, the moisture can travel to the outer surface.

Thermal properties: Of all the manufactured fibres, polyester is most thermoplastic in nature. This implies that it can be most easily heat set to incorporate the desired features like pleats and creases. It would also have a better retention of the incorporated feature, as compared with other synthetics. Safe ironing temperature for polyester is in the range of 120°C–150°C. Its melting temperature falls in the range of 240°C–290°C, which is more than that of nylon.

In flame, polyester burns with sputtering and gives a characteristic black smoke. The smell is that of chemicals and the residue is a non-crushable black bead.

8.8.3   Chemical Properties

Acids: Polyester can withstand the action of weak acids but is destroyed by strong acids.

Alkalies: It is good resistance to weak alkalies, moderate resistance to strong alkalies.

Common bleaches and organic solvents: These are used in stain removal and dry cleaning, respectively, and do not damage the polyester fibres.

8.8.4   Biological and Other Properties

Polyester has excellent resistance to insects and microbes.

Dimensional stability: Polyester exhibits good dimensional stability when laundered or dry cleaned.

Static charge: Being hydrophobic, polyester faces the problem of static charge build-up. This drawback is tackled by modifying polyester and application of finishes.

Sunlight: Polyester has excellent resistance to sunlight.

8.9 USES OF POLYESTER

Polyester finds a wide range of applications since it is the most versatile of the synthetic fibres. The filament yarns are textured and used extensively in the apparel sector. When cut into staple lengths, it is common to blend polyester with cotton, viscose and wool. The proportion varies with the required end use and helps to combine the good properties of both constituent fibres. Apparel applications include outerwear, shirts, trousers, suits, sarees, costumes, leisure wear, lingerie, rainwear, ties and scarves. High strength sewing threads are made from staple yarns. Many other industrial applications are also common. Examples include automobile seat belts, tyre cords, ship sails, geotextiles, artificial blood vessels and other medical textiles. In the home, polyester is commonly used as draperies, as a filling for pillows, mattresses and other quilted articles and for waddings in interlinings. Thus, it can be stated that the versatility of polyester makes it equally suitable for woven, knitted and non-woven constructions. Apart from regular or standard polyester fibre, special types have also been developed for particular end uses. These include high crimp, high tenacity, high shrink, antistatic, heat resistant, flame resistant, profiled and adhesive polyester fibre variants.

8.10 CARE OF POLYESTER

Polyester fabrics are easy to care for. They are hand/machine washable and quick to dry. Temperature during laundry should not exceed 60°C. Being wrinkle resistant, heavy ironing is not required. Care must be taken to avoid high temperatures while ironing, usual range being 150°C. No special precautions are needed for storage of polyester fabrics, since they have excellent biological resistance.

ACRYLIC

8.11 HISTORY AND WORLD PRODUCTION

Acrylonitrile, the starting material for acrylic fibres was first made in Germany in 1893 (Kadolph and Langford, 2007). Scientists figured out that because by itself it has no absorption for water, it needs to be copolymerised.

Du Pont of USA developed acrylic fibre in 1944. Commercial production began in 1950. Modacrylic was also made around the same time (1949). The two were referred to as one group till 1960, when separate nomenclature was evolved. Today, acrylic fibres account for 6.8% of the world's total manufactured fibres. Nearly, all production is done as staple fibres. Just as for nylon and polyester, Asia holds a major share in acrylic also. It contributes to 59.5% of the total global production.

8.12 CHEMICAL COMPOSITION AND MANUFACTURE

The main component of the acrylic polymer is the acrylonitrile monomer. Figure 8.6 shows the acrylonitrile group. The acrylic polymer system is held together by Van der Waal's forces of attraction. There are about 70–80% crystalline regions and 30–20% amorphous regions in acrylic.

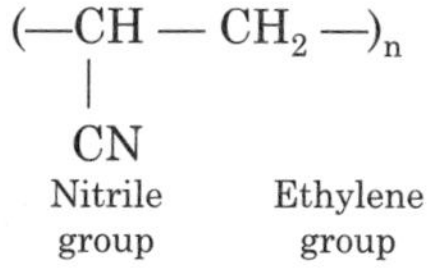

$$(-CH-CH_2-)_n$$
$$|$$
$$CN$$

Nitrile   Ethylene
group   group

Figure 8.6   Acrylonitrile group.

The remaining constituents in the fibres are one or more monomers that combine by addition polymerisation. Table 8.2 sums up the chemical composition of the two poly acrylonitrile fibres. Some of the commonly used comonomers include acrylamide, acrylic acid, halogen monomers, methacrylate, sodium vinylbenzene sulphonate, vinyl acetate, vinylidene chloride and vinyl pyridine.

Table 8.2   Chemical Composition of Acrylic and Modacrylic

Constituents	Acrylic	Modacrylic
Acrylonitrile units	at least 85%	at least 35% but less than 85%
Comonomers	15%	65 to 15%
Degree of polymerisation (approx.)	2000	2000

Manufacturing steps can be summarised as follows:

1. *Polymerisation:* The acrylonitrile is made to polymerise with one or more selected monomers in a reactor.
2. *Resulting polymer is dissolved in appropriate solvent:* It may be mentioned here that choice of solvent will be made on the basis of method of chemical spinning employed. Dry spinning can be done, using DMF, or wet spinning can be carried out using a bath of dimethyl acetamide (for details on chemical spinning, refer to Chapter 9).
3. *Spinning:* i.e. Extrusion of the solution through a spinnerete.
4. *Post spinning operations:* These include, lubrication, imparting waviness and cutting of filaments into staple fibres.

8.13 PROPERTIES OF ACRYLIC

8.13.1 Microscopic Properties

Since acrylic is a manufactured fibre, its microscopic features can be controlled. The fact that it is not melt spun (like nylon and polyester) means that the exact control is difficult. Figure 8.7 shows a representative longitudinal section (L.S.) while Figure 8.8 depicts a round cross section of these fibres. Other options include multilobal, dog-bone and kidney shapes. Striations are a characteristic feature of these yarns. Specks of delustrant are also visible. The microscopic appearance cannot be used to identify acrylic fibres.

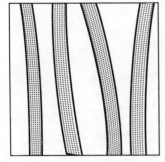 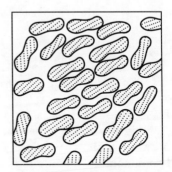

Figure 8.7 Longitudinal section of acrylic.

Figure 8.8 Cross section of acrylic.

8.13.2 Physical Properties

Length, diameter, colour and lustre: These are variable and can be controlled by the manufacturer.

Tenacity: The tenacity of acrylic and modacrylic can be termed as fair to good; under dry conditions it is 2.0–4.2 gpd for acrylic while that for modacrylic is 2.0–3.1 gpd. On wetting, acrylic witnesses a slight drop in its strength. The reason is that water enters the amorphous regions of the polymer and breaks some of the Van der Waals' forces.

Elongation and elastic recovery: Elasticity of these fibres varies. Both have a good elastic recovery. At 2% elongation, acrylic has an elastic recovery of 92%, while modacrylic has a score of 99%.

Resiliency: These fibres are extremely resilient in nature. This property is utilized in the construction of high pile fabrics.

Density: A value of 1.25–1.34 g/cm^3 makes these fibres light in weight.

Moisture regain: Acrylic has low regain of 1.0–2.5 %, owing to its extremely crystalline nature. Modacrylic has a higher value of 2.5–4.0% and the reason can be assigned to a greater percentage of comonomers, some having more polar groups that attract water.

Thermal properties: Acrylics are highly inflammable. Certain modacrylics are made using halogenated compounds that impart superior properties. An example is teklan, which is a chlorine containing modacrylic. Such fibres do not burn but instead they melt, char and disintegrate. Melting point is in the range of 450–490°F, while safe ironing temperature is 300°F.

Burning behaviour conforms to that of synthetics. Both fibres burn with a chemical smell and leave a residue of hard black bead.

8.13.3 Chemical Properties

Acids: Acrylic and modacrylic have good resistant to acids.

Alkalies: These fibres can withstand alkalies but sometimes undergo saponification on the surface. This leads to a yellowing of the fabric.

Organic solvents: The common organic solvents used in dry cleaning do not harm acrylic and modacrylic fibres.

8.13.4 Biological and Other Properties

Acrylic and modacrylic have excellent resistance to clothes moths, carpet beetles, mildew, bacteria and fungi. This is one reason why it is acting as a substitute for wool in winter apparel.

Dimensional stability: When heat set, both these fibres show good dimensional stability. They also do not shrink on wetting. Non-heat set fabrics have a soft handle and this leads to the problem of crushing and stretching. Use of heat while tumble drying in a machine can further aggravate the problem.

Static charge: Being poor conductors of water, acrylic and modacrylic can pose the problem of static charge build-up.

Sunlight: Acrylic and modacrylic can be termed as the most sunlight resistant fibres.

Table 8.3 compares the chief properties of polyester, nylon 6, nylon 6, 6, acrylic and modacrylic—the synthetic fibres in common use.

8.14 USES OF ACRYLIC

The salient points that go in favour of acrylic are that it is light in weight, soft and insulative. An excellent resistance to sunlight, chemicals and insects have made acrylic pose a tough competition to wool. These properties, coupled with lower prices have led to its popularity in winter apparel, including imitation fur, sweaters and even knitting yarns. In the home, acrylic is used as blankets, curtains, carpets and in pile rugs. Acrylic also has industrial end uses. It can be used alone or blended with other fibres.

Some trade names for acrylic are Cashmilon, Orlon, Zefran, Acrilan, Creslan.

Modacrylic

Common applications include simulated fur and pile fabrics, blankets, carpets, curtains and sleepwear. It finds a favourable market in these products because of its inherently flame retardant nature. Among industrial usages, filters of modacrylic are widely used due to their light weight and excellent chemical resistance.

Table 8.3   Comparative Properties of Synthetic Fibres

Property	Polyester	Nylon 6, 6	Nylon 6	Acrylic	Modacrylic
Shape (length and diameter)	can be	controlled	for	these	fibres
Lustre	can be	controlled	for	these	fibres
Strength (dry)	2.5–9.5 gpd	4.6–8.8 gpd	4.9–8.5 gpd	2.0–4.2 gpd	2.0–3.1 gpd
Strength (wet)	2.5–9.5 gpd	4.0–7.6 gpd	4.2–8.0 gpd	1.6–3.8 gpd	2.0–3.1 gpd
Elastic recovery	90–100% at 2% extension	100% at 4% extension	100% at 4% extension	90–95% at 2% extension	80–90% at 2% extension
Resiliency	Excellent	Good–very good	Good–very good	Good	Very good
Moisture absorption	0.4% very low <0.5% and wickable	4.0–4.5%	2.5–5.0%	1.0–2.5%	2.5–4.0%
Acids	Can withstand weak acids, is destroyed by strong acids	Poor resistance to acids	Poor resistance to acids	Good resistance to weak acids, fair but resistance to strong acids	Good to excellent resistance
Alkali	Good resistance to weak alkali Moderate to strong alkali	Good resistance to alkali	Good resistance to alkali	Good resistance to weak alkali Fair resistance to strong alkali	Good resistance
Sunlight	Excellent behind glass, no direct sunlight otherwise	excellent	excellent	excellent	excellent
Biological	Excellent biological resistance	Excellent biological resistance	Excellent biological resistance	Excellent biological resistance	Excellent biological resistance

Table 8.3 Comparative Properties of Synthetic Fibres (*Contd...*)

Property	Polyester	Nylon 6, 6	Nylon 6	Acrylic	Modacrylic
Thermal ironing, melting point	121°C, 240–290°C melting point	151–175°C, 250°C	150°C, 210°C	<160°C, 190°C	Does not support combustion, burns very slowly
Flame	Melts, thermo-plastic, non-crushable bead	Melts, thermo-plastic, non-crushable bead	Melts, thermo-plastic, non-crushable bead	Burns readily with melting, after glow	Shrinks away from flame, is difficult to ignite, self-extingui-shing, drips less

8.15 CARE OF ACRYLIC

Acrylic and modacrylic fabrics can be machine or hand washed, using normal detergents. Precaution must be taken to avoid high temperature in washing, drying and ironing of these fabrics. When blended with wool, dry cleaning can also be a good option. Pilling can pose a problem and can be kept to a minimal by reversing the article to its wrong side while washing. Storage does not require specific conditions as in the case of wool due to superior biological resistance of these fibres.

8.16 OLEFINS

Olefins are aliphatic (open chain) hydrocarbons, containing only carbon and hydrogen atoms. Double-bonded carbons produce structures called **alkenes**. Two such alkenes have been used to make filaments. These are ethylene (C_2H_4) and propylene (C_3H_6). On being given appropriate conditions like heat and catalysts, these alkenes undergo addition polymerisation to yield polyethylene (PE) and polypropylene (PP) polymers which have at least 85% by weight of the starter alkene units.

The use of plastics started around World War II, but production of olefin fibres took another decade. Polypropylene was commercially produced in Italy in 1957. The credit for polyolefin synthesis goes to two scientists—Karl Zeigler of Germany and C. Natta of Italy. In 1963, they were awarded the nobel prize in Chemistry for their work on polyolefin synthesis (Hudson et. al., 1993).

Production

Alkenes are produced from alkanes during the cracking of petroleum. As already mentioned, the monomers yield polymers (Figure 8.9), when supplied the right conditions. Three options exist for conversion of the polymer into filaments. Melt spinning or gel spinning can be carried out. A third way is to extrude the molten polymer in the form of a sheet which is then pulled or cut into network yarns (for process details, see Chapter 9). Of these three methods, melt spinning is the most common one.

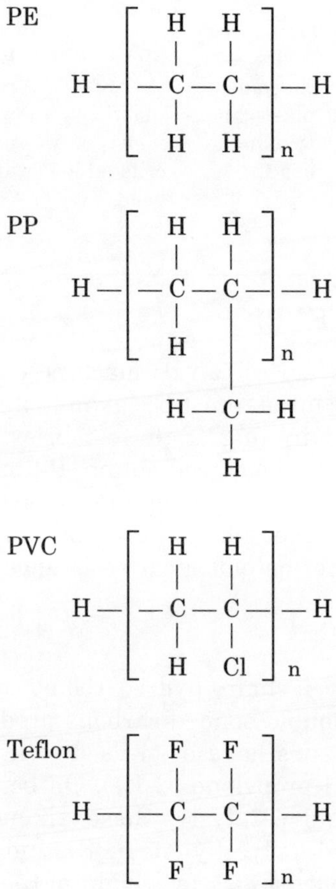

PE

$$H-\left[-\overset{\overset{\displaystyle H}{|}}{\underset{\underset{\displaystyle H}{|}}{C}}-\overset{\overset{\displaystyle H}{|}}{\underset{\underset{\displaystyle H}{|}}{C}}-\right]_n-H$$

PP

$$H-\left[-\overset{\overset{\displaystyle H}{|}}{\underset{\underset{\displaystyle H}{|}}{C}}-\overset{\overset{\displaystyle H}{|}}{\underset{\underset{\displaystyle |}{|}}{C}}-\right]_n-H$$

$$H-\overset{\overset{\displaystyle H}{|}}{\underset{\underset{\displaystyle H}{|}}{C}}-H$$

PVC

$$H-\left[-\overset{\overset{\displaystyle H}{|}}{\underset{\underset{\displaystyle H}{|}}{C}}-\overset{\overset{\displaystyle H}{|}}{\underset{\underset{\displaystyle Cl}{|}}{C}}-\right]_n-H$$

Teflon

$$H-\left[-\overset{\overset{\displaystyle F}{|}}{\underset{\underset{\displaystyle F}{|}}{C}}-\overset{\overset{\displaystyle F}{|}}{\underset{\underset{\displaystyle F}{|}}{C}}-\right]_n-H$$

Figure 8.9 Basic sturctural formulae of olefin polymers.

Properties

Table 8.4 sums up the properties of the two olefin fibres—polypropylene and polyethylene. A comparison reveals that polyethylene has a lower melting point and also has a tendency to get deformed, if subjected to more than 10% stretch. It must be noted that the properties listed are for regular olefin fibres. Many modifications are also carried out to combat undesired properties or introduce desirable features.

Table 8.4 Properties of Olefin Fibres

Properties	Description
Length, diameter, colour and lustre	Can be controlled, also depends on production method
Tenacity	2.5–5.5 gpd, under dry and wet conditions
Elongation and elastic recovery	Excellent elastic recovery, PE may face slight problem of distortion on stretching
Resiliency and abrasion resistance	Good
Density	0.9 g/cm³, lighter than water
Moisture regain	0%, but can transport moisture by wicking
Thermal properties	Burn slowly, continue to burn when removed from flame, residue is a hard bead
Melting temperature PE	125°C
PP	165°C
Chemical properties	Generally good resistance to acids, alkalies and solvents; strong oxidising acids can cause strength loss
Biological properties	Excellent resistance to clothes moths, carpet beetles, mildew, bacteria and fungi
Dimensional stability	Good, if heat set
Static charge	Being non-polar, do not face static problem
Sunlight	Gradual decline in strength, unless given UV stabilization finish

Uses

Polyethylene does not have many textile uses. Its main applications include filters, ropes, nets, packing material, overalls, gloves and plastic sheets.

Polypropylene has wider applications. In the apparel sector, it is used as thermal innerwear, undergarments, hosiery and children's clothing. Good wicking properties help such fabrics give comfort to the wearer. In the home, polypropylene is extensively used in carpets, carpet backing, blankets and as upholstery fabrics. Its ability to repel water borne stains proves very useful here. Industrial uses include filters, nets, cords, sailcloths, coverings for fibre bales and bags. It also has applications in the sector of geotextiles.

8.17 SPANDEX

Spandex is an elastomeric fibre, possessing excellent elastic properties. It was developed as a substitute for natural rubber, which has certain drawbacks. Spandex is a block copolymer, containing polyurethane (—NH—COO—)$_n$. Having one of the most complex structures, spandex has two kinds of regions. The first kind are the rigid sections that impart strength to it. The second are the flexible, amorphous segments which lie coiled up like a spring when the filament is in a relaxed state. On being subjected to stretch, these coiled up structures straighten out. Thus, both kinds of regions have an equally important role to play in allowing a spandex filament to stretch and get back to its original configuration. In 1958, spandex (tradename lycra) was first manufactured in USA. In India, the Thapar group was the first to launch spandex in 1991, by the tradename **Elyxa**.

Properties

The chief properties of spandex are listed in Table 8.5. It is generally considered superior to natural rubber in strength and durability. Natural rubber gets damaged by heat, chlorine, perspiration, suntan oils and solvents. The differences in spandex and natural rubber have also been mentioned in the following table.

Table 8.5   Properties of Spandex

Properties	Description
Length, diameter, colour and lustre	Can be controlled; in comparison to natural rubber, finer diameters can be achieved
Tenacity	0.7–1.0 gpd, under dry and wet conditions; twice that of rubber
Elongation and elastic recovery	600–800% elongation, excellent elastic recovery
Resiliency and abrasion resistance	Good; rubber has poor abrasion resistance
Density	1.0–1.2 g/cm^3
Moisture regain	Less than 1%, but can be dyed; rubber is non-absorbent, hence difficult to dye
Thermal properties	Melting point ranges from 450°F–500°F, while softening and sticking occurs around 350°F. Rubber starts deteriorating at temperatures greater than 22°F
Chemical properties	Generally good, can withstand swimming pool chlorine levels but not chlorine bleaches. Rubber has relatively poor chemical resistance and is also harmed by chlorine in pools
Biological properties	Good resistance to microbes
Dimensional stability	Good
Static charge	Static problem leads to soiling
Sunlight	Good resistance to sunlight, rubber gets deteriorated

Uses

Spandex is generally used in combination with other fibres. Its extraordinary elastic properties make it popular in foundation garments, hosiery, swimwear and clothing for active sports. It is also finding increasing applications in fashionable and decorative fabrics such as nets and laces. Any consumer can vouch for the ease of wearing, snugness of fit and comfort offered by blends of spandex. Over the years, Indian apparel items such as saree blouses and churidars that require a snug fit, have turned to spandex for satisfying results.

The family of manufactured fibres is often divided up into three generations on the basis of the time of their birth. The first generation are the cellulosics or regenerated fibres. Synthetics (nylon, polyester) form the second generation while the youngest or third generation fibres are those developed for specific end uses. These are also referred to as high technology, high performance or super fibres. Members of this generation include aramids, carbon fibres and glass fibres.

8.18 ARAMIDS

Aramids are aromatic polyamides. They are variants of nylon in which more than 85% of their amide linkages (—CO—NH—) are attached directly to two aromatic rings (if this number is less than 85%, then the resultant fibre is a nylon). This leads to molecules that have better crystallinity and high orientation. They are thus, more resistant to higher tem-peratures and also stronger than ordinary nylons. Another difference is that while nylon is melt spun, aramids are produced by dry or wet spinning. Two major aramids are **Nomex**[R] and **Kevlar**[R], both introduced by Du Pont, USA in 1963 and 1973, respectively.

Properties

Nomex is widely known for its outstanding flame resistance property. At temperatures of around 99°F, it decomposes but does not melt. Kevlar is popular for its exceptionally high strength (23 gpd). In general, aramids are used for their excellent abrasion resistance, high resistance to stretch, good chemical resistance, light weight and good resistance to X-rays. Some drawbacks include poor resistance to concentrated acids and alkalies, degradation on prolonged exposure to UV rays and difficulty in dye uptake (moisture regain 4%). However, the unique features possessed by aramids override the few limitations that they possess and hence the use of aramids is growing day by day.

Uses

Salient applications include protective clothing and helmets for defence personnel and astronauts, bulletproof vests, fencing suits, clothing for fire fighters, race drivers, forestry and refinery workers, aircraft furnishings, fibre reinforced plastics and industrial textiles.

It would be of interest to know that the Tata Advanced Materials Limited (TAML) was established in India in 1992. It manufactures light weight, composite based products like bullet proof jackets, helmets and vests. These indigenised ballistic products are supplied to the army, navy, paramilitary and state police forces in India and across Asia.

8.19 CARBON FIBRES

Introduced in the late 1960s, carbon fibres have been a subject of research the world over. PAN fibres are the most important precursor of carbon fibres. Pitch obtained from petroleum, coaltar and PVC is also an important low cost material for their manufacture. Some other starter materials for carbon fibres are glass, rayon and steel.

Production from PAN fibres

These fibres are first treated in an oxidising atmosphere to convert thermoplastic PAN into a non-thermoplastic material which can withstand the excessively high temperature of the next processing step. This second step involves carbonizing of treated (oxidised) PAN to about 1000°C without tension. Further heat treatment to any temperature upto 3000°C is given depending on the required strength of the final carbon fibres. Figure 8.10 shows the carbon fibres produced from PAN.

Figure 8.10   Carbon fibres produced from PAN.

Properties

Salient properties of carbon fibres include their extraordinary heat resistance and strength (15.9 gpd). Carbon also exhibits excellent resistance to concentrated acids, alkalies and solvents. It does face a problem when in contact with strong chlorine bleaches. It has a good moisture regain of 10.0%, which makes it free from the problem of static charge build-up. Being stiff, carbon elongates by about 0.7% and has a 100% elastic recovery. A specific gravity of 1.77 makes carbon a medium weight fibre.

Uses

Carbon fibres are not used for daily apparel but have specific end uses. These cover a wide gamut of areas like protective clothing for occupations that involve exposure to very high temperatures and chemicals, (industrial belts, brushes). Carbon reinforced plastics are extensively used in machine parts, sports equipment, automobile interiors and aerospace industry. In the medical field, bone drafts made of carbon fibres offer strong replacement options.

8.20 GLASS FIBRES

Production

Glass fibres are produced as continuous filaments or as staples. Mineral ingredients such as limestone, silica sand and other selected ingredients are mixed together and then formed into glass marbles, about 1″ in diameter. An electric furnace is used to melt these marbles and the liquid mixture flows out through tiny orifices at the base of the melting chamber. These emerging strands are drawn out by a high speed winding device before they harden to form glass filaments. For the manufacture of glass staple fibres, the drawing out is carried out by high pressure jets of compressed air. A revolving drum collects the staple glass fibres, which are then processed into yarns after drafting and twisting. Figure 8.11 shows glass fibres. Both woven and non-woven materials are made of glass, depending on final use.

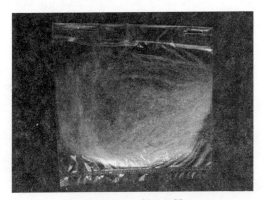

Figure 8.11 Glass fibres.

Properties

Glass fibres possess some special properties. They have a high strength, low density, good sound insulation and excellent chemical resistance. They are also corrosion resistant, incombustible and have electrical properties. It is possible to modify the basic properties of glass fibres by using a host of binders and reinforcing materials. This fact has led to a boom in their production and applications.

Uses

Glass filters are used for high temperature substances as well as strong liquids. Fabrics, webs and paper made from glass are extensively used in chemical, metallurgical, electrical, automotive, engineering and construction material industries. Glass fibres are also being used in composite materials, like glass reinforced plastics. These have a wide and ever-expanding range of uses in the home and the industry. Defence, shipbuilding, railway transport and aircraft industries rely on glass fibres heavily.

8.21 METALLIC FIBRES

The use of gold and silver threads in weaving and embroidery is nothing new to India. There are many examples of traditional textiles that utilise such yarns. Banarasi brocades and Paithani sarees are some of the examples. Metallic threads have also been used in other countries of the world for textiles, bags and footwear. Metals, being malleable and ductile, are used as thin wires or wrapped around a core of flexible fibre. However, there are some drawbacks associated with these, like low strength, high cost and a tendency to tarnish. Gold and silver are being replaced by other metals such as aluminium, steel, iron, nickel and cobalt based super alloys. Another common option is to use aluminium yarn coated with a polyester film. Commonly known as *tested zari*, such yarns need to be handled carefully while ironing. On the whole, such alternatives are inexpensive and stronger than conventional gold and silver threads.

Uses

The first and foremost use of metallic yarns is to impart an attractive and decorative look to a fabric. The metallic yarns may be used in varying proportions to create interest. These yarns also serve a functional purpose of imparting electrical conductivity. Thus, metallic yarns are used in synthetic carpets to solve the problem of static charge build-up. Other common applications include tyre cords, brake linings, medical sutures and the aerospace industry.

8.22 ORGANISATIONS IN THIS SECTOR

- Association of Man-made Fibre Industry of India, Mumbai
- Man-made Textile Research Association (MANTRA), Surat
- Synthetic and Art Silk Mills Research Association (SASMIRA), Mumbai
- Synthetic and Rayon Textile Export Promotion Council (SRTEPC).

EXERCISES

8.1 Give the names and formulae of raw materials used for the manufacture of nylon 6, nylon 6, 6 and polyester.

8.2 Compare synthetics with natural cellulosics with respect to physical and chemical properties.

8.3 "Nylon has superior biological properties as compared to wool". Comment with reasons.

8.4 Define inorganic fibres with examples. Give salient applications of these fibres.

8.5 What are aramid fibres? How do they differ from nylon with respect to chemical structure and properties?

REFERENCES

Gohl, E.P.G and Vilensky, L.D., *Textile Science*, CBS Publishers and Distributors, Delhi, 1987.

Hudson, P.B., Clapp, A.C. and Kness, D., *Joseph's Introductory Textile Science*, 6th ed., Harcourt Brace Jovanovich College Publishers, 1993.

Kadolph, S.J. and Langford, A.L., *Textiles,* 10th ed., Pearson Education, NJ, 2007.

SUGGESTED READING

Collier, B.J., Bide, M.J. and Tortora, P.G., *Understanding Textiles,* 7th ed., Pearson Education, NJ, 2009.

Cook, J.D., *Handbook of Textile Fibres II: Man-made Fibres*, Merrow Rednook Books, Great Britain, 1993.

Editors of American Fabric Magazine, *Encyclopedia of Textiles*, Prentice Hall, Englewood Cliffs, New Jersey, USA, 1960.

Kostikov, V.T., *Fibre Science and Technology*, Chapman & Hall, London, UK, 1995.

Moncrieff, R.W., *Man-Made Fibres*, John Wiley & Sons Inc., New York, 1966.

Vidyasagar, P.U., *Handbook of Textiles*, Mittal Publications, Delhi, 1998.

PART III
Yarns

In the previous section we have familiarised ourselves with fibres of various kinds. Since the ultimate use of most textile fibres is fabric, they have to pass through an intermediate form, yarns. Yarns are the starting material for constructing fabrics through weaving, knitting, braiding and knotting. Non-woven fabrics are an exception since they use fibres and not yarns as a starting material. The appearance as well as performance of any textile fabric is strongly influenced by the properties of the yarns from which it is made.

The next two chapters of this part, will deal with yarn production and yarn properties.

CHAPTER

9 Yarn Production

A yarn is an assembly of fibres or filaments having a substantial length and relatively small cross section, with or without twist. The family of yarns is constituted of:

1. Spun yarns
2. Filament yarns
3. Tape, network or film yarns

9.1 TYPES OF YARNS

9.1.1 Spun Yarns

These are made by a number of staple fibres twisted together. Natural fibres such as cotton, linen, wool and jute can be made into spun yarns. Even manufactured fibres can be cut into staple lengths and processed to give spun yarns. These require mechanical spinning which is quite complex. Spun yarns have a dull, fuzzy look. They soil readily and are prone to pilling. On the positive side, they are comfortable to wear and have less static build-up.

9.1.2 Filament Yarns

These are made by chemical spinning. All manufactured fibres are produced as filament yarns (monofilament or multifilament) by a variety of chemical spinning methods. Monofilaments are made by a single filament which is obtained by a spinneret with one hole. Generally, such a yarn is stiffer and coarser than a multifilament yarn. Multifilament yarn is made from a number of filaments laid together with or without twist. In this case, the spinneret has many holes through which the dope is extruded simultaneously. Multifilament yarns are soft and pliable.

9.1.3 Tape, Network or Film Yarns

These are produced by splitting or slitting of sheets of materials or polymers which are extruded and solidified. One or more strips are made by lengthwise division of the polymer sheet.

Such yarns prove to be cost effective and find extensive usage in industrial textiles for packaging. Polyethylene, an olefin fibre is often made by this method.

9.2   HISTORY

It is difficult to pinpoint the exact time when spinning of fibres for converting them into yarns, began. The fact that it predates recorded history cannot be debated. The present day practices have evolved slowly from spinning without implements, through spinning with simple implements, to spinning with machines. Hand spinning relied heavily on the spinning wheel which was invented in India (*charkha*) and dates back to AD 500–1000. It was introduced to Europe around the fourteenth century. Subsequent mechanisations took place in the West and paved the way for the industrial revolution that impacted all spheres of human life. Salient among these inventions were the spinning jenny (invented by James Hargreaves, 1764), water power spinning frame (by Richard Arkwright, 1769), spinning mule (by Samuel Crompton, 1769) and the ring spinning machine (John Thorp, 1828).

9.3   SPUN YARN PRODUCTION

Before proceeding with discussion of spun yarn production, it is necessary to be introduced with the terminology. Table 9.1 gives a skeletal draft of various production methods employed for spun yarns. The subsequent sections will use this format for discussion.

Table 9.1   Yarn Production Methods

Spun yarns		
Mechanical/ conventional spinning	Non-conventional spinning	Spun yarns from manufactured fibre
• Cotton system • Woollen system • Worsted system • Linen system	• Open end spinning • Friction spinning • Integrated composie spinning • Fasciated yarns • Self twist yarns	• Tow to top • Direct tow to yarn

As clearly laid out in Table 9.1, spun yarns can be produced by either of the three techniques, viz., conventional spinning, non-conventional spinning and from manufactured filaments that have been converted into staple fibres.

9.3.1   Conventional/Mechanical Spinning

This has been a commonly practiced method of yarn production, hence the term 'conventional'. The phrase 'mechanical' implies that the fibres are made to pass through a series of machines that eventually convert them into yarn. The kind of machinery and at times, the number of runs through it is decided by the fibre length. Many kinds of mechanical spinning systems are used—cotton system, woollen system worsted system and linen system. The first three are more common and are discussed in this chapter. It must be carefully noted that the length, and not the fibre type, decides the system employed. Table 9.2 gives the steps involved and the length of fibres that are processed by the three common mechanical systems of spinning.

Table 9.2 Mechanical Spinning Systems

Mechanical spinning system	Length of processed fibres	Steps involved
Cotton	Short staple, 0.5–2″	Opening Cleaning and blending Picking Carding Drawing out and Drafting Combing (optional) Twisting Spinning (twisting and winding on bobbins) Winding on larger packages
Wool (like carded cotton)	Long staple, less than 2.5″	Sorting Scouring Carbonising Carding Spinning
Worsted (like combed cotton)	Very long staple, more than 2.5″ in length and usually of finer diameter	All steps of woollen system, with the additional step of combing carried out after carding

Cotton spinning system

The steps listed in Table 9.2 for the conventional ring spinning process are described now:

1. Opening, cleaning and blending: Cotton fibres arrive at the spinning mills in the form of large bales which are compressed packages of nearly 225 kg of fibres. These need to be loosened and disentangled by the process of opening which is done by hands or machines. Metal cylinders with protruding fingers are used to effectively pluck out smaller tufts of fibres. In this step, blending can also be done to obtain uniformity of fibre quality. Bales from different sources also need to be homogenously blended together, though two generic types of fibres can also be blended. The loose and fluffy tufts are passed through high velocity air currents which remove trash, dirt, burrs, leaves and any remaining seeds.

The three process of opening, cleaning and blending are carried out in a **blowroom**.

2. Picking: The separated fibre mass is taken to a **picker frame** which carries out additional cleaning and then forms the fibres into a mat, called a **lap** which is 45 inch wide and 1 inch thick. The fibres are arranged randomly and resemble a roll of absorbent cotton sold in the market. Some units employ a chute feed hopper, which sucks the fibres using compressed air and delivers them to the carding unit. This is also referred to as *pneumatic transfer of the material.*

3. Carding: This is an important step which continues the cleaning process, removes the fibres which are too short for yarn, separates the fibres and partially straightens them, so that their longitudinal axis are somewhat parallel.

The picker lap is drawn on a carding roller or **card**. It is a rapidly revolving cylinder covered with very fine hooks or wire brushes. A moving belt of wire brushes slowly, moves concentrically above this cylinder (Figure 9.1).

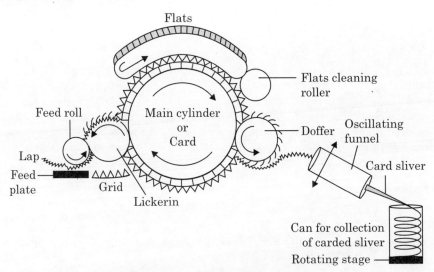

Figure 9.1   Schematic of carding.

A thin uniform web is formed in this machine. It moves into a funnel shaped device where it is formed into a soft rope-like strand of fibres called a **card sliver**. It is similar to a broom stick in diameter (3/4″–1″).

A card sliver produces **carded yarns** and **carded cottons** which are inexpensive. The cheap cotton fabric used for lining and in binding of books belongs to this category.

4. Combing: This is an optional step. When yarns of high quality, which are smooth, fine, even and strong are desired, the sliver is put through an additional step called **combing**. In this operation, several card slivers are combined and once again spread into a web. Fine toothed combs are used to straighten the fibres till a point when they become highly oriented (parallel to the longer axis) and short fibres are removed from the long fibres. The combed web is again passed through a funnel-like device to form a **combed sliver**, made of the longest fibres.

The wastage in the form of short fibres (noils), is nearly one fourth of the raw material. This is used for the manufacture of regenerated fibres, like rayon and acetate. Cost of combed yarns is more but so are the advantages. Fabrics produced from these are smoother and stronger. They also have a greater lustre and durability.

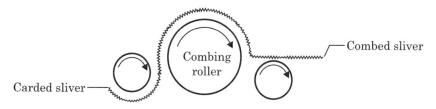

Figure 9.2 Combing (schematic).

5. Drawing and drafting: The **draw frame** has four pairs of rollers, each revolving at a progressively faster speed. This action pulls the stapled slivers length wise over each other, producing longer and thinner slivers. Slivers from six to eight cans are fed to the draw frame, which consists of roller pairs and polished steel table (Figure 9.3). Blending can also be done by introducing two generic types of fibre slivers from the cans.

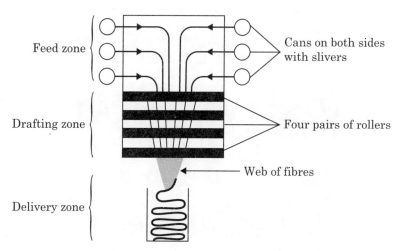

Figure 9.3 Schematic of drawframe.

In this way, by combining several slivers (carded or combed), irregularities are eliminated. The number of passages in the draw frame can vary from 1–3, depending on the desired result.

6. Roving: The drawn sliver is taken to a **roving frame** when it is passed through rollers similar to those in the draw frame. These attenuate (thin out) the sliver from 1/4th–1/8th of its original diameter (like a pencil lead). Also, a slight amount of twist is given to the fibre strand which helps to hold it together. It is then wound on bobbins.

7. Spinning: This is the final process in the manufacturing of spun yarns. The **spinning frame** draws, twists and winds the yarns in one continuous operation (Figure 9.4a and 9.4b).

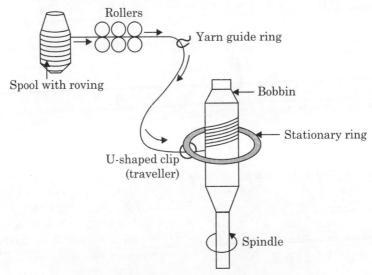

Figure 9.4(a)   Ring spinning.

Figure 9.4(b)   Actual ring spinning frames.

The strand of fibre or roving is fed from the bobbin through the rollers. The rollers draw and elongate the roving which passes through a yarn guide and then through a traveller. This is a U-shaped clip which moves freely around a stationary ring. The sliver moves through it and onto a bobbin which is mounted on a spindle that turns at a constant speed. The turning of the bobbin and movement of the traveller imparts a twist to the yarn.

The basic step of ring spinning remains the same since its invention even today. However, advances in technology have led to highly sophisticated and automated processing equipments with monitoring devices which produce yarns at much higher speeds, less noise and dust than the older machines. Ring spun yarns are produced by the oldest and most common method. Yarns are strong, even and have a good orientation.

Table 9.3 summarises the conventional spinning (cotton spinning)

Table 9.3   Summary of Cotton Spinning

Step	Machine	Input	Output	Function
1.	Blowroom	Bales	Fibre tufts	Opening of bales Cleaning Blending
2.	Picker	Fibre tufts	Lap	Further opening and cleaning Formation of a lap
3.	Card	Lap	Carded sliver	Individualising the fibres Cleaning Orientation Sliver formation
4.	Draw frame	Sliver	Sliver	Improvement in regularity in one to three passages Blending; cross mixing of slivers
5.	Comber	Sliver	Sliver	Removal of short fibres Further cleaning Parallelisation
6.	Roving frame	Sliver (broom stick thickness)	Sliver (pencil lead diameter)	More attenuation Slight twisting
7.	Ring spinning frame	Roving	Ring spun yarn	Attenuation to the required fineness Twisting Winding

After the bobbin is full, it is removed from the spindle and replaced by a new bobbin.

In a **winding** process, yarns from various bobbins are wound onto larger packages of the size desired for weaving or knitting.

Long staple spinning systems

These include the wool and worsted systems.

Sorting is the first step done at mills. Various criteria used include length, fineness, spinning quality and trash present.

This is followed by **scouring** to remove water soluble impurities and grease. Neutral detergents and water is used for this step. Several scouring treatments may be required followed by rinsing and drying.

Carbonising follows, which employs dilute sulphuric acid to burn out (carbonise) the vegetable matter such as burrs and leaves, that may be entangled in the fibres. A final rinse removes the acid and the carbonised matter.

Carding is the next step which uses a series of card cylinders with longer needles than in the cotton system. This cleans up the fibres and separates them out. Wool fibres less than 5 cm (2″) are used to produce woollen yarns (Figure 9.5). However, fairly long fibres, which usually have finer diameters are converted into worsted yarns (Figure 9.6). These are taken from the card to the comber.

The step of **combing** helps in further aligning the fibres i.e., arranging the fibres in a parallel form, removes trash as well as short fibres (noils). The combed sliver φ, called **tops**, are then sent for **pin drafting**. This reduces the diameter and evens out irregularities. A slight twist is imparted to the strand.

Spinning follows, for which carded or combed silver is directly taken, omitting the steps which are followed in the cotton system. This involves further twisting and winding on bobbins mounted on a rotating spindle (similar to ring spinning frames of cotton system).

Figure 9.5 Woollen yarn with short, randomly arranged fibres.

Figure 9.6 Worsted yarn with long and parallel fibres.

9.3.2 Non-conventional Spinning

Apart from the conventional ring spinning process, there are some non-conventional processes as well. These include:

- open end systems, which make use of mechanical motors, rotors, air or water to form yarns at very high speed;
- friction spinning;
- integrated composite spinning;
- fasciated yarns; and
- self-twist yarns.

1. Rotor spinning (open end spinning)

This process was introduced nearly a century after ring spinning. It omits the step of forming a roving. After drafting, the sliver is fed into a rotary beater. This device ensures that the fibres are beaten into a thin supply which enters a duct and gets deposited on the sides of the disc (rotor) (see Figure 9.7). The transportation of the fibres is achieved through air currents. Turning of the rotor introduces twist in the fibre strand. On top of the rotor is a tube through which the twisted yarn leaves to join the previously formed yarn. Simultaneously, more fibres enter the machine and deposit in the grooves of the rotor. Winding of the ready yarn is done on larger packages than in ring spinning.

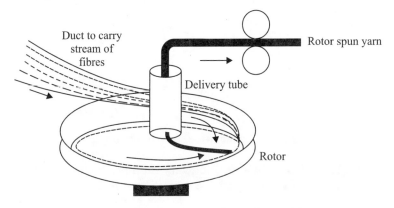

Figure 9.7   Rotor spinning (schematic).

Advantages of open end spinning are as follows:

- less labour required
- less floor space
- final package can be of any size
- increased production speed due to elimination of steps
- yarns produced are bulky, absorbent, have greater covering power and excellent dye uptake. They have fewer knots or neps and are thus, more smooth in appearance. They are also less prone to pilling.

Some drawbacks of rotor spun yarns are that they have lower strength than ring spun yarns. Extremely fine yarns cannot be produced. It is also not possible to spin combed yarn or 100% manufactured staple by this method.

2. Friction spinning

This process was developed by Dr. Ernst Fehrer of Austria in the early 1970's and the machine was named after him (DREF). It consists of two perforated drums of the same diameter, moving in the same direction. Carded fibres are transported by air current to the nip (point of contact) of the rollers (see Figure 9.8). They become compressed and twisted due to friction between rollers and strong air suction through the perforations. Amount of twist inserted is related to the rotation of the drums (upto 100 twists per rotation is possible). The final yarn is pulled out from below the roller and wound on a package placed at the top of the drums.

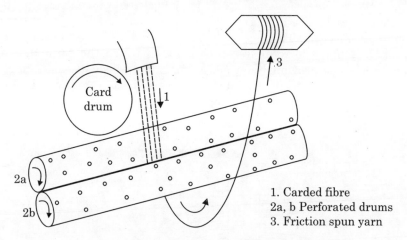

1. Carded fibre
2a, b Perforated drums
3. Friction spun yarn

Figure 9.8 Schematic of friction spinning.

Advantages of this method include very high production rates, lower costs, no limitation of yarn package size, soft handle and high evenness.

Drawbacks include poor orientation leading to lower tenacity of final yarn and limitation of count (yarns produced are finer than rotor but coarser than ring spun yarns). There is also a limitation of length of fibres used since long fibres tend to curl and loop while being transported through the air current.

3. Integrated composite spinning

This is also referred to as twistless spinning. In this method, a strong and uniform core of monofilament is coated with a bonding agent (e.g., molten polymer resin). It is then covered with staple fibre slivers which give it the desired appearance and texture (Figure 9.9).

1. Filament base
2. Coat of bonding agent
3. Staple fibre outer core

Figure 9.9   Integrated composite spinning (ICS).

4. Fasciated yarns

These are a bundle of parallel fibres which are wrapped by other relatively long fibres (see Figure 9.10). Fasciated yarns have poor abrasion resistance since surface fibres are not well anchored. This is not very popular today.

Figure 9.10   Fasciated yarn.

5. Self-twist yarns

A pair of rovings is passed through two rollers which are oscillating as well as rotating in opposite directions (Figure 9.11). Each is imparted a twist in a direction opposite to the other and converted into a yarn. After leaving the rollers, the two yarns are held together. Their opposite twist direction makes them wind around each other to form a 2-ply yarn.

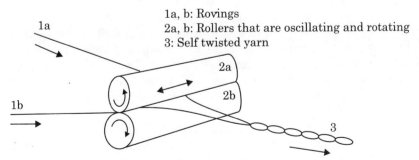

1a, b: Rovings
2a, b: Rollers that are oscillating and rotating
3: Self twisted yarn

Figure 9.11   Self-twist yarns.

Salient advantages include low production costs owing to less space, labour and energy consumption as compared to conventional ring spinning.

To summarise, it can be stated that various approaches can be used to consolidate fibres and form yarns. These are:

(i) Twisting   (ii) Wrapping
(iii) Entangling   (iv) Bonding

9.3.3 Spun Yarns from Manufactured Fibres

1. Tow to top (convertor system)

The spinnerets are modified to produce a tow or bundle of filaments with fine diameter. The tow is stretched so that it breaks at the weakest points or cut to produce staple lengths. These are processed through the conventional spinning systems to form spun yarns and the method is called **tow to top**.

2. Direct tow to yarn (direct spinning)

The extruded tow is fed to a special draw frame. The drafting rollers stretch it to the required thinness and break it into shorter lengths. All steps prior to drafting are omitted. This is followed by ring spinning (twisting and winding). The name *direct spinning* refers to the fact that conversion of tow to yarn takes place in a single process.

9.4 PRODUCTION OF FILAMENT YARNS (CHEMICAL SPINNING)

In 1862, Ozanam invented the **spinning jet or spinneret** which was a small thimble-like nozzle with one or many holes, through which the fibre solution (dope) could be pumped out. Platinum or gold was the metal used due to the fact that these are inert. Today, however, stainless steel is commonly used. Laser beams are used to make holes which can be round or of any desired shape. While studying the properties of manufactured fibres in the last section, you have read that physical features of these fibres (including length, diameter, cross sectional shape) can be controlled. It is with the design of the spinneret that these properties can be manipulated. For production of filaments, about 350 holes are punched on one spinning jet. Filament tow is an untwisted rope of thousands of fine filaments. It is made by extruding the dope through 100 or more spinnerets, each with about 3,000 holes. This rope is then cut into desired length and used for producing spun man-made yarns.

The process of chemical spinning could be broken down into three components, viz., pre-spinning steps, actual spinning and post-spinning steps (Table 9.4).

Table 9.4 Steps in Chemical Spinning

Pre-spinning operations	Chemical spinning	Post-spinning operations
Addition of • Delustrant • Bleach • Optical brightening agent • Dye pigment	• Melt • Dry • Wet • Emulsion • Gel	• Drawing • Washing • Spin finishing • Heat setting

Pre-spinning operations

These include addition of delustrants (for reducing the bright lustre of manufactured fibres) with manufactured fibres. Bleaches, whiteners or optical brighteners and sometimes even dye pigments (solution dyeing). Addition of dye pigment is called dope dyeing and is commonly used for fibres that have a very low moisture regain, e.g. Olefins.

Chemical spinning

For any kind of chemical spinning, there are three common steps. The manner in which these are executed forms the basic distinction between the various types of chemical spinning (melt, dry and wet). These steps are:

- Conversion of a polymer into a liquid or spinning solution, also called a **dope**.
- Extruding the solution through a spinneret i.e., pumping the dope.
- Solidification of the liquid into filaments (solid).

Post-spinning operations

These are common to all methods of chemical spinning and include washing, drawing (i.e., stretching) to improve orientation and heat setting. Spin finishes are also applied to counteract the problem of static charge build-up.

Drawing: A newly formed filament contains both amorphous and crystalline molecular arrangements. Before the filament is fully solidified, it can be stretched or drawn (Figure 9.12). This makes the molecules more parallel to the longer axis. Oriented molecules are longer, narrower and stronger than as-spun (undrawn) yarns.

Molecules get oriented

Figure 9.12 Drawing.

Each filament yarn has an inherent potential for stretching. When all of this is used up, the yarns produced are referred to as **fully oriented yarn (FOY)**. However, it is a common practice to leave a portion of this potential stretch which can be utilised in subsequent processes like texturing. Such yarns are called **partially oriented yarns (POY)**.

Heat setting is done for thermoplastic fibres. They shrink on application of heat and remain in that position, imparting dimensional stability.

9.4.1   Melt Spinning

Figure 9.13 gives a schematic diagram for the melt spinning process. Polymer is heated and it melts to form a liquid spinning solution. Chips of polymers are fed to a hopper which is heated. There is a grid (sieve) at the base which permits only molten liquid to pass through.

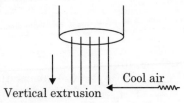

Figure 9.13   Melt spinning.

Extrusion is done through a spinneret vertically. Solidification is done by cooling, for which cool air currents are used. Nylon and polyester are produced by melt spinning.

For polymers which cannot be converted into a molten stage, two options exist—dry or wet spinning.

9.4.2   Dry Spinning

In this case, a volatile solvent is used to dissolve the raw materials and form a solution. Extrusion is once again in a vertical position. Solidification by evaporation occurs when the filaments come in contact with warm air currents (Figure 9.14). There is a one way mass transfer which occurs in the form of movements of the solvent from the extruded filaments. The volatile solvent is recovered and recycled. Acetate is produced by dry spinning. The volatile solvent used is acetone.

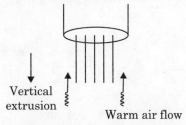

Figure 9.14   Dry spinning.

9.4.3 Wet Spinning

This is the oldest, most complex and also the most expensive method of man-made yarn manufacture. A non-volatile solvent is used to convert the raw material into a solution. Extrusion is done in a horizontal position, in a water bath (Figure 9.15). Solidification occurs through coagulation. There is a two way mass transfer with entry of water into the filament strand and exit of the non-volatile solvent. This explains why regularity of cross section is so difficult to achieve in the case of wet spinning. Viscose, the first manufactured fibre, is spun by this method. Table 9.5 compares the three common chemical spinning methods.

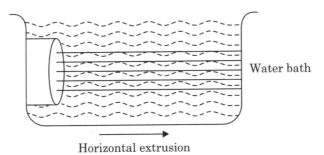

Figure 9.15 Wet spinning.

Table 9.5 Comparison of Melt, Dry and Wet Spinning Methods

Feature	Melt spinning	Dry spinning	Wet spinning
Polymer converted into liquid	By heating to high temperature and melting	By dissolving in a volatile solvent	By dissolving in a non-volatile solvent
Extrusion through a spinnerete	Vertically, in a cold air chamber	Vertically, in a warm air chamber	Horizontally, in a water bath
Solidification	By cooling of the molten polymer (one-way mass transfer)	By evaporation of the volatile solvent (one-way mass transfer)	By coagulation and precipitation (two-way mass transfer)
Cross section	Uniform, controllable	Slightly irregular	Highly serrated, difficult to control
Cost of process	Least cost	Medium cost	Most expensive
Complexity of process	Simplest method	More complex than melt spinning, less than wet spinning	Most complicated

9.4.4 Gel Spinning

The polymer is mixed with a solvent to form a gel. This is passed through the same equipment as for melt spinning. The solvent is then extracted and the fibres are drawn.

9.4.5 Emulsion Spinning

If the polymer is such that it has a very high melting point or is insoluble, then it cannot be melt, dry or wet spun. Neither can it be gel spun. The only option then is emulsion spinning. The polymer is made into an emulsion, forced through a narrow tube to align it, then fused without melting by application of heat. This is followed by extrusion into a coagulating bath through a spinnerete and subsequently stretching to impart orientation.

9.5 SOME VARIATIONS IN CHEMICAL SPINNING

Bicomponent and Biconstituent yarns can be made by chemical spinning. The term bicomponent refers to two variants of the same generic type (e.g., nylon 6 and nylon 6, 6). Biconstituent means two different generic fibre types (e.g., nylon and polyester).

When more than one type of molten polymers are extruded, there are many arrangements that are possible. These are referred to as *sheath core*, *bilateral* and *matrix fibril arrangement*. In sheath core, one component forms a central core around which the second component is present as a sheath (Figure 9.16).

In the bilateral arrangement, the two components are present side by side (Figure 9.17).

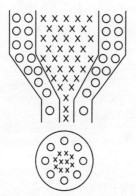

Figure 9.16 Sheath core.

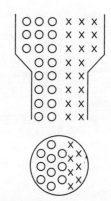

Figure 9.17 Bilateral.

In the matrix fibril arrangement, the matrix forms a background in which round or elongated droplets of the fibril (second component) are present. Figure 9.18 depicts the matrix fibril arrangement. You might have noticed this in plastic trays which have tiny glass pieces embedded in them. These enhance the strength of the structure considerably, since the path of break is no longer straight but around the fibril pieces.

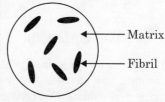

Figure 9.18 Matrix fibril.

Bulky yarn is made from fibres which have variations in cross-sectional shapes. These may be obtained by vibrating spinnerets. If on the other hand, an air duct is used to add bubbles in the extruded dope, then hollow fibres are produced which will form bulky yarns and fabrics.

Thick and thin yarn can be produced through modifications in chemical spinning. By varying the pressure of extrusion through the spinneret, the filament gets an uneven diameter, thus forming thick and thin filaments.

EXERCISES

9.1 Enumerate the processing steps of cotton and woollen spinning system.

9.2 Differentiate between ring spun and open-end spun yarn.

9.3 "Worsted yarn is stronger and smoother than woollen yarn". Give reasons to support this statement.

9.4 Describe ring spinning with a diagram.

9.5 Compare the chemical spinning method employed for nylon with that used for viscose rayon.

9.6 Write a note on dry spinning. Give two examples of fibres that are produced with this method.

SUGGESTED READING

Collier, B.J., Bide, M.J. and Tortora, P.G., *Understanding Textiles*, 7th ed., Pearson Education, NJ, 2009.

Corbman, B.P., *Textiles Fibre to Fabric*, 6th ed., McGraw-Hill, 1983.

Goswami, B.C., Martindale, J.G. and Scardino, F.L., *Textile Yarns Technology, Structure and Application*, John Wiley & Sons, USA, 1977.

Joseph, M.J., *Essentials of Textiles*, 4th ed., The Dryden Press Saunders College Publishers, 1988.

Kadolph, S.J. and Langford, A.L., *Textiles,* 10th ed., Pearson Education, NJ, 2007.

CHAPTER

10

Yarn Properties

In the last chapter, we have studied the methods of producing short staple, long staple, filament and tape yarns. There are some other criteria which can be used to classify yarns. Alternatively, these can also be referred to as yarn properties. In the present chapter, the following concepts related to yarns are discussed:

1. difference between a thread and a yarn;
2. yarn twist—its amount, direction and degree of balance;
3. yarn count/number/size—its two systems;
4. yarn structure—single, ply and cord yarns;
5. yarn appearance—smooth and textured; and
6. yarn function—durability and design (simple and complex yarns).

10.1 DIFFERENCE BETWEEN A THREAD AND A YARN

A thread is a product used to join pieces of fabrics together. It is frequently of plied construction. Yarns which are fine, even and strong, qualify for usage as threads. Thus, a thread is always a yarn, but a yarn may not always be a thread.

Characteristics considered important for a thread include adequate elasticity, smooth surface, high strength, resistance to snarling as well as damage by friction, dimensional stability and colour fastness. Threads can be used for machine or hand stitching. These can also be employed for embroidery and lace making. An additional property of attractive appearance is important in the latter usages.

Sewing threads can be made of cotton, linen, silk, rayon, polyester or nylon. These could have various structures like simple, ply, cord, monofil, multifil or elastic.

10.2 YARN TWIST

Fibres are given a twist to hold them together and impart strength to a yarn. One end of the fibre strand is held stationary, while the other end is revolved. The fibres then assume a spiral position around the yarn axis. There are three important aspects of yarn twist, viz., amount, direction and balance of twist.

10.2.1 Amount of Twist

The unit of twist is twist per inch (tpi) of yarn length. Generally, filaments need a twist of 3-6 tpi while staples require a higher tpi of 10–20. More twist is required for staple, fine yarns and warp yarns. Twist is also qualitatively described as low, medium and high.

Here are some concepts related to amount of twist:

1. It is a tool for bringing variations to fabrics.
2. Amount of twist has a direct bearing on the cost of the yarn. Higher twist would mean lower productivity, as the length gets shortened with twist incorporated. The cost is transferred to the consumer too.
3. Higher the twist, more compact and fine will be the yarns.
4. In general, twist increases the strength of a yarn. The relationship of direct proportionality holds good upto a point. This is termed as the *optimum twist*. Beyond an optimum point, however yarns can kink, become brittle and weak. It is thus, important to know the optimum twist for a yarn.
5. High twist imparts elasticity to yarns.
6. Twist makes yarns resistant to abrasion.
7. Twisted yarns shed soil easily since there is less space between fibres for soil to settle and the surface is smoother. Thus, maintenance of fabrics made from high twist yarns is easier for the consumers.
8. A good amount of twist produces yarns which are uniform, smooth and have a subdued lustre.

Low twist yarns are soft, fluffy, warmer, have more surface texture but show less resistance to abrasion and wearing due to lower strength. Figure 10.1 depicts low and high twist yarns.

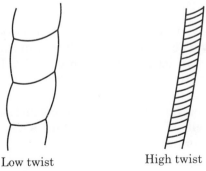

Low twist   High twist

Figure 10.1   Low and high twist yarns.

10.2.2   Direction of Twist

In order to understand the **direction of a twist**, lets perform a simple experiment. Lay a scarf or dupatta flat. Then gather it up and hold it in both hands. Keep the left hand on top in a stationary position and rotate the lower part with the right hand in an anti-clockwise direction. Observe what happens to the structure. It acquires a twist with the spirals conforming to the slope of the central portion of the alphabet 'S'. From the base, the diagonal lines move towards the left hand side. This is referred to as the *counter-clockwise twist, S-twist* or *left handed twist* (see Figure 10.2).

Next, straighten the scarf and repeat the experiment with a clockwise movement of the right hand at the lower end. The spirals now resemble the central bar of the alphabet Z and the diagonals move to the right hand. This direction of twist is thus, named *clockwise, Z-twist* or *right hand twist*. The Z-twist is more common (Figure 10.3).

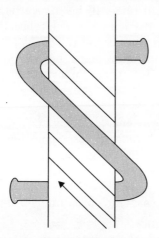 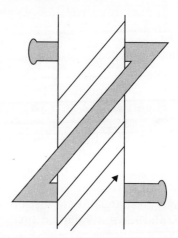

Figure 10.2 S-twist or left-hand twist.   **Figure 10.3** Z-twist or right-hand twist.

10.2.3 Degree of Balance

The degree of twist given can result in yarns that have a torque and are, thus, **twist lively**. This is the result of an unbalanced twist. Alternatively, yarns can be given a balanced twist. Let us get back to the scarf experiment. Hold the two ends after gathering them in your hands. Start twisting them. After a few twists, hold the scarf in a U-position. Observe how the structure maintains its loop without doubling or twisting upon itself. When this is true for a yarn, it is said to be **balanced**. Such yarns produce smooth fabrics. Now give a very high amount of twisting and repeat the exercise. You will notice that the scarf kinks and twines around itself. Such a phenomenon makes a yarn unbalanced or twist lively. This is desired for crepe yarns and textured effects (Figure 10.4).

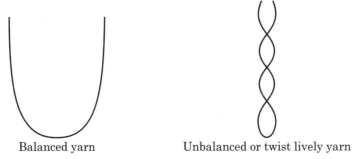

Balanced yarn   Unbalanced or twist lively yarn

Figure 10.4   Balanced and unbalanced yarn.

10.3   YARN NUMBER (YARN COUNT OR YARN SIZE)

This is an indicator of yarn thickness. There exists a mathematical relation between the length of a yarn and its fineness. This is quantitatively expressed as a number, hence the term *yarn number*. There are two systems which can be employed to denote yarn fineness. These are the direct and indirect systems.

10.3.1   Direct Yarn Number

These are commonly used for filaments, which express fineness as mass per unit length of yarn. Denier and tex are the two units which comprise direct yarn number.

Denier is the weight in grams of 9000 metres of yarn.

Tex is the weight in grams of 1000 metres of yarns.

In the **d**irect system, **d**enier (and tex) is **d**irectly proportional to the **d**iameter (call it the 4 D rule). Thus, if the yarn A is 4d, while yarn B is 6d, then yarn B will be thicker than yarn A.

10.3.2   Indirect Yarn Number

This system uses length per unit mass of yarns as an indicator of fineness. There are many kinds of indirect yarn numbers which are commonly used for spun yarns.

Cotton count (Ne):   number of 840 yard hanks that weigh one pound
Woollen count: number of 300 yard hanks that weigh one pound
Worsted count: number of 560 yard hanks that weigh one pound
Metric count: number of 1 km hanks that weigh 1 kg

In this system, the count of a yarn is indirectly proportional to the diameter. Thus, a high count means a low diameter or greater fineness of the yarn.

Yarns with cotton count upto 20 are considered coarse; between 20 and 60 are medium while yarns with count exceeding 60 are fine.

To understand this concept better, let us take a hypothetical situation. Imagine a weighing scale with 1 pound weight in a pan. You have to calculate the indirect yarn number (cotton count) of two yarns—A and B. These have been wound on packages such that each has 840 yard length. You start with yarn A and add hanks till the scale is balanced. Now remove and count the number of 840 yard hanks you needed to weigh one pound. Let this number be 5. Now repeat the same exercise with yarn B and find that you need 8 hanks to balance the scale. Thus, cotton count of yarn A is 5 (or 5s), while that of yarn B is 8 (or 8s). Can you figure out which yarn will be heavier and, thus, have a greater diameter?

Obviously, yarn A, with a lower count has a greater diameter or is less fine.

10.4   YARN STRUCTURE OR SUB PARTS

A common way of classification of yarns is based on the number of constituent parts that go into the making of a yarn. Yarns can be single, ply or cord.

10.4.1   Single Yarn

A single yarn is made up of filament or staple fibres. Such yarns are used for a uniform look. Very few textile applications employ single yarns. When amount of twist is increased, interesting effects can result. Crepe yarns are one such example.

10.4.2   Ply Yarn

A ply yarn is made up of two or more singles. Ply yarns are named on the basis of the number of singles that join to make them. For example, 3 ply and 4 ply. Ply yarns are less flexible, more coarse and heavy than single yarns.

10.4.3   Cord Yarn

A cord or a cable yarn is composed of two or more ply yarns. Figure 10.5 depicts single, ply and cord yarns.

For naming cord yarns, the number of plies as well as the number of single yarns in those plies is used. For example, 3, 2 ply cord yarn represents the use of 3 plies in yarn construction, each composed of 2 single yarns.

10.5   ON THE BASIS OF VISUAL APPEARANCE

Yarns may be classified as smooth or textured.

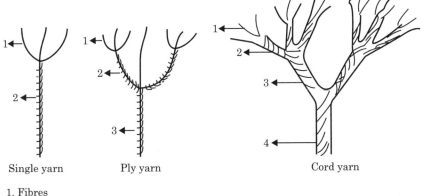

| Single yarn | Ply yarn | Cord yarn |

1. Fibres
2. Single yarn
3. Ply yarn
4. Cord yarn

Figure 10.5 Structure of yarn.

10.5.1 Smooth Filament Yarns

These have regular surface and cross sections. They feel slippery and clammy. Fabrics made from these lack warmth and comfort since, filaments have a poor score in bulk, absorbency, pilling resistance and stretch properties. Aesthetic appeal of such filaments is also low.

10.5.2 Textured Filament Yarns

Texturing can be defined as the permanent introduction of loops, coils, crimps or other distortions in an otherwise straight, smooth filament. This process imparts stretch, bulk, improved handle and greater absorbency to the filaments. Crease and pill resistance also get enhanced. Textured yarns have greater covering power or apparent volume, than similar conventional yarns with normal twist. Increased softness and warmth contributes to greater comfort. There are many methods employed to impart texture. Most of these, with the exception of air-jet texturing method, require the property of thermoplasticity.

1. Air-jet texturing

No heat is applied and processing of non-thermoplastic fibres (e.g., rayon or blends) can also be done. The process is a very versatile one since multi-filament yarns with count ranging from 60 to 3000 denier can be textured. Due to absence of any heat application, the internal structure remains unchanged and the effect is obtained by altering the outward appearance only. Air-jet textured filaments have a matte lustre and loopy, hairy appearance, thus resembling natural yarns most closely.

The machine consists of an inlet for the yarn at the base and one or more inlets for compressed air currents (see Figure 10.6). The yarns and air-jet mixture reaches the top into the funnel which is the area of turbulence. The filaments are tossed around to form numerous loops. As the yarn hits against the battle plate (a disc at the mouth of the funnel), the entanglements get fixed. Yarn is withdrawn by rollers and wound onto a package.

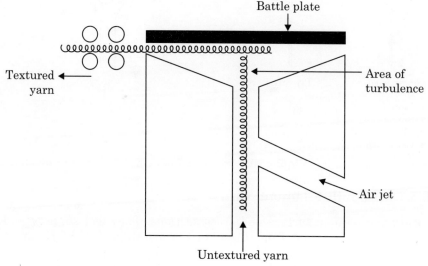

Figure 10.6 Air-jet texturing.

2. False twist process

Thermoplastic yarns are twisted and heated, followed by untwisting to produce yarns with sinusoidal crimps. A second set of heaters is used to stabilise these distortions (Figure 10.7).

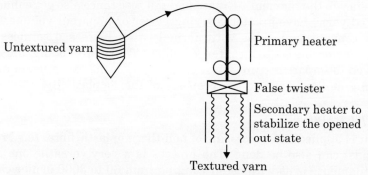

Figure 10.7 False twist.

3. Gear crimping process

This involves feeding yarns under controlled temperature and tension, between rotating intermeshing heated gears that impart gear tooth configuration to the filaments (see Figure 10.8).

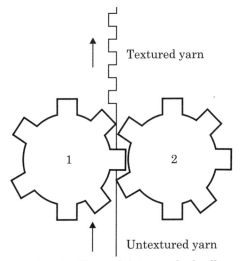

1, 2: A pair of heated, intermeshed rollers

Figure 10.8   Gear crumping.

4. Knife edge or edge crimping process

Heated thermoplastic filaments are drawn over a sharp knife edge. This causes certain areas to fuse slightly, imparting a spiral like curl to the yarn. You would have seen florists curling tapes while packaging bouquets. They use the blunt edge of a scissor and quickly pass the tape over it. The process is schematically represented in Figure 10.9.

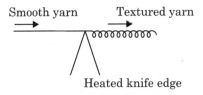

Figure 10.9   Knife edge texturing.

5. Knit-deknit process

Filament yarns are knitted into a fabric; it is heat set and then unravelled. The yarns acquire a permanent crimp.

6. Stuffer box process

Smooth filament tow is forced into a narrow stuffer box with an overfeed which makes it hit against the lid and buckle upon itself. This creates a saw-toothed crimp, which gets heat set by the heating coils in the walls of the box. Yarn keeps entering from the base till its push can displace the weighed lid. A crimped yarn is drawn out (see Figure 10.10).

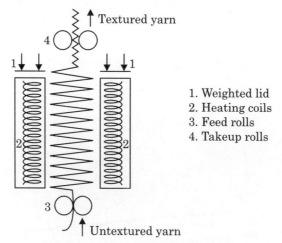

1. Weighted lid
2. Heating coils
3. Feed rolls
4. Takeup rolls

Figure 10.10   Stuffer box process.

7. *High bulk*

Such a textured yarn is produced by combining high shrinkage fibres with non-shrinkage fibres in a single yarn. Heat is then supplied leading to shrinkage of one component while the second component gathers up to produce a high bulk yarn. Many interesting effects are produced by this technique.

10.6   BASED ON YARN FUNCTION: DURABILITY OR DESIGN

Yarns may be simple in appearance and contribute to strength or add design to a fabric by virtue of their structure (fancy/novelty/complex yarns).

10.6.1   Simple Yarns

As the name suggests, simple yarns have a uniform size, regular surface and are relatively smooth in appearance. They have an equal number of twists per inch throughout their length. This uniformity makes them durable and helps prevent snagging and tearing. Such yarns are also relatively easy to maintain.

10.6.2   Complex Yarns

Fancy yarns bring an unusual look, variation and interesting effects into the fabric. Such yarns do not have a uniform thickness throughout their length. This in turn implies that they may show uneven performances in strength and wear. Complex yarns may be single or ply, though occasionally they may even have a cord structure.

Their three components are:

- Base or core which controls the length and stability of the yarn.
- Fancy or effect part which contributes to the design and
- Binder or tie which holds the fancy yarn in place during use and care.

Durability is related to each of these three components. For e.g., if the size of the fancy part is larger, it may have a greater tendency for snagging, pilling and abrasion. Similar result may also occur if the binder part does not succeed in holding the fancy part firmly to the yarn.

We will now look at some of the fancy yarns in common use. Their description will indicate their structural details (i.e., single, ply, cord or modified cord). For each category, many names exist and there is an overlap of information when you compare various books. A comprehensive list is as follows.

1. Loop, curl, boucle: A ply construction, there are closed loops at regular intervals along the base yarn (Figure 10.11).

2. Ratine: There is a base yarn around which an effect yarn is twisted. At intervals, the effect yarn forms a longer loop which is conspicuous and then continues to twine around the ground yarn (Figure 10.12). The tie or binder holds the effect yarn to the base (ply yarn).

Figure 10.11 Loop.   **Figure 10.12** Ratine.

3. Spiral/corkscrew: This is produced by choosing two plies that vary in twist or count. These are twisted together to produce a spiral effect (Figure 10.13).

Low twist

Figure 10.13 Spiral or corkscrew.

4. Knot/spot/nub/knop: At intervals, an enlarged spot is visible (Figure 10.14). This is produced by twisting the effect yarn many times in the same place around the base yarn). When the spot is tiny and at regular intervals, it is referred to as a seed effect.

5. Spike/snarl: On either side of the base yarn, the effect yarn forms alternating enclosed loops (Figure 10.15).

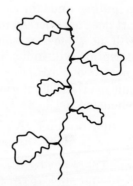

Figure 10.14 Knot (also called knop, nub or spot).

Figure 10.15 Spike or snarl.

6. Slub effect: Slub literally means a lump in a yarn. This effect can be obtained by two methods. The first is by inserting fibre tufts at regular intervals into a yarn while it is being twisted. The second is to alter the twist being given to a yarn. Low twist areas will have a greater diameter and fluffy structure than high twist areas (Figure 10.16).

Figure 10.16 Slub.

7. Metallic yarns: In earlier times, pure metals were extensively used in fabrics. Pure silver and gold were beaten, and then drawn into wires before being used for weaving. Naturally, the prices of such materials were high. Today, there are two processes commonly used to produce low cost, non-tarnishable, light weight, washable imitation metallic threads, also referred to as *tested zari* or *imitation zari*. In the metalizing process, a polyester film is deposited with aluminium which is vapourised under high pressure. It is then given a coating with lacquer to further increase its lustre. In the laminating process, a colourless film of polyester or acetate is laminated with aluminium foil to give it a glitter.

8. Chenille yarn: This is an interesting process since first a fabric is woven which has a pile construction, i.e., a raised nap which is shiny (like velvet). It is then slit into strips which are used in weaving interesting upholstery fabrics.

EXERCISES

10.1 Differentiate between the following pairs (with suitable illustrations):
   (i) Single and ply structures
   (ii) Thread and yarn
   (iii) Balanced and twist lively yarn
   (iv) S and z twist
   (v) Simple and complex yarn

10.2 Draw a schematic diagram to represent a 3, 5 ply cord yarn.

10.3 Why is yarn count an important indicator of a yarn? Which two systems are used for its expression?

10.4 Define texturing. Give its salient functions.

10.5 Describe air-jet texturing. What is its chief advantage over other methods of texturing?

SUGGESTED READING

Collier, B.J., Bide, M.J. and Tortora, P.G., *Understanding Textiles*, 7th ed., Pearson Education, NJ, 2009.

Goswami, B.C., Martindale, J.G. and Scardino, F.L., *Textile Yarns Technology: Structure and Application*, Wiley & Sons, USA, 1977.

Hudson, P.B., Clapp, A.C. and Kness, D., *Joseph's Introductory Textile Science*, 6th ed., Harcourt Brace Jovanovich College Publishers, 1993.

Selvakumar and Yuvaraj, A Study on Effect of Twist and Count on Sensory Properties of Shirting Fabric, *JTAI*, Vol 66, No. 2, pp. 100–104, July–August 2007.

Wingate, I.B., *Fairchild's Dictionary of Textile Terms*, 6th ed., Fairchild Publications, New York, 1988.

PART IV
Fabrics

In this part, fabric construction processes will be discussed. If you look around, you would notice that in everyday life you use many kinds of fabrics. Simple observation would reveal that fabrics vary greatly in their look, texture and performance. You would also agree that an apparel textile is so very different from an upholstery fabric. Even among the broad category of apparel, a salwar-kameez fabric looks quite different from a T-shirt. This difference stems from the fabric construction method employed in each case.

Broadly speaking, fabrics can be made from yarns or even from fibres directly. Fabric construction is done by the following methods:

1. Weaving: Two sets of yarns interlace at right angles to each other in patterns which are basic or fancy.
2. Knitting: A single yarn loops (either crosswise or lengthwise) to produce a fabric.
3. Felts and non-wovens: These are made from fibres directly without passing through the intermediate yarn stage.
4. Other methods: Nets, laces, braided fabric, tapa cloth, multi-component fabrics (quilts, bonded, laminated).

Chapters 11 and 12 will cover weaving and knitting respectively. Chapter 13 will discuss felts, non-wovens and other miscellaneous methods of fabric construction.

CHAPTER

11

Weaving

Weaving is the oldest method of fabric construction. Ancient Indian texts have references of woven fabrics. *Kabir*, a well-known Indian poet and philosopher, belonged to a family of weavers and many verses composed by him have references of this process.

11.1 LOOM: PARTS AND MOTIONS

A loom is a device used in weaving. Figure 11.1(a) carries a schematic diagram of a basic handloom. At its back is placed the **warp beam** or a roller with the warp yarns wound on it. These pass through the eye or hole in a metal wire or thin strip, called a **heald**. A number of healds are set in a rectangular wooden frame called a **harness** or **shaft**. In the simplest loom, there are two harnesses and alternate warps pass through them. Thus, all odd warps pass through the healds of the first harness, while all even warps pass through the healds of the second harness. If the first harness is lifted, all odd numbered warp yarns would be raised to create a space called a **shed**. This motion is called **Shedding** and is a primary motion of a loom.

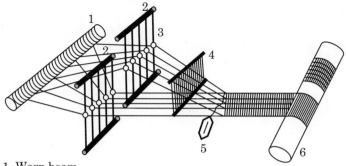

1. Warp beam
2. Harness
3. Heald
4. Reed
5. Shuttle
6. Cloth beam

Figure 11.1(a)   Schematic diagram of a simple handloom.

The weft yarns or pick is wound onto small **bobbins** (pirns) and placed inside a **shuttle** [Figure 11.1(b)]. This shuttle has a boat-like shape, with pointed ends. After shedding is done, the pick is laid in the second operation called **picking** (another primary motion). For this, the shuttle travels through the shed and waits at the other side.

Figure 11.1(b)   Bobbin and shuttle.

It is important to weave a fabric which is compact and firm. This is achieved by using a **reed**, which is a comb-like device placed towards the front of the loom. It has fine metallic wires with spaces called **dents**, through which the warp yarns have been passed prior to weaving. The reed is pressed against the weft in the third primary motion, called **beating**.

At places where the warp yarn is lifted, it will be visible. At other points, it is the weft yarn that will be seen in an interlacement. After the first pick is laid, the odd numbered warp yarns will be seen on top, while the even numbered warp yarns will be covered with the weft. For the next pick, the frist harness is lowered and the second harness is lifted up.

As the weaving proceeds, the warp yarns keep getting converted into a woven cloth after interlacement by the weft yarns. It is then time for the secondary motions of weaving. These are actually a pair of motions: **take up** and **let off**. The woven cloth is taken up or wound on the cloth beam placed in front of the loom. This pulls the warp yarns from the warp beam at the back of the loom. In other words, the warp beam lets off yarns and makes them available for weaving. Table 11.1 sums up the motions of a loom, along with the parts that help carry them out.

Table 11.1   Motions of Weaving

Category of motion	Name of motion	Parts employed
Primary	Shedding	Harness frame
	Picking	Shuttle
	Beating	Reed
Secondary	Take up	Cloth beam
	Let off	Warp beam

11.2   TYPES OF LOOMS

Classification of looms can be done on two criteria, viz., source of power and mechanism of laying the weft yarn.

11.2.1   Handlooms and Powerlooms

On the basis of the first criterion, looms can be divided into handlooms and powerlooms. As the term suggests, looms that are manually operated are referred to as *handlooms*. These are cheaper but have a comparatively slower rate of production. However, in a country like India, handlooms still occupy an important position. A variation of such looms is the *treadle loom* that uses foot levers which help lift the harness when pressed with feet. In the *pit loom*, the weaver sits with his legs inside a pit from where he controls the harness action through foot movement. In the *loin-loom*, the strap controlling the shaft movement passes through the lower back of the weaver who squats on the floor. This is common in the North-Eastern part of India.

The powerloom is run by mechanical energy. It is faster than a handloom and is employed by the mill sector.

11.2.2   Shuttle and Shuttleless Looms

The loom that has been discussed in Section 11.1 uses a shuttle for laying the pick [Figure 11.1(b)]. It is thus, referred to as a *shuttle loom*. Hand driven shuttle looms have more or less retained their traditional character over the years in various states of India. However, major milestones have been achieved in looms that are power driven. Some of these include automatic weft and warp stop motions, automatic pirn changing devices and computer operated designing features.

In many places, shuttle looms have given way to *shuttleless looms*. The pick is laid across the shed using a variety of mechanisms. The name of the loom clearly indicates which device is used. Shuttleless looms have lower noise levels and greater production speeds.

The *rapier loom* employs a long rod which carries the weft yarns across the shed. The *gripper or projectile loom* uses a small metal hook which carries the weft through the shed. *Air jet looms* employ compressed air which forces the strand of weft to pass the entire width of the fabric. *Water jet looms* have thin water streams which move with a force enough to place the weft. Only hydrophobic yarns can be woven into fabrics on such looms.

11.3   WOVEN FABRICS: SOME CONCEPTS

Whichever may be the shedding device or degree of automation employed, there are certain characteristics typical of woven fabrics. **Warp** or **end** refers to the yarns laid lengthwise on the loom. Cross wise yarns are called **weft, pick** or **filling** yarns. Warp yarns are generally stronger than weft yarns and are given a sizing (stiffening) treatment since they have to face a lot of wear and tear in the weaving operation.

Bias refers to a direction which is at 45° angle to the warp and weft. There is maximum stretch along the bias of a fabric. This is made use of in apparel construction, e.g., for a churidar pyjama. Before cutting any fabric, the grain is checked. This is the position of the warp and weft yarns. Ideally, these two set of yarns should be perpendicular to each other. If a woven fabric exhibits skewing or bowing (incorrect relative positioning of the warp and weft) it would not result in good quality apparels.

Fabric count (or thread count) is an indicator of the compactness of a weave. It is defined as the number of warp and weft yarns per square inch of a woven fabric. A fabric with 50 warps and 40 wefts in one inch will have a fabric count of 50 × 40 or 90.

Balance is the ratio of the warps to wefts in one square inch. A balanced fabric is one in which this ratio is 1:1. On the other hand, an unbalanced fabric might have a yarn ratio of 2:1.

Fabric count can be judged by any of the two methods:

(i) Unravelling method, which involves 'unweaving' a defined length and width of a fabric to get yarns and counting them. This damages the fabric and is, thus, less popular.

(ii) Pick-glass method which uses a small device with a one inch square window at one end and a magnifying glass at the other end (Figure 11.2). It is placed properly and the numbers of warp and weft yarns are counted through it.

Figure 11.2   Pick glass.

High fabric count indicates fineness, body, stability, strength and cover. Such fabrics are wind and water repellent, fire retardant and have reduced seam ravelling. On the other hand, a low fabric count gives better drape, flexibility, permeability, higher shrinkage potential and more seam ravelling.

A balanced fabric will exhibit less seam slippage and an even wearing out in both directions than an unbalanced one.

Selvedge or selvage is the 'self edge' of a woven fabric. Observe a woven sari or dupatta. You would notice that the two longer sides have edges that do not need any kind of finishing. These portions are also slightly thicker than the rest of the fabric. While weaving fabrics on handloom, the weaver uses a greater density of warp yarns in the edges to produce a distinct selvedge.

In the case of shuttleless looms, selvedges pose a problem and need to be made afterwards. If the fabric is thermoplastic, it may be given fused selvedges by applying heat and causing the yarns to fuse with each other.

Grainline is a straight line with arrows which is drawn parallel to the selvedge to represent direction of the warp yarns. Figure 11.3 depicts the various concepts of a woven fabric discussed earlier.

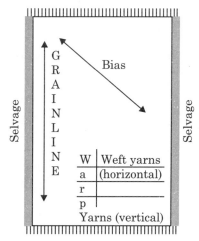

Figure 11.3   Concepts of a woven gabric.

11.4 WEAVES

The interlacement of the warp and weft yarns produces designs called **weaves**. Various factors such as number of harnesses, threading pattern of warps through the healds, number of picks laid together and lifting plans of harnesses can be regulated to obtain a wide variety of weaves. Broadly, these can be classified into basic and fancy or decorative weaves. Table 11.2 gives a classification of weaves, which will be followed in subsequent discussions.

Table 11.2   Classification of weaves

Weaves	
Basic	**Fancy**
Plain weave	Dobby
Variations	
• Rib weave	Jacquard
• Basket weave	
	Surface figure weave
Twill weave	• Spot
• Regular twill	• Swivel
• Irregular twill	• Lappet
Satin and sateen weave	Pile weave
	• Weft pile
	• Warp pile (cut and uncut)
	Leno weave
	Double weave

Point paper diagrams are representations of a weave in a 2-D form. Graph papers can be used by students or these can be made on a plain paper after making a vertical and horizontal framework of lines. Vertical lines depict the warp and horizontal lines depict the weft. Small squares formed depict the interlacement of the two sets of yarns. In order to represent the warp as being above the weft, the square is shaded or crossed. A blank square signifies that the weft has been placed over the warp in that interlacement. Let us go back to the example discussed in the simple handloom model. The first harness, with all the odd numbered warps is lifted, the pick is placed in the shed and beating up is done. The point paper depiction of the first pick is shown in Figure 11.4 (a). In this manner, if you keep representing the weave, you would obtain a point paper diagram [Figure 11.4(b)].

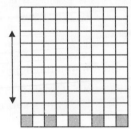

Figure 11.4(a) Reprsentation of first pick. **Figure 11.4(b)** Plain weave with repeat marked.

Repeat is the area of the point paper which depicts the "seed" of the entire weave. It is often marked on the point paper diagram with a dark outline. If this piece is replicated, it would yield a bigger representation of the weave (Figure 11.4(b)]. The number of times a pick passes in a repeat equals the number of harnesses required to make it.

Along with a discussion on weaves, point paper diagrams will be given for basic weaves while schematic diagrams will be used to describe fancy weaves.

For the sake of ease of understanding, some basic weaves are discussed in points. These cover the number of harnesses, interlacement patterns, special features and examples.

11.4.1 Basic Weaves

1. Plain weave

  (i) Simplest and most inexpensive weave
 (ii) Only two harnesses are required
(iii) The weft yarn goes under and over one warp across the width of the fabric
 (iv) It can be represented by the symbol 1 × 1

Examples of fabrics with plain weave are organdie, muslin, cambric, poplin, flannel and canvas.

Point paper diagram has been shown in Figure 11.4(b).

The plain weave has two variations, viz., rib and basket.

Rib weave: Instead of a single yarn, a group of yarns is used (as one unit). Figure 11.5(a) and (b) depicts the rib weave which can be produced in either direction. It may be noted that a weft rib weave is obtained due to grouping of warp yarns, while a warp rib weave results due to the grouping of weft yarns.

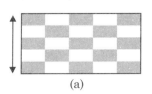

(a)

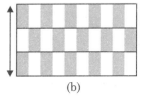

(b)

Figure 11.5   Rib wave.

Sometimes, grouped yarns are followed by single yarns during loom setting. When this is done in any one direction, the resulting weave is called a **striped dimity** [warp or weft, see Figure 11.6(a), (b) and (c)]. **Cross bar dimity** is formed by using group of yarns and single yarns in both warp and weft direction. The resulting fabric is very pleasing and commonly used in apparel (Figure 11.7).

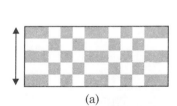

(a)

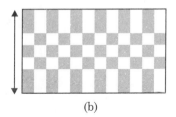

(b)

Figure 11.6   Striped dimity.

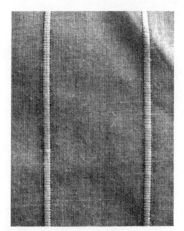
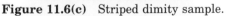

Figure 11.6(c)   Striped dimity sample.

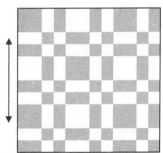

Figure 11.7   Cross bar dimity.

Here's a tip for making point paper diagrams—first make the skeletal structure carefully. Then show interlacements following 1 × 1 formula.

Basket weave

   (i) The fabric design resembles the familiar pattern of a chessboard or a basket with equal sized squares.
  (ii) Two or more warp yarns interlace with one or more filling yarns.
 (iii) The fabric produced is flexible, loosely woven, somewhat wrinkle resistant, suitable for covering and drapery.
 (iv) The width of the combined yarns in any one direction will be equal to the corresponding yarns in the other direction.
  (v) Formula for basket weave depicts the number of warp yarns and weft yarns that interlace as a single unit. The yarns lie side by side and can even be counted with the naked eye.

Examples include hopsacking (jute packaging bags), oxford and monks' cloth. Figure 11.8 shows the point paper diagram for a 3 × 2 basket weave.

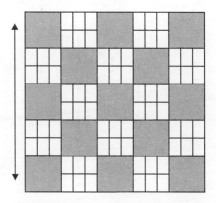

Figure 11.8   3 × 2 basket weave.

2. Twill weave

Table 11.3 gives a classification of twill weaves. Broadly speaking, twill weaves can be divided into regular twills, characterised by uninterrupted diagonal lines on the face and back of the fabric. The second category comprises irregular twills, in which the diagonal line changes its path to create interesting effects. Regular twills can be sub-classified on the basis of angle of the diagonal. The angle of this line can be 45° (regular/medium twill), lower (15°—reclining twill) or higher (75°—steep twill). Various other terms will be explained in this section.

Table 11.3 Classification of Twill Weaves

Regular twill	Irregular twill
• Angle of diagonal lines	• Diamond twill
(i) Reclining twill	• Curved twill
(ii) Normal twill	• Zig zag twill
(iii) Steep twill	• Herringbone
• Direction of diagonal lines	• Pointed twill
(i) Right hand twill	
(ii) Left hand twill	
• Evenness of face and back	
(i) Even faced or reversible twill	
(ii) Uneven faced or irreversible twill	
(warp or weft faced)	

But first, it is important to know the basic characteristics of this weave. These are as follows:

(i) Twill weave requires a minimum of three harnesses.

(ii) The filling yarn interlaces more than one but not more than three warp yarns. In the next picking, the weft yarn moves the design one step to the right or left. This forms the diagonal pattern. In regular twills, this runs uninterrupted but in irregular twills, the diagonal changes its course to produce many interesting effects.

(iii) The fabrics with twill weaves are attractive, durable and strong. Being tightly woven, they do not get as dirty as plain weaves but once soiled, they are more difficult to clean.

Examples include denim, gabardine, drill, some tweeds and many suiting fabrics.

The formula for depicting twill weave resembles a fraction. Thus, 3/1 represents a twill weave in which at 3 points, the warp yarn is visible, followed by the weft at 1 point. The number of harnesses required for constructing regular twill is calculated by adding the numerator and denominator. This is also equal to the repeat of this weave. Let us now represent a twill weave using a point paper diagram (Figure 11.9). Continuing with the example of 3/1 twill, let us mark the intersection on the first pick.

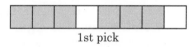

1st pick

While laying the 2nd pick, the shaded area moves one block to the right or left. If you continue like this, you would get a point paper diagram which has diagonal lines moving from the bottom to the top right corner [right handed twill Figure 11.9(a)] or to the top left corner [left handed twill, Figure 11.9(b) and (c)].

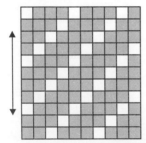 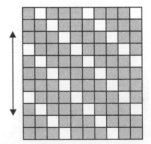

Figure 11.9(a) 3/1 right handed (warp faced twill). **Figure 11.9(b)** 3/1 left handed (warp faced twill).

Figure 11.9(c) Twill weave (left handed).

It must be remembered that the sum of the numerator and denominator cannot exceed 6, since the twill weave can have a maximum float length of 3. But there are many combinations which are possible. For example, 2/1, 1/2, 3/1, 1/3, 2/2, 3/2, 2/3 and 3/3 can all be made by twill weave. The number of harnesses required will be 3, 3, 4, 4, 4, 5, 5 and 6, respectively.

When the number of warps and wefts appearing on a fabric is equal, it is an **even faced twill**. Thus, twill weaves with formulae 2/2 and 3/3 will form reversible fabrics. If the numbers in the formula are unequal, then the resulting weave is called an **uneven twill**. It can be further described as **warp faced** (when greater number of warps are visible, e.g., 2/1, 3/1, 3/1) or **weft faced** (when greater number of wefts are seen, e.g., 1/3, 2/3 and 1/2).

The family of irregular twills also has many members like diamond twill, curved twill, zig zag twill, herringbone and pointed twill. Point paper diagrams for herringbone (Figure 11.10) and pointed twill (Figure 11.11) have been given. These are commonly seen in men's suiting materials.

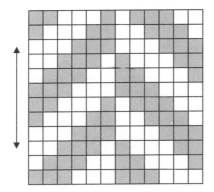

Figure 11.10   Herringbone twill 3/3 herringbone weave.

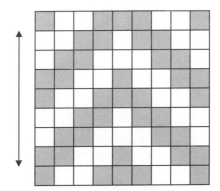

Figure 11.11   Pointed twill.

3. Satin weave

The third basic weave is satin. Known for its rich sheen and soft handle, satin weave has been long considered a symbol of luxury and feminity. Its salient features are as follows:

(i) There is a predominance of warp yarns on the surface of the fabric. These appear as continuous lengths (called **floats**) and are tucked in by the weft yarn. The diagonal of the satin weave is purposely interrupted in order to produce a smooth and lustrous surface.

(ii) Float length varies from 4 to 11 and number of harnesses required vary from 5 to 12 (float length + 1 = no. of harnesses needed).

(iii) Satin has high lustre, smooth and slippery feel due to long floats.

(iv) On the other hand, these floats can snag and get pulled easily, making satin weave fabrics less durable and weaker than plain or twill weave fabrics.

(v) Satins find wide usage as lining fabric and in sarees.

Sateen is a variation of this weave. There is a predominance of the weft yarns in the form of floats with very few warps visible.

Figure 11.12 depicts a satin weave. You can interchange the shaded and unshaded area to get a depiction of sateen weave.

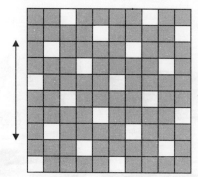

Figure 11.12   Satin weave with 5 harnesses.

11.4.2   Fancy weaves

1. Dobby weave

This is characterised by small, geometrical or floral repeat figures. The loom may have 24–30 harnesses and is called a **dobby loom**. A simplified version of the jacquard looms, it uses wooden cross bars with metal pegs. Every cross bar determines which warp yarns will be raised to form the shed in a given row of pattern.

Examples include honeycomb [Figure 11.13(a) and (b)] and birds' eye (Figure 11.14). It is not possible to remove the design without unravelling the fabric. This helps beginners distinguish between surface figure weaves on one hand and dobby or jacquard weaves on the other.

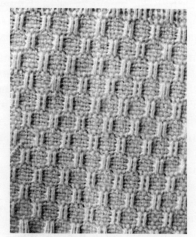

Figure 11.13(a)   Honeycomb weave.

Figure 11.13(b)   Dobby weave sample.

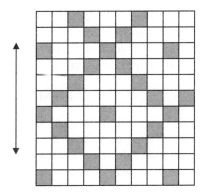

Figure 11.14 Birds' eye weave.

2. Jacquard weave

The loom used is also called **jacquard loom**, after its inventor, Joseph Jacquard. This is one of the most elaborate weave, made by combining plain, twill and satin weaves even in the same crosswise yarn. It has elaborate patterns and scenes that make it extremely attractive and also expensive. Such fabric weaving is also possible due to the loom's ability of controlling each warp yarn individually. Today, a lot of jacquard weaving is done with the help of computers. Manually operated jacquard looms involve intensive labour and skill. The design is first made on a graph paper and colours as well as the weaves for each part are decided. Next, the position of each warp yarn (raised or lowered) is analysed. A small rectangular cardboard is prepared for each of the weft yarns by punching it. A punched hole will indicate that the warp corresponding to it will be raised before the pick is laid. The punched cards are laced together, their number being equal to the repeat size of the pattern.

The warp yarns are tied with cords, which are attached to hooks. These hooks are in contact with needles. For each picking, one card assumes position. When a needle hits against a hole in the card, it moves through, thus engaging and lifting a hook. This raises the cords attached to that hook and subsequently the warp yarns from a shed. When the weft has been placed, the needles retract and the cards rotate to bring the next one in position.

Brocades and damask are made on jacquard looms. Such weaves are used for formal clothes and upholstery as well. Some of the silk sarees produced in India like Baluchari of Bengal are examples of jacquard weave. These have elaborate hunting scenes and depiction from the epics—all executed through jacquard weaving. Figure 11.15(a) and (b) shows jacquard weave samples.

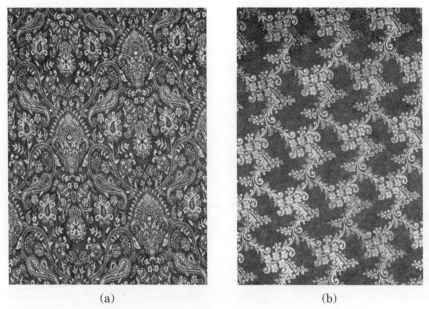

(a)   (b)

Figure 11.15   Jaquard weave samples.

3. Surface figure weaves

Extra set of warp and/or weft yarns are used to create many interesting designs on fabrics. There are three members in this family:

Spot or dot: Extra yarns are used in one or both directions, to produce designs. Generally, these differ in colour and/or weight from the base fabric, thus making them prominent.

    When you see the reverse of a spot weave, you will either see floats between two spots [unclipped spot, Figure 11.16(a)] or the cut edges of yarns along the sides of the design [clipped spot, Figure 11.16(b)]. The 'eyelash' patterned fabric (dotted swiss) is one example of clipped spot.

Figure 11.16(a)   Spot weave (unclipped).

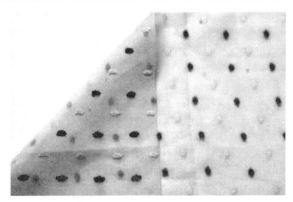

Figure 11.16(b) Spot weave (clipped).

Swivel weave: Extra filling yarn is used to create beautiful motifs. The yarn is wound on a small spool which intermediated with the warp yarns, turning back at the ends of the motif. If you see the reverse side of a swivel weave, you would notice two yarn cut ends—one at the beginning and the other at the end of the motif (Figure 11.17). The extra weft is firmly held in place and this method permits the use of different colours even across one width of the fabric (unlike spot designs with extra weft yarns).

Cotton sarees from Calcutta are a common example of swivel weave. It is also common in women's fabrics for salwar kameez.

Lappet weave: Extra warp yarn is used to create a pattern which is securely fastened to the ground weave. Fabrics with this weave are durable and expensive. The second warp is rolled on a beam and placed with the warp roll at the back of the loom. One way to recognize lappet weave is to observe the path of the design yarn. If it travels along the entire length, then it is lappet weave (Figure 11.18). The effect sometimes resembles hand embroidery or machine hakoba embroidery.

Figure 11.17 Swivel weave front and back.

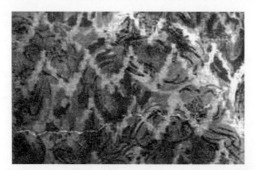

Figure 11.18 Lappet weave.

4. Pile weave

Originating from the Latin word *pilus* meaning hair, these weaves have a soft projecting surface of fibres. One set of yarns, called **ground warp** and **weft**, form the base fabric in plain or twill weave. An extra yarn forms floats which are then cut and brushed to form the pile. Weft pile fabrics are made by using an extra weft yarn. It floats over three or more warp yarns of the ground fabric. On being removed from the loom, these floats are cut to form a raised surface. Corduroy and velveteen are examples of weft cut piles. Corduroy exhibits ridges and furrows to produce a ribbed effect. Velveteen on the other hand, has an overall effect. It is also possible to produce figured velveteen by cutting and raising of pile in predetermined design areas.

We could depict pile weave construction with the help of diagrams [Figure 11.19(a) and (b)] which schematically represent yarns before and after cutting.

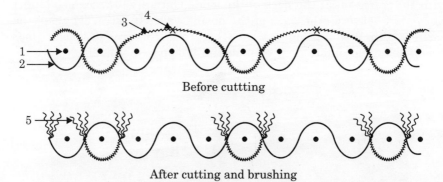

Before cuttting

After cutting and brushing

Figure 11.19(a) Corduroy (weft cut pile).

Before cuttting

After cutting and brushing

1. Ground warp	2. Ground weft
3. Extra weft to make pile	4. Points at which extra weft is cut
5. Cut weft pile	

Figure 11.19(b)   Velveteen.

Warp pile weaves are made by using an extra warp yarn. Salient examples are terry pile (looped towel) fabric and velvet. Notice the surface of a towel. You would observe many loops on both sides. Terry pile weave can also be described as an **uncut warp pile**. The second warp yarn is wound on a beam which is placed above the weaving surface. The pile warp has a slack tension which makes it buckle up and form loops on both sides after the beating up. The reed gets into action after 3, 5 or 7 picks have been laid. The longer the gap, the greater is the length of loops formed [Figure 11.20(a) and (b)]. This means a better water absorbing surface but at the same time, longer loops are more prone to snagging and are, thus, less durable.

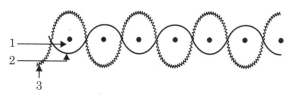

1. Ground weft
2. Ground warp
3. Extra warp yarn which makes loops

Figure 11.20(a)   Uncut warp pile.

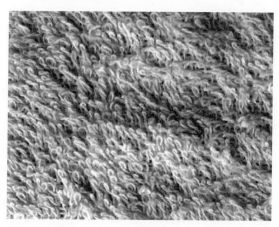

Figure 11.20(b)   Uncut warp pile (terry towel) sample.

The second kind of warp pile is the **cut pile** (e.g., velvet). There are two methods of preparing it:
  (i) Wire cut pile method and
  (ii) Double cloth method, whose names describe the process used.

In the wire cut method, special wires are inserted during weaving in the shed created by raising of the pile warp. The wires have a razor edge on the side. After weaving, these are pulled up from the fabric. This action cuts through the floats formed over them. The pile is brushed and sheared. As a variation, wires without blade edges may be used. They are removed by pulling from one side after the weaving is complete. The pile fabric, thus, formed has loops only on one side. The length of the loops is decided by the circumference of the wires used.

In the double cloth method, five sets of yarns are used. One set of warp and weft forms one ground fabric and a second set of warp and weft forms the second ground fabric. A fifth yarn (warp) travels between the two by interlacing in a V- or W-manner. Figure 11.21(a) and (b) give a schematic representation of these interlacing patterns. The W interlacement yields more durable results as the pile yarn is held in the base fabric at two points instead of one. The double fabric made on the loom is then cut through to produce pile which is brushed and sheared. Two widths of velvet fabric are thus made simultaneously and wound on separate rollers (Figure 11.22). This method yields good quality velvet at greater speeds.

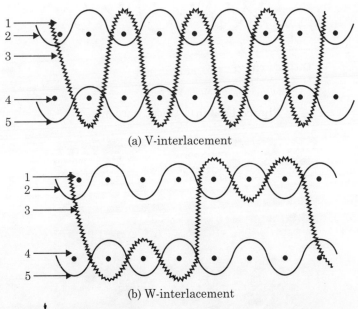

(a) V-interlacement

(b) W-interlacement

1. Ground weft (first fabric)   2. Ground warp (first fabric)
3. Extra yarn far warp pile   4. Ground weft (second fabric)
5. Ground warp (second fabric)

Figure 11.21 Double cloth method of contructing warp pile (before cutting).

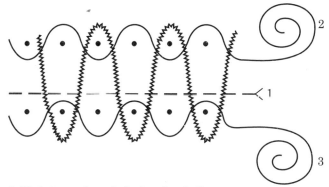

1. Blade to cut through the interlaced pile warp yarn.
2, 3: Two separate rolls of cut warp pile fabric.

Figure 11.22   Double cloth method (after cutting)

5. Double weaves

These are made with 3, 4 or 5 sets of yarns. Double cloth which is made from 3 yarns is also called a **double faced** or **backed fabric**. There could be 2 sets of warp yarns, which share 1 filling yarn. It is also possible to have 2 sets of filling yarns which use one common warp.

When double weaves with four yarns are used, one pair of warp and weft forms one fabric while another pair forms a second fabric. These two layers are held together by the periodic cross-over of their weft and/or warp yarns between the two layers. Such fabrics can be identified by the fact that they are reversible and exhibit a 'pocket' effect in some parts of the design. This happens when the weft yarns have returned to their original sides (double cloth). A third kind of double fabric is made by using five sets of yarns. Such constructions are expensive and hence not very common. The process has already been described in the warp pile weave method. The finished product is used as a single, heavy, reversible fabric without being sliced through (as for velvet construction).

Double cloth weave constructions are used in apparel, upholstery and draperies. Salient uses for double faced or backed fabrics include satin ribbons, interlinings of coats and reversible blankets.

6. Leno weave

This is characterised by an open mesh structure which is achieved through a doup attachment on the loom. This controls the warp yarns by moving vertically as well as horizontally. The weave is also sometimes referred to as *doup weave*. Fabrics produced with such crossed yarn arrangements exhibit superior strength, reduced shrinkage and slippage. Figure 11.23 depicts the leno weave.

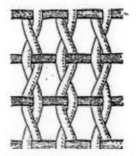

Figure 11.23   Leno weave.

Notice the alternating 'dominant' and 'recessive' positions that the warp yarn takes when interlacing with the weft and the second warp yarn.

Difference between gauze and leno weave

Gauze is an open mesh fabric which has a plain weave construction and a very low fabric count. It is made on a two harness loom without any attachment. Chief use includes surgical bandages.

11.5   SOME INNOVATIONS IN WEAVING

In the last section on weaves, we have looked at biaxial, flat and single shed weaving processes. Technology is rapidly advancing and other options are available today. As a student and consumer of textiles, it is important to know some of the new developments in the field.

11.5.1   Triaxial Weaving

As the term suggests, yarns interlace in all the three axes, viz., horizontal, vertical and bias. Two sets of warp yarns and one set of weft yarns interlace at 60° to each other. This produces fabrics with extraordinary tear and burst resistance, uniform strength and durability in all directions. Salient uses include industrial, geotextiles and aerospace applications. Selected apparel and home textile usages are also being explored.

11.5.2   Circular Weaving

Circular weaving is done on circular looms to produce tubular fabrics. End uses include sacks and pillow slips which do not require any stitching on the sides.

11.5.3   Multiple Shed Weaving

Multiple shed weaving produces fabrics at double the speed of single shed looms. A number of sheds are created along one length of warp yarns. As many as twenty wefts can be laid simultaneously in a multiple shed loom.

EXERCISES

11.1 Name and describe the primary motions of a loom.

11.2 What do you understand by the term shuttleless looms? Give examples.

11.3 Draw point paper diagrams for the following weaves:
   (i) 5 × 3 basket weave
   (ii) 3/2 right handed twill
   (iii) 2/3 left handed twill.

11.4 Define fabric count and balance. How are these parameters related to the durability of a woven fabric?

11.5 Explain the method of constructing pile weaves with diagrams and examples.

11.6 Differentiate between the following pairs of weaves:
   (i) Lappet and swivel
   (ii) Dobby and jacquard
   (iii) Even and uneven faced twill
   (iv) Striped and cross bar dimity.

SUGGESTED READING

Adanur, S., *Handbook of Weaving*, Technomic Publishing Company Inc., USA, 2001.

Behera, B.K. and Mishra, R., Three Dimensional Weaving, *IJFTR*, Vol. 33, no. 3, pp. 274–287, 2008.

Collier, B.J., Bide, M.J. and Tortora, P.G., *Understanding Textiles*, 7th ed., Pearson Education, NJ, 2009.

Hudson, P.B., Clapp, A.C. and Kness, D., *Joseph's Introductory Textile Science*, 6th ed., Harcourt Brace Jovanovich College Publishers, USA, 1993.

Murphy, W.S., *Handbook of Weaving*, Abhishek Publications, Chandigarh, 2000.

Schwartz, P., Rhodes, T. and Mohamed, M., *Fabric Forming Systems*, Noyers Publications, Park Ridge, NJ, 1982.

CHAPTER

12

Knitting

In the last chapter, we have learnt about weaving, a very old method of fabric construction. Another method which is fast catching up is knitting.

12.1 HISTORY OF KNITTING

Knitted fabrics are made from interlocking loops, formed from one or more yarns. The origins of hand knitting cannot be dated, but it is believed to be quite old. Hand knitting uses two needles or pins (which are available in a range of diameters). One or more yarns may be used in a variety of stitches to produce weft knitted fabrics. The process requires time and skill. In machine knitting, loops of yarns are formed with the help of thin, pointed needles. As new loops are formed, they are drawn through the previous ones, thus producing a knited fabric. The salient inventions in the field of machine knitting are listed in Table 12.1.

Table 12.1 Inventions in the Field of Machine Knitting

Year	Inventor	Equipment
1589	Reverent William Lee (Germany)	Mechanical knitting frame (flat bed) which uses spring beard needles
Late eighteenth century	John William Stint	Ribbing device
1775	Crane of England	Warp knitting machine
1816	Sir Mare Isanband Brunel	Circular knitting machine
1849	Sir John Scaly Edward Townshend	Patented the latch needle and then the compound needle
1863	William Cotton	Machine which could add or drop stitches, to shape the garment parts
Mid 1950s		Basic frames for modern knitting were developed
Late 1970s and early 1980s		Computerisation of knitting process

12.2 KNITTING: SOME CONCEPTS

12.2.1 Stitches

Loop or stitch is the basic structural element of a knit construction. Each loop has one head, two legs and two feet (Figure 12.1).

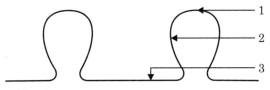

1. Head
2. Legs
3. Connecting part (feet)

Figure 12.1 Loop.

Wale: vertical column of loops which runs parallel to the length of the knitted fabric. It can be compared to the warp in a woven fabric (Figure 12.2).

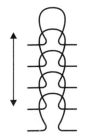

Figure 12.2 Wale.

Course: horizontal row of loops which runs perpendicular to the length of the knitted structure. It can be likened to the weft in a woven structure (Figure 12.3).

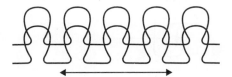

Figure 12.3 Course.

12.2.2 Gauge or Cut

It is an indicator of the fineness or coarseness of a knitted fabric which in turn is related to the number of needles used on the machine. Units of gauge are *number of needles per inch on the machine* (npi) or *number of needles per centimetre* (npcm). The stitches (or loops) of a fabric can also be counted to determine its gauge since one needle will form one loop.

12.2.3 Technical Face and Technical Back

These are the terms used for the two sides of a knit structure. The appearance of the technical face and back serves an important function of identifying the type of knit stitch in a fabric. Sometimes, for designing purposes, the technical back is used as the front in a garment.

12.2.4 Needles

Just as hand knitting employs long, thin needles which come in various diametres, so also machine knitting uses many types of needles. The diagrams for four knitting needles are given below.

(i) Latch needle

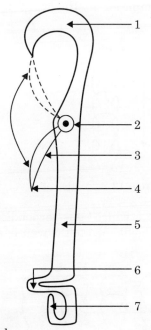

1. Hook
2. Rivet
3. Latch blade
4. Latch spoon
5. Stem
6. Butt
7. Tail

Dotted line depicts the closed position of the needle

Figure 12.4 Latch needle.

(ii) Spring beard needle

For finer fabrics with smaller loops.

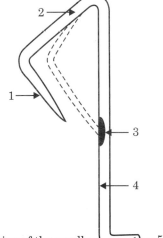

1. Beard
2. Hook/head
3. Groove/eye cut in the stem
4. Stem
5. Shank
Dotted line shows closed position of the needle

Figure 12.5   Bearded/spring needle.

(iii) Compound needle

Knit at greater speeds than latch needles.

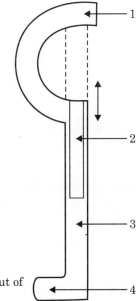

1. Head
2. Sliding latch
3. Stem
4. Butt
Dotted line depicts sliding latch out of
the stem to close the needle

Figure 12.6   Compound needle.

(iv) Double latch hook

These are used in purl machine.

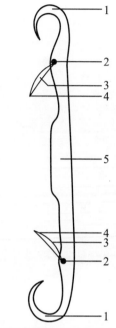

1. Head
2. Rivet
3. Latch blade
4. Latch spoon
5. Stem

Figure 12.7 Double latch hook.

12.3 WEFT AND WARP KNITS

Knitted fabrics can be classified into weft knit and warp knit structures. Table 12.2 lists the differences in the two constructions.

Table 12.2 Comparison of Weft and Warp Knitting

Weft knitting	Warp knitting
One continuous yarn forms courses across the width.	Many yarns form wales along the length.
The yarn is fed crosswise to the length of the fabric.	The loop forming yarn is fed in the direction of the length of the fabric.
Can be done by hand or machine.	Only through machine.
Can produce straight fabric (on flat bed machines) or tubular fabric (in circular machines).	Only flat bed machines are used to produce straight fabric.
Can be unravelled; may ladder.	Cannot be unravelled, usually does not ladder
Knitting needles can work sequentially (one at a time) or simultaneously (all together)	Knitting needles always work together as a unit.

(Contd...)

Table 12.2   Comparison of Weft and Warp Knitting

Weft knitting	Warp knitting
Latch needles are used.	Compound needles and sometimes spring-beard needles are used.
Loops have an open structure.	Loops have a closed structure.
Yarn specification is not very stringent and hence weft knits are comparatively cheaper.	Yarn specification is more stringent and hence cost is more.

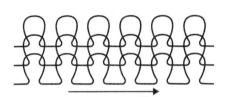

Figure 12.8   Weft knitting.

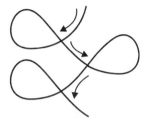

Figure 12.9   Warp knitting.

12.4   WEFT KNIT STITCHES

There are four weft knit stitches, viz., plain, purl, rib and interlock. Two variations can also be made (tuck and float) using weft knitting. Each of these is described below.

12.4.1   Plain, Single, Jersey

- Made with one needle bed and one set of needles
- Basic stitch, most commonly seen in knitted structures
- Technical face has flat, vertical wales of loops whose legs are prominent [Figure 12.10(a)]

Figure 12.10(a)   Plain or jersey knit (face).

- Back has dominant horizontal rows formed by heads and feet of loops [Figure 12.10(b)]

Figure 12.10(b)   Plain knit (back).

- Salient advantages include greater speeds and lower costs of production, possibility of knitting light to medium weight fabrics
- Drawbacks include tendency to 'run' or formation of 'ladder' in case of yarn breakage and tendency to curl towards technical back
- Common uses include sportswear, sweaters and T-shirts

12.4.2   Purl Fabric

- Made with two needle beds and one set of needles which are double hooked
- Fabric has the same appearance on face and back, which resembles the technical back of a single jersey [Figure 12.10(b)]
- Fabrics produced are thick, bulky and do not curl
- Machine maintenance is expensive and production is slow, thus escalating the cost of the final product
- Mainly used for infant and children's sweaters, stoles

12.4.3   Rib Fabric

- Made with two needle beds and two sets of needles which are arranged in an alternating manner (Figure 12.11)
- Fabric has same appearance on face and back with columns of loops interspersed with ridges of loop heads

Figure 12.11   Rib knit.

- Structure can be 1 × 1 (one column of wales and one ridge), 2 × 2 or 3 × 3
- Fabrics have excellent crosswise stretch and do not curl
- Commonly used in sleeve bands, waist bands and necklines of sweaters to give a snug fit

12.4.4   Interlock Fabric

- Made by two needle beds and two sets of needles, which are placed directly opposite to each other. These work alternately
- Made by two rib fabrics (1 × 1) intermeshed with each other to produce a double fabric which is reversible and resembles the face side of a single jersey
- Fabric produced is firm and does not curl

12.4.5   Variations in Stitch

(i) Tuck stitch

Comprises a held loop and a tuck loop, both intermeshed in the same course. A needle receives a new loop but does not shed the old one. These accumulated loops are knitted together to produce 'blister' effect [Figure 12.12(a)].

The fabric has a soft handle and lofty appearance, though less extensible.

(ii) Float/Miss stitch

It appears as a length of yarn not received by a needle. It connects two loops of the same course that are not in adjacent wales. Miss stitch is formed by holding a needle in a non-working position so that it misses a loop, the yarn being carried as a float past it. Figure 12.12(b) depicts a float or miss stitch.

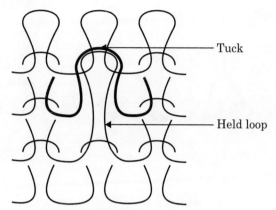

Figure 12.12(a) A tuck stitch.

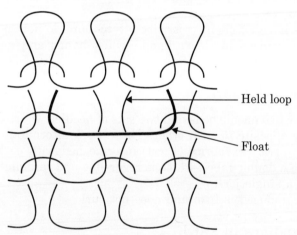

Figure 12.12(b) Float/miss stitch.

12.5 WARP KNITTING

In warp knitting, one or more sets of warp yarns are wound on warp beams. Each individual yarn is drawn through a yarn guide to the hook of the knitting needle which is mounted on a guide bar that extends across the width (lapping) of the machine. This bar moves, to cause the yarn to be lapped around the needle. Next, the needle bar moves to form loops simultaneously through all needles, across the course. The guide bar then moves sideways (shogging) to be positioned one or more needles away from the previous point. Thus, each needle loops its own yarn, producing parallel rows of loops simultaneously that are interlooped in a zig zag pattern. More the guide bars, greater is the design flexibility.

The warp knitting machine resembles the weaving loom in some ways, though it is much wider than most looms. The stitches on the face of the fabric appear vertically, though at a slight angle. The back shows horizontal floats (also called **laps** or **underlaps**) which appear to be at a slight angle.

There are four salient warp knits, viz., tricot, raschel, milanese and simplex. More than 95% of warp knitting goods are made by tricot or raschel knitting machines. The rest are made using simplex and milanese knits. A brief description of warp knits follows.

12.5.1 Tricot

Tricot in French means, *to knit*. The simplest tricot is made with one set of needles and two guide bars. Some machines can have 3 or 4 guide bars (the number indicating the number of sets of warp yarns used). Spring beard or compound needles are used in these machines. Machine widths can be 168 inches and the speed of production is quite high. Filament yarns of nylon, polyester, acetate or triacetate are generally used. Technical face has vertical wales and finer appearance than the back which has horizontal courses. Being run-proof and non-ravelling, tricot knits have high resiliency and elasticity (higher in crosswise direction) as well as high tear strength.

Its chief uses include lingerie, women's dresses and blouses, men's shirts and sleepwear.

12.5.2 Raschel

These machines have 1–2 needle beds with latch needles in a vertical position and upto 30 guide bars. Fabric comes out of the knitting frame vertically instead of horizontally. A large number of guide bars implies great design possibilities. Speeds of such machines are, however, lower (almost half) than tricot machines. Spun yarns can be used in the construction of raschel knits. A very diverse range, from very heavy to sheer structures, is possible. Uses of raschel knits span from women's dresses, men's tailored suits, sportswear, laundry bags, carpets, curtains, upholstery to nets and laces.

12.5.3 Milanese Knits

These can be recognised by the interlooping pattern which produces a visible diagonal path at the technical back. Such fabrics have greater regularity in structure, higher elongation and tear strength than tricot knits. They are also highly run-resistant.

Limited design possibilities have made milanese knits capture only a small share in total knit production.

12.5.4 Simplex

This is a heavier, thicker version of the tricot which finds limited applications in hand bags and gloves.

12.6 VARIATIONS IN KNITTING

Many interesting effects can be achieved in weft knits. Salient among these include:

(i) **Transfer stitch, spread stitch and cross stitch** are some variations which produce a variety of patterns in weft knitting.

(ii) **Use of coloured yarns or fancy yarns** to produce stripes, cables and open mesh structures.

(iii) **Knitted terry fabric** is made by introducing an extra yarn which forms loops extending above the plane of the fabric.

(iv) **Knitted velvet fabric** is obtained by cutting and brushing the loops formed with the extra yarn. In general, knitted pile fabrics are soft and quite absorbent but have poor shape retention as compared to woven piles.

(v) **Fake fur or silver knit** is obtained by feeding fibre slivers to the needles. These get entrapped and stay in position by the intermeshing loops. The technical back exhibits a pile or fleecy effects. Printing with an animal hide pattern creates the fake fur.

(vi) **Jacquard patterns** are formed by using jacquard mechanisms which employ various stitch types and colours. Circular knitting machines are equipped with electronic controls which create elaborate patterns.

(vii) **Inlay or weft insertion** is a technique in which an extra yarn is inserted at the back and tucked at regular intervals. Its purpose may be to impart design or strength and stability to the knitted structure. Sometimes it is brushed and raised to form a nap/fleece.

Just as in the case of weft knitting, many variations are possible in warp knitting. Some salient ones include warp knitted terry and velvet, nets, laces, thermal cloth, insertion warp knits and satin knits.

12.7 COMPARISON OF KNITTING WITH WEAVING

Let us compare the two processes of fabric construction

1. Knitting is 'younger' to weaving as a fabric construction process.
2. Yardage as well as garments can be made on knitting machines while looms produce only yardage.
3. Knitting is two to five times faster than weaving.

4. Knitting involves formation of loops, thus a greater length of yarn is used up to form loops across the width and along the length of a knitted fabric.

5. Knits have greater porosity but lesser cover than wovens.

6. Fineness of construction is indicated by gauge or cut in knits, as against fabric count or thread count in wovens.

7. Wide knitting machines run as fast as the narrow ones; in weaving, wider looms have a slower speed of production.

8. Yarn specifications for knitting are more stringent than for weaving. This escalates the cost of raw material. However, no yarn preparation like sizing, washing or pirn making is needed in knitting.

9. Knit fabrics exhibit upto 5% shrinkage as against 2% in the case of wovens.

10. Looping imparts stretch to the knit fabric, while wovens do not stretch to any marked degree (unless specially made using stretch yarns). Only the bias direction of a woven construction exhibits some stretch.

11. Design can be changed very rapidly, especially in weft knitting. Thus, the pulse of prevailing fashions can be reflected more effectively in knitting than is possible in weaving.

12.8   PROPERTIES OF KNITS

Knits are known for their excellent drape, fit and comfort. They give warmth due to the insulative air pockets. Other positive features include high absorption, light weight and wrinkle resistance and recovery. The other side of the coin is that knits are costly and some fabrics tend to sag and loose shape. Some weft knits also face the problem of ladder formation. If one loop breaks, then a hole is made which starts to 'run' or slip down the wale. It was perhaps this phenomenon which started the idiom, "a stitch in time saves nine!".

12.9   USES AND CARE OF KNITS

Today, knits (especially warp knits) compete closely with products of the loom. Their properties make them the preferred choice for sportswear, casualwear, undergarments, and socks. A whole range of fibres is being used for construction of knits for a gamut of end uses. These include wool, cotton, rayon, silk, metal yarns and textured synthetics like nylon and acrylic. Apparel uses of knits predominate other categories. Curtains, cushion covers, upholstery and carpets are common applications of knits in the home. In India, Ludhiana produces a vast range of knitted home textile products.

Care of knits will depend on the fibres that have been used in their construction. Thus, woollen knits will have to be laundered and stored very carefully. On the other hand, acrylic knits can be machine washed and are not even threatened by attack from carpet beetles and clothes moths.

EXERCISES

12.1 "Weft knits are cheaper than warp knits", give reasons.

12.2 What makes a knitted fabric warm and absorbent?

12.3 Enumerate weft knit stitches. Explain the most common of these.

12.4 Describe the following terms:
   (i) Gauge
   (ii) Courses and wales
   (iii) Latch needle
   (iv) Compound needle
   (v) Beard needle.

12.5 Name and explain two problems commonly faced by weft knits.

SUGGESTED READING

Collier, B.J., Bide, M.J. and Tortora, P.G., *Understanding Textiles*, 7th ed., Pearson Education, NJ, 2009.

Hudson, P.B., Clapp, A.C. and Kness, D., *Joseph's Introductory Textile Science*, 6th ed., Harcourt Brace Jovanovich College Publishers, 1993.

Mohashi, P.D., Imperfections in Knitted Fabrics, *JTAI*, Vol. 67, No. 2, pp. 55–62, July–August 2006.

Lakra, D., Growth of Knitting Industry, *JTAI*, Vol. 67, No. 4, pp. 165–167, November–December 2006.

Schwartz, P., Rhodes, T. and Mohamed, M., *Fabric Forming Systems*, Noyers Publications, Park Ridge, NJ, 1982.

CHAPTER 13

Non-wovens and Other Methods of Fabric Construction

13.1 INTRODUCTION

Broadly speaking, non-wovens include those fabric structures which are made by some means other than weaving or knitting. This means a partial or complete elimination of conventional textile processes such as sliver formation, attenuation, spinning, weaving or knitting. This, in turn, leads to large saving of time and cost. Today, non-wovens are witnessing a phenomenal spurt in applications and demand. This industry also has a significant potential for growth.

There are some steps common to the formation of any non-woven. Table 13.1 enlists the four steps followed for their preparation.

Table 13.1   Steps in Non-Woven Production

Step	Sub-steps
1. Preparation of fibres	Blowroom processes like opening, cleaning and blending
2. Formation of web	Mechanically (with card) Aerodynamically Hydrodynamically Electrostatically By other special techniques
3. Bonding	Mechanical (felting, needle punching) Physical (heat and pressure) Chemical (dry or wet adhesives) Direct methods (spun bonding, melt blowing)
4. Finishing	Dyeing, printing, embossing, resin finishing, imparting relevant finishes

13.2 NON-WOVEN CATEGORIES

Non-wovens are commonly divided into two groups, viz., felts and bonded fabrics (Table 13.2). It is interesting to note that while felts are perhaps the oldest of fabrics made by man, bonded fabrics are the "youngest". Over the years, bonded fabrics have become synonymous with non-wovens and felts are considered a separate category. It is possible to further categorize felts into wool felts (or true felts) and needle felts. Bonded fabrics can also be divided into sub-groups, based on the method of bonding employed.

Table 13.2 Classification of Non-Wovens

Non-Wovens			
Felts	Bonded fabrics made by		
Wool felts Needle felts	Thermal treatment. Thermoplastic spun bonded	Chemical treatment (adhesive bonded). Dry powder. Liquid adhesive	Direct Method • Spun Bonded • Melt Blown

13.3 FELTS

13.3.1 Wool Felts

These are fabric structures made by the interlocking of scales present on wool fibres. Technically, any animal hair fibre can be used for felt construction. However, the most commonly used and practical option is sheep hair or wool. Today, wool fibres are also blended with other non-felting fibres to reduce cost of production but the proportion of wool in such blends is at least 50%.

Production

Scales present on the wool fibres have a tendency to interlock and shrink when subjected to heat, moisture, friction and agitation. It is believed that wool felts may have been accidentally discovered by primitive man as he stuffed some sheep hair tufts into his footwear. The combined effects of heat, perspiration and friction would have yielded a matted structure at the end of the day. Textile historians agree that felt production preceded spinning and weaving. This method is followed even today, though as a controlled process, which comprises the following steps:

   (i) Wool fibres (alone or along with small proportion of non-felting fibres) are cleaned, blended and carded.
  (ii) Two or more layers are placed, one on top of the other, at right angles to attain the required thickness. The thickness, in turn, is decided by the end use of the felt.
 (iii) These layers (batts) are trimmed and rolled. Heat and moisture is applied and the batts are consolidated into a felted fabric on a felting machine. This has a pair of heavy, reciprocating boards between which the wool fibre structure is placed.
  (iv) The fulling machine then repeatedly beats, compresses and squeezes the wet web to a felt of required density. Sometimes, soap or dilute sulphuric acid is also used while fulling.

(v) The felt is neutralised, scoured, rinsed and dried after putting it on a stenter frame. It is stretched to its required dimensions.
(vi) The structure is then steam pressed to obtain a smooth surface.
(vii) Felts can be imparted finishes to make them moth proof, fireproof, water repellent and resistant to fungi. Choice of finish would be decided by the end use planned.
(viii) The prepared felt fabric can be decorated by a variety of means like dyeing, printing, embroidery or appliqué.

Properties and uses

These are dependent on the raw material used i.e., type of animal hair and non-felting fibres which may have been added.

Some general features include good insulation properties, easy shaping, good shock and sound absorbance and good resilience. On the other side are poor elastic recovery, low breaking elongation and difficulty in mending holes (as done by *rafugars* in woven fabrics).

Felts are used in apparel (collar backs for coats and jackets, hats), home furnishings, rug pads, insulation materials, billiard cloths and have industrial applications. The *'Namda'* of Kashmir is an example of felt fabric. Figure 13.1(a) shows a traditional Kashmiri floor mat. Figure 13.1(b) depicts a more contemporary application.

Figure 13.1(a)   Kashmiri floor mat.

Figure 13.1(b)   Contemporary usage of felt.

Care

Felts are mostly dry cleaned. Even when home laundered, it is important never to pull or twist the felt fabric. Other conditions such as choice of detergent, temperature and method of washing will be similar to that of wool fibres. For the same reason, their storage will require the use of moth repellent naphthalene balls. Some wool felts are imparted finishes that make them moth proof and hence easy to maintain.

13.3.2   Needle Felts

These 'felts' are made wholly or mainly from fibres other than wool. Almost any type of fibre can be used, though synthetic fibres are commonly used. Fibre entanglement is achieved by the mechanical action of barbed needles. Needle punched volume in 2007 was 23,050 tonnes and accounts for half of all non-woven production in India (Butler, 2007).

Production

Fibres are cleaned, blended and then prepared into a batt or web. This enters the needle punching machine or needle loom in which many barbed needles are fixed on a needle board which repeatedly penetrates the web (see Figure 13.2).

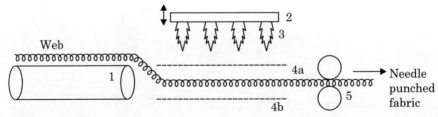

1. Feed apron
2. Needle board
3. Barbed needles
4. (a) Stripper and (b) Bed plates
5. Take up rollers

Figure 13.2   Needle punching machine.

At each stroke, the barbs drag the fibres to the lower side of the web, thus, entangling the structure. New trends include the use of needle boards on both sides of the web and also the use of several such boards [Figure 13.3 (a), (b)]. Experiments with slanted needles have also been done in order to make the process more efficient. Sometimes, supplementary fibre bonding techniques may also be used to impart additional strength to the needle felt.

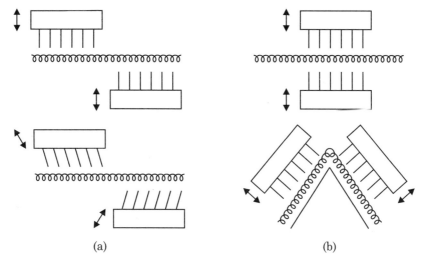

Figure 13.3   Possible arrangements of needle boards.

Properties and uses

The properties of needle felts depend on a host of factors. Machine parameters such as fineness of needles, number and size of barbs play a crucial role in the final product. Web variables such as type of fibres, their lengths and orientation also have a direct bearing on the kind of needle felt produced. In general, it can be stated that needle punched fabrics are light in weight, warm and offer ease of care and maintenance since synthetic fibres are normally used.

Chief uses include pre-moistened wipes, medical/surgical products, decorative fabrics, blankets, interlinings, waddings, floor coverings, carpet underlays, upholstery materials, mattress covers, packaging materials and industrial filters. Some protective apparel and outerwear is also made using needle felts.

13.4   BONDED FABRICS

These are flexible materials which have been formed directly from fibres and rely on thermal or chemical treatments for their construction.

Production

As listed in Table 13.1, the production process can be broken down into various steps:

1. Preparation of fibres: Fibres are cleaned and blended. The raw material requirement is not stringent and, thus, fibres of different chemical and physical compositions can be combined in a single structure.

2. Formation of web: A fibre web or batt is made by any of the following four methods:

(a) Mechanical web formation   Webs are layered in either **oriented, cross-laid, combination of oriented and cross laid** or **random arrangement**. In oriented webs, fibres are parallel to the longitudinal axis (Figure 13.4). Cross laid webs are made by combining two or more layers of web, each placed at right angles to the previous one (Figure 13.5). A combination arrangement implies that webs are oriented and sets of such webs are placed at right angles in subsequent rows. Random webs are the most popular and have fibres arranged randomly.

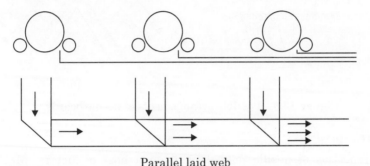

Parallel laid web

Figure 13.4   Oriented webs.

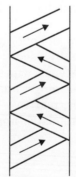

Web from the card is turned by cross-lapper

Figure 13.5   Cross-laid webs.

(b) Aerodynamic web formation   Dry laid webs are made by either collecting fibres into a suction drum or separating them on carding machines.

(c) Hydrodynamic web formation   Wet laid webs are made by mixing the fibres with a liquid (generally water). This slurry is transported and cast onto a perforated cylinder or moving screen. Water is removed by vacuum, followed by drying.

(d) Electrostatic web formation   The alignment of fibres in the web can be controlled by application of an electric field.

3. Bonding: The web is flattened and bonded. The method of bonding serves as a basis of classifying the bonded fabrics (Table 13.2). This can be done by thermal, chemical (dry and wet adhesive) or direct methods. These are described as follows:

(a) Thermoplastic fibres may be uniformly blended in the fibre web or used in small areas at regular intervals. On application of heat, these soften and fuse. As the web cools, the fibres are all held securely together. In spun blown webs, biconstituent filaments can be spun from two different polymer types extruded at the same spinneret. On heating, one component melts and fuses to bring about bonding.

(b) An adhesive may be applied. It may be either in a dry powder form such that the thermoplastic particles may fuse and bond the web on application of heat. Alternatively, a liquid adhesive solution can be used. Application can be done by impregnation or saturation bonding. This is done between screens or rollers [Figure 13.6(a), (b)]. In spray bonding, the adhesive is sprayed on both sides of the web (Figure 13.7). In print bonding, the print paste contains the adhesive which may also serve the purpose of imparting design to the non-woven fabric. It is important that the distance between the print is less than the length of the fibres used in the web.

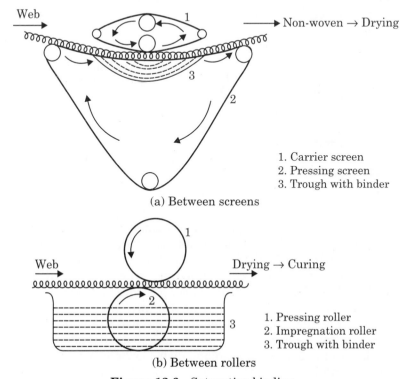

1. Carrier screen
2. Pressing screen
3. Trough with binder

(a) Between screens

1. Pressing roller
2. Impregnation roller
3. Trough with binder

(b) Between rollers

Figure 13.6   Saturation binding.

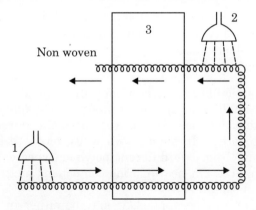

1, 2. Spray guns of adhesive
3. Hot air drier

Figure 13.7 Spray bonding.

(c) Direct methods include those techniques which combine web
formation and consolidation in a single step i.e., the non-woven
is directly manufactured. In **spun bonding**, rotating spinneretes
extrude synthetic filaments. Air currents lead to entanglement
and these randomly laid molten filaments fuse at cross over points,
forming a non-woven fabric (see Figure 13.8). The conveyer belt
carries it for collection.

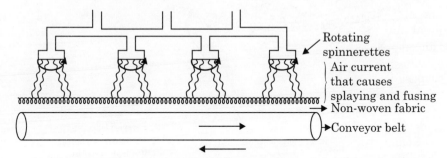

Figure 13.8 Spun bonding.

In **melt blowing**, the polymer is heated for micro seconds at
very high temperature to lower its viscosity. It is then blown out
as a spray of extremely fine molten fibres. These are gathered on
a collector in the form of solidified non-woven fabric and wound
onto rollers (Figure 13.9). It is also possible to produce moulded
articles by using a collector of appropriate shape.

The non-wovens made by the direct method are not very strong
but can be used as filters since their porosity is controllable.
Today, in India, spun bonded and melt-blown techniques comprise
the second most important technology (after needle punching).

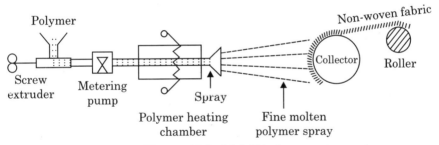

Figure 13.9 Melt blowing.

4. Finishing: Drying of bonded webs is the next step. This is followed by curing i.e., treatment at very high temperature using hot air ovens or infra red light. This is especially required when liquid adhesives are employed for bonding and the bonding agent has to be set by chemical or thermal action.

The prepared bonded fabric can be dyed and printed, if required.

Properties and uses

Bonded non-wovens are known for their low cost, 100% cover and use of any kind of raw material. They also possess isotropic properties (same in all planes) which make them the preferred choice for filtration and geotextiles.

Properties like form, stability, crease resistance, air permeability and stability to washing as well as dry cleaning make bonded fabrics ideal for use as interlinings, facings and paddings in garments. Cut edges do not fray, making the finishing of apparel very simple.

Other applications include tissues, diapers, bandages, sanitary towels, disposable napkins, mats, bed pads, lampshades, teabags, cloths for wiping and polishing, industrial textiles, medical textiles, electrical insulations, padding, packaging, roofing, blankets, carpets and carpet underlays, decorative fabrics for crafts and outerwear.

Some of their drawbacks are poor draping qualities, difficulty in mending and tendency to lose shape or open up on washing.

Care

In many cases, the products made are disposable, thus, doing away with any care or maintenance steps. At times, this could in itself create problems for the environment. If laundry is required, minimum agitation should be given.

13.5 OTHER METHODS OF FABRIC CONSTRUCTION

13.5.1 Braided Fabrics

A braid is made by interlacing three or more yarns to form a plait (as seen in hair). These can be used for trimmings or joined together to form a fabric. Braided textiles stretch considerably in length. Craft items and bags made of jute or coir braids are made in the coastal areas in India [see Figure 13.10(a) and (b)]. Braided constructions are also used in shoelaces, wicks and electrical wire coverings.

Figure 13.10(a)   Braided jute bag.   **Figure 13.10(b)**   Closer view of braid.

13.5.2   Laces

The hand lace industry became quite popular in Italy during the fourteenth century. Although a machine for lace making was introduced in seventeenth century, it was only in 1813 that John Leavers made a commercially efficient lace machine. This led to increased production and saving of labour. The starting material for lace is generally a thread and not a yarn. If, however, a yarn is used then it is given enough twist to strengthen it. Construction of a lace includes thread twisting, intertwining and knotting, thus producing sturdy products. Some types of commonly used laces are bobbin lace, embroidery lace and raschel lace. All laces are characterised by an open mesh structure and decorative design. Patterning can be done in laces using jacquard mechanisms. Figure 13.11 shows a lace.

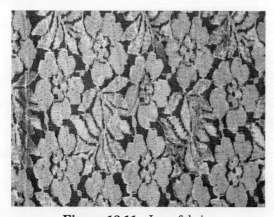

Figure 13.11   Lace fabric.

End uses include lace trimmings in variety of apparel (dresses, lingerie) and home textiles (pillow covers, napkins). Lace fabrics can also be made up into dresses, curtains and table cloths. Care procedures include careful handling while washing or dry cleaning to retain the shape.

13.5.3 Laminated Fabrics

The American Society for Testing and Materials (ASTM) defines laminated fabrics as a layered fabric structure in which a face or surface fabric is joined to a backing fabric with an adhesive that does not add significantly to the thickness of the combined fabric.

13.5.4 Nets

Before 1800, all netting was done by hand. In 1809, a machine was developed for this purpose. Nets are open work fabrics made by threads or yarns, on bobbinet machines in which the bobbin yarns are looped around the warp yarns in a spiral formation. This produces large geometric open gaps between yarns with no designs. Applications include veils, curtains, fishing nets, sports equipments and hammocks. Price and quality of a net are dependant on the complexity of design, type of fibre used and whether it is handmade or machine made. Care procedures are decided by the fibre used. However, an open mesh structure requires careful handling while washing and drying. Figure 13.12 shows a net construction.

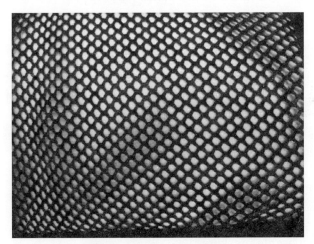

Figure 13.12   Net fabric.

13.5.5 Stitch Bonded Fabrics

An assembly of fibres or yarns are held together (bonded) by stitching along the length direction. Their chief advantage is high production rate with a low capital investment. Applications include filling materials for winter clothing, cleaning cloths and low cost furnishings.

13.5.6   Tufting

This method of fabric construction aims to simulate pile fabrics, at a fraction of their cost. A woven fabric acts as the base and a set of pile yarns is inserted into it to form tufts or loops on one side. These may be cut and brushed also (see Figure 13.13). Tufting was originally done by hand. Around the beginning of the twentieth century, a tufting machine was made that employed needles for tuft insertion. Fibres generally used for the base include cotton, linen and jute. Tufts are made from a wide variety of natural as well as man-made fibres such as cotton, wool, rayon, acetate, polyester, nylon and acrylic. A latex coating is then given at the back to enhance the stability of the tufted structure. End uses include warm lining materials, bedspreads, blankets, rugs and carpets.

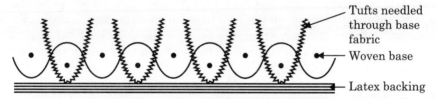

Tufts needled through base fabric

Woven base

Latex backing

Figure 13.13   Tufted construction.

EXERCISES

13.1 Classify non-wovens. Distinguish between their sub-categories.

13.2 Explain the working of a needle punching machine with the help of a diagram.

13.3 Enumerate the steps of bonded fabric preparation. Describe the methods employed for consolidation of the fibre web.

13.4 Describe direct methods of non-woven production with the help of diagrams.

13.5 State the advantages and drawbacks of felts.

13.6 Write a note on applications of non-wovens in the disposable and non-disposable markets.

REFERENCE

Butler, I., Outlook and Prospects for Non-Wovens in India, *ITJ*, Vol. 118, No. 1, pp. 84–87, October 2007.

SUGGESTED READING

Agrawal, Y., Malik, T., Mohanta, R. and Kapoor, R., Spunbond and spunlace: Two Advance Technologies for Non-wovens, *JTAI*, Vol. 67, No. 3, pp. 111–115, September–October 2006.

Alexander, P.R., *Textile Products: Selection, Use and Care*, Houghton Miffflin, USA, 1977.

Martin, G. (Ed.), *Encyclopedia of Textiles, Fibres and Non-Woven Fabrics*, Wiley & Sons, USA, 1984.

PART V
Finishing

In the previous section you have studied various methods of fabric construction. However, a fabric cannot hit the market immediately after its construction. There are a host of processes that a fabric needs to undergo to alter and/or improve its aesthetics as well as performance properties. These processes come under the blanket term 'finishing', which will be discussed in this part. Chapter 14 gives the definition, classification and details of basic and special finishes. The two processes of colour application, viz., dyeing and printing are described in Chapter 15.

CHAPTER

14

Basic and Special Finishing

Finishing is the last stage of fabric processing. It covers a wide range of processes which make an unattractive,'greige' fabric turn into an attractive one. It is possible to carry out finishing at different stages of textile production. Thus, a fibre, yarn, fabric or garment can be subjected to the finishing process, though most efficient results are obtained at the fabric stage.

14.1 CLASSIFICATION OF FINISHES

Finishes can be classified in various ways:

14.1.1 On the Basis of the Life of a Finish

(a) **Temporary:** a finish which is lost after a couple of washing or dry cleaning cycles. Some of these may be renewable e.g., starching of cotton fabrics, while others may be non renewable e.g., printing with gold dust.

(b) **Durable:** a finish which lasts for most of the life of a product. For example, the heat set pleats of a nylon skirt may remain perfect for about a year and then open out.

(c) **Permanent:** a finish which stays throughout the lifetime of a product. A well-dyed fabric does not lose its colour even if it wears off. Similarly, stiffening imparted to a fabric by use of resins is a permanent finish.

14.1.2 On the Basis of Mode of Action

(a) **Mechanical** finishes which employ use of mechanical equipment like perforated machines, copper plates and rollers. Examples of mechanical finishes are calendering and raising.

(b) **Chemical** finishes which use acids, alkalis, bleaches, detergents, resins and other chemicals to attain the desired result. These may either act on the surface (external finishes) or penetrate and combine chemically with the substrate (internal finishes). Thus, if a coating of fire retardant chemical is deposited at the surface, it is an external finish while use of cross linking agents (urea formaldehyde), to impart crease proof finishes, is an example of an internal finish.

14.1.3 On the Basis of Achieved Results

This is the most common classification method which is based on achieved results and will also be followed in this chapter. There are three categories of finishes, viz., basic, special and colouration finishes.

Finishing could be likened to the process of getting ready before we leave our homes each day. There are certain activities like brushing our teeth, bathing and combing our hair which are 'basic'. Similarly, there are some 'basic/routine' finishes which all fabrics have to undergo.

For special occasions such as weddings and parties, one takes more time to get ready. A person may apply foundation to look fairer, curl up otherwise straight hair or wear high heels to appear taller. It is, thus, possible to alter (enhance/subdue) or impart a feature which is otherwise absent. Similarly, in the field of finishing, certain functional or special finishes are imparted, based on the intended end use of the fabric.

(a) **Basic/Routine/General Finishes:** All fabrics undergo these finishes to make them acceptable to consumers and prepare them for subsequent processes like special finishes and colouration. Hence, these finishes are also referred to as *preparatory finishes*. These include singeing, desizing, scouring, bleaching, basic calendering, beetling, mercerisation, sizing, weighting, tentering and inspection. Not all fabrics undergo each of these processes. The final list is decided by the finisher on the basis of the market requirement.

(b) **Special/Functional Finishes** are aimed at aesthetics and/or performance. These can be further divided into four categories, described below:

   (i) Finishes that alter appearance by mechanical means: This list includes special calendering (schreinering, moiré, embossed surface, friction calendering) and raising and finishing of fibre surface (gigging, napping, sueding, flocking, emerising, brushing and shearing).

   (ii) Finishes that alter appearance by chemical means: These include the finishes imparted by the use of delustrants, optical brighteners, acids (burned out designs, parchmentisation) and alkali (plissé). The softening, stiffening and fading finishes also come under this head.

   (iii) Finishes that enhance comfort and after care properties: Finishes imparted for this purpose include absorbent, antistatic, abrasion resistant, antislip, stain and soil resistant, durable press and shrink resistant finishes.

   (iv) Finishes that impart safety and protection: This group includes flame resistant, water repellent and water proof, antipesticide finish, light reflectant finishes, moth proofing and bacteriostatic finishes.

(c) Colouration finishes give colour to an otherwise white fabric. These are further divided into two groups: dyeing and printing, and will be discussed in the next chapter. Table 14.1 summarises this classification.

Table 14.1   Classification of Textile Finishes

Basic/ routine finishes	Special/functional finishes				Colouration finishes	
	For aesthetics		For performance		Dyeing	Printing
	Mechanical finish	Chemical finish	Safety and protection	Comfort and after care properties		

14.2   BASIC/ROUTINE FINISHES

14.2.1   Beetling

A mechanical finish used for linen and cotton fabrics. The fabric is pounded by heavy hammers. This action closes the interstices of the weave, flattens the yarns and gives a greater area for reflection of light, thus increasing the fabric lustre.

14.2.2   Inspection

This involves careful examination of the fabric for any imperfections (Perching). Some of these can be repaired quite inconspicuously (burling). A few flaws may require greater repairs (mending). Figure 14.1 shows a fabric being inspected with the help of lights from behind.

Figure 14.1   Inspection of fabric.

14.2.3 Singeing

'Singe' means to burn the surface slightly. An unfinished fabric has protruding fibre ends on the surface, some loose fibres and dust. Brushing is first done to remove the lint and dust. Then the fabric is passed in full width over heated copper plates or gas flames at very high speeds (100–200 metres per minute) to burn off the protruding ends.

To prevent any damage from afterglow or sparks, the fabric immediately enters a water bath after leaving the singer.

14.2.4 Desizing

Preparatory processes for weaving include sizing, i.e., application of a stiffening agent (generally starch) on the warp yarns. This has a waterproof property which will hamper in application of subsequent finishes and colouration. Desizing is the removal of this sizing.

It is generally done with the aid of enzymes which digest the stiffening agent.

Silk fabrics undergo 'degumming' since the sericin gum imparts stiffening to the silk fabrics.

14.2.5 Scouring

In common language, scouring means thorough washing. A 'gray' fabric may have certain inherent impurities as well as the acquired ones. For example, a cotton woven fabric may contain natural waxes and pigments (inherent) as well as dirt and oil (acquired) due to handling by hands and loom processing.

These can be removed by scouring. For cotton, boiling water, soaps/syndents, alkaline builders as well as wetting agents are all used proportionately to obtain clean fabrics.

Protein fabrics are treated with neutral or slightly acidic chemicals since alkaline reagents can harm them.

14.2.6 Bleaching

This finish produces white fabrics by chemically removing any colour present in them. Generally speaking, natural fibres have greater degree of unwanted colour as compared to manufactured ones. Bleaches can either be oxidising or reducing. Commonly used oxidising bleaches include sodium hypochlorite (or Javelle water), hydrogen peroxide, sodium perborate and potassium permanganate. Sunlight and ozone are also examples of oxidising bleaches.

Salient among reducing bleaches are sodium hydrosulphite, sodium bisulphite and sodium thiosulphate.

The effect of oxidising bleach is more permanent than reducing bleach.

The choice of the bleaching agent and other conditions is made on the basis of the substrate and the degree of whitening required. Treatment with bleach must always be followed by washing.

This finish can also be applied by consumers on white fabrics. Commercially available brands such as 'Ala' are easy to use and produce quite satisfactory results.

14.2.7 Stiffening, Weighting

This finish imparts firmness and body to fabrics. Although a basic finish, stiffening may be done after colouration.

Cellulosic fabrics can be stiffened with starch (temporary) or resins (permanent). Consumers today have easy-to-use stiffening agents such as 'revive' which can be applied after washing.

Silk fabrics undergo a sizing process called **weighting**. After complete degumming, silk fabrics become soft and light (silk gum sericin, which is removed, contributes to 25% of the total weight). This loss in weight is compensated by treating silk with suitable organic and inorganic compounds such as salts of tin, aluminium, iron and tannic acid. Silks weighted 'at par' acquire a fuller handle and appearance. However, as a malpractice, some silks are weighted 'above par'. This is harmful as it lowers the strength and lustre of silk.

14.2.8 Basic Calendering

It is a finish similar to ironing except that it is carried out by using two big rollers. In home ironing, the heated metallic iron presses the cloth which is placed on a padded surface like the ironing board. In basic calendering, one of the rollers is metallic and heated, while the other is padded. Fabrics pass in open width between these two and get a smooth surface.

14.2.9 Tentering

This finish follows any wet treatment. As the fabric leaves the liquid bath, it is stretched between two parallel chains with pins or clips (This may leave small holes in the selvedge). The distance between the chains is adjusted to get the desired width and the fabric is carried to the drying chambers.

This is a basic but important finish since improper tentering can lead to "off grain" fabrics which will affect the appearance and performance properties.

14.2.10 Mercerisation

In 1851, John Mercer discovered the effect of caustic soda (alkali) treatment on cotton. It led to a change in the cross section from kidney or bean shape (℃) to circular (O) shape, thus enhancing lustre.

Such cottons had greater tensile strength, increased affinity for moisture and dyes but a shrinkage in length.

In 1889, Lowe discovered the variation of this process, viz., mercerising cotton under tension. This produced fabrics which retained the good properties mentioned earlier without undergoing any shrinkage. Some additional properties such as softer handle and greater capacity to respond to mechanical finishing processes were also obtained. This paved the way for commercial usage.

Mercerisation involves immersing cotton (yarn or fabric) in an alkali solution (16–23% NaOH or KOH) for a controlled period of time, followed by thorough rinsing and neutralisation.

This finish is given to cotton prior to dyeing. However, there is a market for unmercerised cotton as well. 'Markin' is such an example. It is used for making quilt or mattress covers and for draping by students of clothing courses.

The finishes already discussed are generally used for cellulosics. Wool fibre has to undergo some special treatments like carbonising, crabbing, decating and fulling. Table 14.2 enumerates these with a brief account for each finish.

Table 14.2   Some Basic Finishes for Wool Fabric

Finish	Mechanism
Carbonising (chemical finish)	Burning off vegetable impurities by use of dilute H_2SO_4.
Crabbing (mechanical finish)	Wool fabric is subjected to hot water, then cold water followed by passing it between the rollers. This helps to set the weave and may also eliminate shrinkage in wool fabrics.
Decating (mechanical finish)	Helps to set lustre and develop permanent sheen.
Fulling (mechanical finish)	Makes wool more compact and soft. A combination of moisture, heat and friction is used to bring about felting shrinkage.

14.3   FUNCTIONAL FINISHES THAT ALTER APPEARANCE

The following finishes employ mechanical means.

14.3.1   Special Calendering

Just like basic calendering, this is a mechanical finish imparted with the aid of rollers. What is different is that a design is introduced in the fabric. It is temporary when applied to cotton but can be made permanent by treating cotton with resins or use of thermoplastic fabrics.

(i) Schreinering

Here the fabric is pressed by a roller which has fine diagonal lines etched out on the surface. This produces smooth fabrics with a soft lustre. Figure 14.2 gives a schematic diagram for this process.

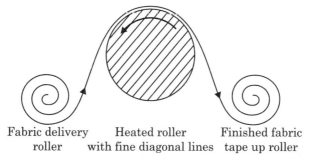

Fabric delivery   Heated roller   Finished fabric
roller   with fine diagonal lines   tape up roller

Figure 14.2 Schreinering.

(ii) Moire'

Ribbed fabrics are doubled in such a way that thick yarns of one side press and produce impressions on the other side. Thus, a 'watered' design is created due to difference in light reflection.

(iii) Embossed surfaces

This finish produces the most visible effect in the form of 3-D designs. The metallic design roller has a pattern which is embossed (raised) on the surface. The corresponding soft roller could be covered with a pad of paper or cloth. With motions of the two rollers, the design is first made to impress into the soft roller. Now the fabric is passed and it acquires the 3-D pattern on coming out of the rollers. Figure 14.3 gives a schematic diagram for embossing finish.

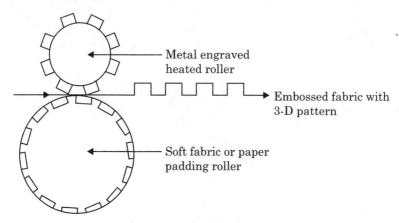

Metal engraved heated roller

Embossed fabric with 3-D pattern

Soft fabric or paper padding roller

Figure 14.3 Embossing.

(iv) Friction calendering

Friction calendering produces fabrics with a highly polished surface. In glazing, fabric is impregnated with resins, while in ciréing, wax is used before passing the fabric through a series of calendering rollers (friction calender) Figure 14.4.

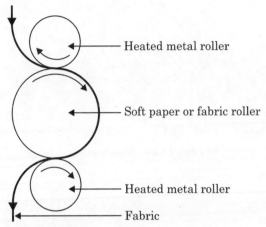

Heated metal roller

Soft paper or fabric roller

Heated metal roller

Fabric

Figure 14.4 Friction calendering.

14.3.2 Raised Surface Finishes

There are many finishes which employ mechanical means to raise fibre ends from the surface of the fabric.

(i) Napping

A series of cylinders with fine, bent, metallic hooks are used to pull loose fibres from the surface (Figure 14.5). A soft, hairy look is obtained which covers up the ground fabric. Flannel is an example of napped finish. Such fabrics are warm and soft, thus, common in children's apparel and sheets.

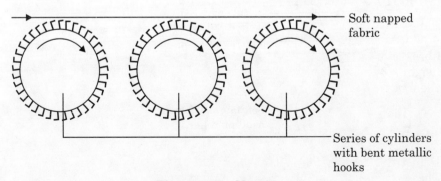

Soft napped fabric

Series of cylinders with bent metallic hooks

Figure 14.5 Napping.

(ii) Gigging

Teasels from the thistle plant (a plant with prickly stems and leaves) are fixed to a cylinder which brushes against a fabric. This action (gentle than napping) produces a short, soft nap without lowering the fabric strength.

(iii) Sueding

In this finish, the fabric comes in contact with a sandpaper covered roller. This abrading surface produces a fuzzy surface due to cutting of fibres on the face of the fabric.

The name of this finish is derived from the velvety nap which resembles suede (a leather product).

(iv) Emerising

In recent years, polyester fabrics with "peach skin" look and feel have hit the market. These are produced by abrading the fabrics with emery paper (having a coating of hard rough substances). An attractive fabric is produced, though at the cost of fabric strength.

(v) Flocking

In the four raising finishes discussed so far, a nap was raised from the fabric surface in varying degree by various means. In flocking finish, very small pieces of fibres known as flocks are attached to the fabric surface with an adhesive. Drying follows and the flock is held securely in place.

Processes used for flocking could be mechanical or electrostatic in nature [see Figure 14.6(a) and (b)]. It is possible to obtain an overall flocked surface or patterned flocking. In the latter case, the adhesive is only applied in the design areas.

Such fabrics require careful handling since care treatments should not damage the adhesive.

(vi) Brushing and shearing

This is a routine finish which is followed for all pile fabrics, whether produced by the weaver or by the finisher. Brushing removes loose fibres and even any dust caught in the pile. Shearing evens out the pile height. It is also possible to bring in design variations like patterned shearing and varying heights of pile through shearing.

The following finishes rely on **chemical means.**

14.3.3 Delustrants

Delustrants are added to the spinning dope of manufactured fibres. These are finely ground particles of Titanium dioxide (TiO_2) or Geranium dioxide (GeO_2) which hamper in light reflection, thus, lowering the sheen of such fibres. Figure 14.7 shows the cross sections of two manufactured fibres.

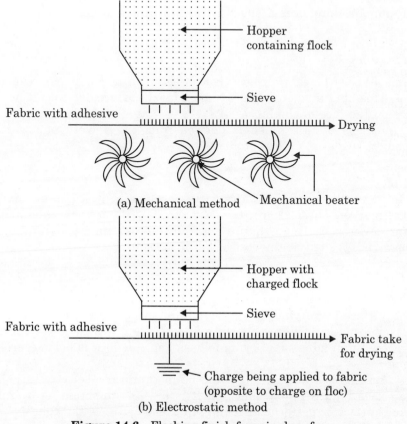

Figure 14.6   Flocking finish for raised surface.

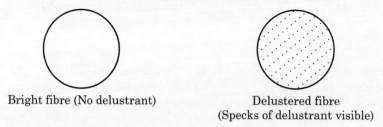

Bright fibre (No delustrant)   Delustered fibre
                                            (Specks of delustrant visible)

Figure 14.7   Cross sections of two manufactured fibres.

14.3.4   Optical Brightening Agents (OBAs)

OBAs are also known as **fluorescent brightening agents** (FBAs). They help provide a "whiter than white" fabric. OBAs are chemicals that coat a fabric. They absorb light from the invisible spectrum (ultraviolet) and re-emit it in the visible spectrum.

Ultraviolet ← 4Å VIBGYOR   7Å →   Infrared
(invisible spectrum)   (visible spectrum)   (invisible spectrum)

This finish can also be renewed by consumers at home. Brands such as Ranipal are OBAs that are applied in home laundry.

14.3.5 Acid Finishes

Two salient finishes obtained by the use of acids are burned out designs and parchmentisation.

Cellulosic fibres are harmed by acids. This fact is used to produce interesting designs on fabrics made from a blend of cellulosic and non-cellulosic fibres. By using controlled concentration, temperature and treatment time with acids, some areas are 'burned out' or made to appear transluscent. Such fabrics are commonly used for ladies suits and blouses.

In parchmentisation, cotton is treated with dilute sulphuric acid to make its surface gelatinous and soft. This is followed by washing with water, a process which causes the gelatinous surface to harden permanently. The fabric now appears to be stiff, transluscent and parchment like (hence the name). Organdy is an example of this finish.

14.3.6 Alkali (Basic) Finishes

As discussed in the mercerisation finish, cellulosics absorb alkalis like NaOH to swell up and cause resultant shrinkage in length. This property is used to obtain plissé effect i.e., a crinkled look in fabric (see Figure 14.8). A thick paste of sodium hydroxide is applied in a predetermined area. The printed areas shrink while the unprinted areas pucker to accommodate this shrinkage.

Figure 14.8 Plisse finish.

A similar crinkled look can also be produced on nylon fabrics by using phenol. The plissé fabric must not be confused with seersucker. The latter is produced by varying the tension of yarns in weaving which causes the slack (loose) yarns to bubble up after the beating up operation.

14.3.7 Softening Finishes

This may be given after certain finishes which produce a rough and harsh feel. Softeners include quarternary ammonium salts, oils, fats, wax emulsions and silicone compounds. Such finishes reduce the static build-up but may also decrease the absorbency and flame resistance.

14.3.8 Stiffening Finishes

A non-chemical stiffening finish is starch, which was discussed under the 'sizing' finish. Chemicals like thermosetting resins can be used to impart permanent stiffness to fabrics. Apart from giving the fabrics a crisp look, such finishes also reduce abrasion and yarn slippage.

14.3.9 Fading Finishes

Fading, once a property of old, worn out fabrics is now in fashion! The finishing industry has come out with many interesting fashion denims. These are achieved by stone washing (washing while tumbling with pumice stones saturated with selected chemicals in a chamber) or chemical wash with enzymes, alkalis or oxidizing agents (see Figure 14.9).

Figure 14.9 Faded jeans.

For fabrics like silk, milder conditions are used to produce "sanded silks". Pumice stones are replaced by fabrics to produce controlled abrasion.

14.4 FUNCTIONAL FINISHES THAT ALTER PERFORMANCE

The following finishes affect the comfort and after-care properties of fabrics.

14.4.1 Absorbent Finishes

Such finishes enhance the fabric's moisture-holding power. Chemicals such as ammonium compounds, humectants and wetting agents are generally combined to impart absorbent finish. Wicking and moisture transport properties are important as they leave the body feeling dry and comfortable. Such fabrics readily absorb perspiration and have a reduced static cling. Dye uptake also improves but these fabrics take a longer time to dry. Common applications include hosiery, sportswear, sleepwear, aramid underwear for race car drivers, towels, infant care, nursing home/senior care products and diapers.

Finishes like beetling and soil release aid in enhancing the absorbency of a fabric. On the other hand, some softening finishes which employ waxes or oils would hamper the absorption capacity of the treated fabric since these agents are hydrophobic.

14.4.2 Antistatic Finishes

Static charge build-up is a problem encountered by synthetics at the manufacturers' level as well as by consumers. There are many ways to tackle this problem. Finishes may be applied to neutralise the charges on the fibre or make it hydrophilic. Water is a good conductor of electricity and can diffuse the static build-up. Chemicals like quarternary ammonium compounds and phosphate esters are used for this purpose.

Blending is another solution to this problem. In products such as carpets, metallic wires are woven in to help conduct electric charges.

14.4.3 Abrasion Resistant Finishes

Abrasion is the wearing-off of fabric surfaces. In man-made fibres, it leads to the problem of pilling which is aesthetically unappealing. Soft thermoplastic resins are used to hold the fibres securely.

Blending is another way of solving this problem.

14.4.4 Antislip Finishes

Yarn slippage is a problem that leads to fraying at the seams. This is a problem faced by smooth filaments as in rayon. A low fabric count, unbalanced construction and tight-fit in garments can further aggravate this problem. Resins of urea or melamine formaldehyde are applied to bind the yarns in their places.

14.4.5 Stain and Soil Resistant Finishes

These help to maintain a 'clean' look of a textile product like carpets or upholstery. Chemicals such as fluorocarbons and organosilicone compounds are used to coat the fabric surface. Thus, a protective coating is formed which inhibits penetration of stains and soil. Another approach is to increase the surface tension so that the liquid based stains roll-off in a manner similar to droplets on lotus leaves.

14.4.6 Durable Press Finish

As the term suggests, fabrics with this finish do not show creases even after use, washing or tumble drying. Today's jet-set pace of life makes consumers look around for convenient clothing. Clothes that can be washed in a machine and worn without any ironing have a great appeal for consumers. Fabrics that have been imparted the durable press finish retain the pressed look for most part of the product's life (as is conveyed by the term 'durable').

In general, creasing is a greater nuisance in cottons since most manufactured fibres can be heat set to impart dimensional stability.

Resins are widely used to impart this finish. Examples include dimethyl dihydroxy ethylene urea (DMDHEU), dimethyl ethylene urea (DMEU), urea formaldehyde and melamine. The functional groups of the resins react with adjacent cellulose molecules. Cross linking occurs in which the weak hydrogen bonds of cellulose are replaced by strong covalent bonds with resins, leading to greater stability. After distortion, the molecules are pulled back to original positions, thus maintaining the smooth, pressed appearance. Silicone based finishes are also used sometimes.

Resin application is followed by treatment at very high temperature, known as **curing**. There are two stages at which curing can be done to seal the resin finish into the fibres i.e., before converting the fabric into garments (pre-curing) or after constructing garments (post-curing process).

Pre-curing

Resin is applied from a water bath → fabric is dried → cured i.e., treated at high temperature to set it in the fabric → fabric is washed to remove unabsorbed chemicals → dried → cut and sewn into 'durable press' garments.

Post-curing

Resin is applied from a water bath → fabric is dried → cut and sewn into garments → curing is done → final wash may be given to remove excess chemicals.

14.4.7   Shrink Resistant Finishes

It is important to first understand the term 'shrinkage' before learning how it can be tackled. The term implies reduction in the length or width of a fibre, yarn or fabric. There has been some discussion in the chapter on fibre properties (Chapter 4), but let us have a recap.

In the weaving operation, warp yarns are held under tension on the loom. When a woven fabric is immersed in water, it relaxes with the warp yarns jumping back to their original length. This causes warpwise shrinkage referred to as **relaxation shrinkage**. Generally, the first wash leads to some shrinkage and fabrics are stable in their dimensions after that. In other words, a major part of the **potential shrinkage** is exhausted in the first wash. However, in some fabrics, certain degree of shrinkage still remains. This is referred to as **residual shrinkage**, and may be exhibited in subsequent washes (**progressive shrinkage**).

While cellulosics have to combat with relaxation shrinkage, wool woven fabrics have to deal with the dual problems of relaxation and **felting shrinkage**. The latter is caused by intermeshing of scales in the presence of moisture, heat and agitation.

Shrinkage control in cotton, linen

1. In the simplest treatment, the fabric is immersed in water and left for a while. It is then wrung and dried in a tensionless state. Ironing or basic calendering follows.

   You might have noticed that fabric bought for lining of ladies suits is pre-shrunk by this method by consumers themselves or the tailor is instructed to do the same. In case of cheaper fabrics, this step also serves a second purpose i.e., removal of unfixed dye.

2. Compressive shrinkage control or **sanforisation** is the most common method employed on a commercial scale. Fabrics given this treatment are often stamped as 'sanforised'.

Fabrics are first dampened with water and then placed over a machine that has continuous woollen or felt blankets. In some machines, these are replaced by rubber pads. The blankets or pads (carriers) can stretch and compress, transferring this movement to the damp fabric that they carry. First the carrier stretches over a curve, thus stretching the fabric placed on it. It then moves to a concave area, where it has to compress into a smaller, flat area. This leads to compressing of the fabric which is set in position by heat application. This alternate stretching and compressing uses up the potential shrinkage of the fabric, thus producing sanforised fabrics with a residual shrinkage of less than 1–2%.

Figure 14.10 schematically represents the compressive shrinkage control process.

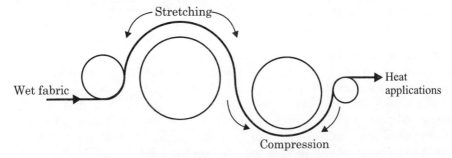

Figure 14.10   Sanforisation.

Shrinkage control in rayons

Rayons cannot be sanforised as they have a very low wet modulus. Resins are applied and these cross linking agents help to stabilise the fabric.

Shrinkage control in synthetics

Synthetics are made shrink resistant by heat setting them. It is important to observe that they are not brought to heat setting temperatures in washing or handling as this will negate the set given to them.

Shrinkage control in woollens

For relaxation shrinkage: In the steam or damp relaxation method, the woollen fabric is steamed and then dried in a tensionless position. This uses up most of the potential shrinkage. The process is also called **London shrinkage**. As a variation, jets of steam may be thrown on wool fabric through perforated cylinders.

For felting shrinkage: There are mainly two approaches for solving the problem of felting. The first is to coat the surface comprising scales with a synthetic polymer finish. A smooth surface will not exhibit intermeshing.

The second approach is to partially degrade the scales by oxidative treatment. This is done by use of chlorine either in gas state or in liquid state (as sodium hypochlorite, NaOCl). The process is termed **chlorination** and is carried out under carefully controlled conditions to ensure that only the scales get affected. These partially degraded scales can no longer felt. Neutralising with dilute acetic acid (antichlor) and rinsing follows the treatment.

In recent years, vapour phase ozone treatment is also catching up as a means of making wool shrink resistant.

The following finishes are imparted for reasons of *safety and protection*.

14.4.8 Flame Resistant Finishes

Such finishes impart safety to the individuals using them. They do not propagate the flame and are self-extinguishing, even if they happen to catch fire when in direct path of the flame. As in the case of other finishes, many options exist. Some finishes are temporary in nature, for example, borax can be used provided it is reapplied after every wash. Apart from water soluble compounds, there are certain insoluble salts that are applied after dissolving in a suitable solvent. Substances containing phosphorous or chlorinated hydrocarbons are commonly used to impart flame resistant properties to fabrics.

But the best results are obtained by using substances that react with the fibres, produce molecular changes and, thus, make them flame resistant.

Possible uses of such fabrics include children's garments, fire-fighter uniforms, mattresses, carpets and furnishings intended for public buildings.

14.4.9 Water-repellent and Waterproof Finishes

Water-repellent finishes resist wetting by water. The surface has been treated in such a way that tiny beads of water are formed and these roll-off without passing through. The treatment given is such that the fabric retains its porosity to air, thus maintaining its comfort properties. Depending on the chemicals and process, the life of the finish could vary. There are temporary (renewable) and durable finishes. Table 14.3 lists these categories with chemicals used.

Table 14.3   Types of Water-Repellent and Waterproof Finishes

Life of finish	Chemicals used
Temporary (renewable)	Wax emulsions
	Aluminium compounds
Durable	Flurochemicals
	Quarternary ammonium compounds
	Silicone compounds

Waterproof finishes do not allow water to pass through. The barrier is such that even air cannot pass through making the fabric uncomfortable to wear. Coating with rubber can make a fabric waterproof, although it will also become heavy and warm.

Waterproof and water-repellent finishes are used for products such as umbrellas, raincoats, shower curtains, automobile seats and other such areas where protection from water is needed. Uniforms for army and certain sportswear for water events also need such finishes.

14.4.10   Antipesticide Finishes

These impart protection to workers who handle pesticides. A kind of coating is given which stops any penetration of the pesticides.

14.4.11   Light Reflectant Finishes

Surfaces given a reflectant finish will shine when light falls on them. The effect is quite pronounced in the dark. Jackets worn by construction workers for metro rail in Delhi, workers of the Municipal Corporation, traffic police as well as early morning joggers have strips of fabric treated with microscopic reflective particles. This ensures that the individual is visible and, thus, protected from automobiles moving in the dark.

14.4.12   Moth Proof Finishes

Larvae of clothes moths and carpet beetles attack protein in fibres like wool and silk, thus damaging them. At the consumer level a two pronged strategy can help combat this menace. Firstly, these fabrics should be cleaned (by washing or dry cleaning) to ensure that there are no food stains which would hasten an attack by unwanted organisms. Secondly, naphthalene balls can be packed along with the articles in air-tight containers. The balls of naphthalene vapourise with time, thus emanating odours which are pungent enough to repel the adult moths. There have been instances when spurious products have damaged clothes and discoloured them. Thus, a consumer should only opt for reputed brands. It is also a good idea to put the balls in old socks or hankies, rather than in direct contact with the woollens. In an older practice, dried *neem* leaves were used for a similar action.

   At the finishers' level, more radical steps can be taken. Moth-proofing finishes may be given by using inorganic or organic compounds which can be of natural or synthetic origin. Alternatively, chemicals could be used to alter the wool composition, since wool's sulphur containing amino acid is the main reason of attack by moths. This would, however, affect other properties of wool also.

14.4.13   Antimicrobial Finishes

These are also referred to as *bacteriostatic* or *antiseptic finishes*. As the terms suggest, these suppress growth of microbes, including disease and rot causing bacteria as well as mildew producing fungi. Such fabrics serve very important purpose in everyday life and also in special situations.

   Shoe linings are given this finish to prevent the 'athlete's foot', an ailment common in sports persons after hurting their feet. Socks are given the antimicrobial finish to combat the problem of foul odour caused by heavy perspiration. Home textiles benefit from this finish since it curbs the musty odours and discolouration brought about by microbe attack. Thus, towels, bedsheets, pillow covers, blankets and carpets are given this finish. Infant garments, especially reusable diapers also benefit immensely from this finish.

The 'special situations' mentioned above include medical textiles and uniforms for war soldiers. It is easy to understand that a "zero germ" environment is important for speedy recovery of surgeries and injuries.

Chemicals used to impart this finish include quarternary ammonium compounds, melamine resins with zinc nitrate, hydrogen peroxide along with acetic acid and zinc acetate, copper zirconium compounds and at times even antibiotics. Some natural dyes too have inherent antimicrobial properties, making fabrics dyed with them resistant to germs.

At the home level, a last rinse after washing can be given in water that has a disinfectant added. Savlon or dettol can be used for this purpose. As can be understood, such treatments would fall in the category of temporary (renewable) finish. Even a thorough drying in natural sunlight is believed to combat the growth of microbes.

14.4.14 Microencapsulation Finishes

A capsule is a miniature container that protects its contents from evaporation, oxidation and contamination until its release on friction or agitation. During encapsulation, tiny droplets of products like fragrances, moisturizers, vitamins, deodorants or repellents are prepared. These are then deposited on the fabric.

Of the various options mentioned, fragrant finishes have caught on really well with consumers. The fabric is coated with microscopic capsules which contain perfumed oils that are gradually released when one brushes against them. Perfumed lingerie and aroma emitting T-shirts are today available to consumers, thanks to the technology of microencapsulation.

Some other new finishes include imparting resistance to fume fading, UV light and heat.

14.5 NANOTECHNOLOGY IN FINISHING INDUSTRY

Originating from the Greek word *nanos* meaning *dwarf*, nanotechnology refers to the technology on an atomic or molecular scale while *nano* means a factor of one thousand millionth (10^{-8}).

The finishing industry is benefiting to a larger extent by the use of nanotechnology. Some of the commercially available nanofinishes are being described below. These are all registered trade names:

NanoCare is a finish for imparting stain-proof qualities. It can last for about 50 washes.

NanoDry is a finish given to polyester fabric in order to impart better wicking properties. Leading apparel as well as home furnishing brands are using this technology.

Nano Touch is a finish that is given to obtain a cotton-like feel on synthetic fabrics.

Nanotechnology helps to produce wrinkle and stain resistance, flame retardant, anti-microbial, deodorant as well as anti-pollen fabrics.

14.6 INTERRELATEDNESS OF FINISHES

A processing chart has to be carefully drawn out for fabrics by the manufacturer. Generally, a combination of finishes is applied. It is important to ensure that the effect produced by one finish is not negated by another. In most instances, a particular property may be imparted by a finish but at the same time, certain undesirable characteristics may creep in. For example, application of resins solves many problems and is widely used. However, some undesirable traits like offensive odour, reduced tensile strength, poor abrasion resistance and increased affinity for oil stains may now crop up. These necessitate the application of other finishes to ameliorate the situation. Thus, finishes for abrasion resistance and soil release may have to follow the resin treatment.

In other situations, a finish may be imparted to solve a particular problem, but may also positively influence other performance properties. For example, a stiffening finish will impart a better handle and body to the fabric and at the same time reduce abrasion and yarn slippage. Similarly, the soil release finish also enhances the absorbency of a fabric.

Today's consumers demand clothes and other textile products which look good, are comfortable, stay clean, keep fresh, smell nice and have simple care instructions. This might have seemed an impossible task for the manufacturers a decade ago but is a reality today. Chemical manufacturers world over continue to update their product lines with textile chemicals that are more efficient, environmentally friendly and economical. However, the search for new fabric finishes continues with an ever-increasing emphasis on multifunctional processing additives.

EXERCISES

14.1 Give various criteria used for classification of finishes with one example for each group.

14.2 Name five finishes that are specific to wool and silk fabrics.

14.3 Enlist and explain three recent finishes.

14.4 Write a note on the action of resins for imparting durable press finishes.

14.5 Describe the following finishes:
  (i) Antimicrobial finish
  (ii) Special calendering
  (iii) Flame resistant finish

(iv) Mercerisation

(v) Water-repellent and waterproof finishes.

14.6 Make a list of finishes that would be helpful for the following end uses:

(i) Infant wear

(ii) Table cloth

(iii) Hospital gowns

(iv) Curtains

(v) Uniform for defence persons.

SUGGESTED READING

Ammayappan, L. and Moses, J.J., Functional Finishes for Woollen Textiles, *ITJ*, Vol. 118, No. 1, pp. 25–32, October 2007.

Andrew, W., Wrinkle Resistant Cotton and Formaldehyde Release, *Colourage*, Vol. 41, 1995, pp. 87–93.

Goyal, R. and Prabha, C.N., Flame Retardant Fabrics: Need for the Time, *Colourage*, Vol. 4, No. 6, pp. 116–120, 2008.

Mairal, A.K. and Vaidya, A.J., Role of Some Speciality Chemicals in Formaldehyde Free Durable Press Finishing of Cotton, *The Textile Industry and Trade Journal*, pp. 25–27, January–February 2008.

Partiban, M. and Kumar, M.R., Eco-friendly Crease Resistant Finishing for Silk, *IJFTR*, Vol. 118, No. 3, pp. 47–52, December 2007.

Rouette, M.J., *Encyclopedia of Textile Finishing*, Vols. 1, 2 and 3, Springer, Germany, 2001.

Thilagavathi, G. and Kannaian, T., Dual Antimicrobial and Blood Repellent Finishes for Cotton Hospital Fabrics, *IJFTR*, Vol. 33, pp. 23–29, March 2008.

CHAPTER

15

Finishing with Colour: Dyeing and Printing

As discussed in Chapter 14, the most widely used classification of finishing divides them into basic, special and colouration finishes. The first two categories have been discussed in the previous chapter, while colouration finishes are described in the present chapter.

15.1 INTRODUCTION

Finishing with colour comprises processes of applying colour on fabrics and fixing it. It is further categorised into two techniques, viz., dyeing and printing. **Dyeing** is the irreversible application of colour on a textile substrate (fibre, yarn or fabric). **Printing** is a kind of 'localised' dyeing. Here, a concentrated dye paste with other additives is applied to a fabric.

Man has known colour since his creation. Nature has been like an artist with an inexhaustible colour palette and breathtakingly beautiful compositions—ever inspiring man to emulate and capture a bit of colour in his surroundings, on the self and on clothes that adorn his body. Primitive man began colouring the caves that sheltered him and soon began smearing his body with pigments that he discovered.

Natural dyes, obtained from plants, animals and minerals were extracted and applied on fabrics. Not all of these dyes formed bonds readily with fabrics and, hence, mordants began to be used. These substances had better affinity for the natural dyes and, thus, acted as bridges between the dyes and the substrate (fabric).

India with its vast reservoir of natural resources and unmatched craftsmanship developed an entire spectrum of shades obtained from natural dyes. These were used in textile crafts which were specific to each state.

In his account of the shawl industry of Kashmir, Moorcraft has mentioned that there were more than 300 tints in regular use during the Mughal times. The Patolas of Gujarat, prints of Baghru and Sanganer, as well as Kalamkaris of Andhra Pradesh were some more examples of the mastery of the Indian dyers.

Evidence points to the use of natural dye (idigo blue) in Egypt around 3000 bc. This is a colour obtained from the leaves of the indigo plant.

In 1856, Sir William Henry Perkin invented the first synthetic dye (basic mauve). This paved the way for further research and led to the introduction of various classes of dyes. A near elimination of natural dye stuffs was a fallout. A majority of dyes used today in the field of textiles are chemically synthesised in the laboratory. However, the recent emphasis on environmental consciousness has brought natural dyes back in focus—even if in limited pockets.

15.2   DYE CLASSES

Dye is a compound with two components: chromophore, which imparts colour and auxochrome that helps in substantivity and enhances the colour intensity.

The range of dyes available today can be classified on the basis of their chemical composition. These are:

- Acid dyes
- Basic dyes
- Disperse dyes
- Vat dyes
- Azoic dyes
- Direct dyes
- Reactive dyes

Apart from dyes, pigments are also used for textile colouration. These are insoluble and lack an affinity for fibres. Hence, they require binding agents such as adhesives and resins to fix them on the surface. The adhesive can alter the handle of the fabric and its durability will control the colour fastness. Pigments are commonly used in dope dyeing and printing. Their use saves time, effort and cost.

15.2.1   Acid Dyes

These acquire their name for the fact that an acidic bath is needed for their application. This also rules out their use for cellulosics since an acidic bath would harm them. Protein fibres (wool and silk), acrylics and nylons are dyed in this category. Acid dyes have a wide spectrum of colour range with varying fastness properties.

15.2.2   Azoic Dyes or Napthol Dyes

These are widely used on cellulosics but find a limited application on acrylic, nylon and polyester. They are also referred to as *ice colours* since their application sometimes involves use of ice to lower the temperature. Bright colours are produced at relatively low cost, with the added advantage of good colour fastness to washing and light. Batik, a resist printing technique by use of wax, uses azoic dyes since subjecting the waxed piece to high temperature of the dye liquor would cause it to melt.

15.2.3 Basic or Cationic Dyes

These are the oldest dyes since they mark the birth of 'synthetic dyes'. They are cationic (positively charged) in nature—hence the name. Known for their brilliant colours and good colour fastness, basic dyes are used for acrylics, modified nylons and polyesters. When used on proteins and cellulosics, these dyes are not quite fast, though they enhance the brilliance of a colour.

15.2.4 Direct Dyes

Direct dyes are so named since they are water soluble and can be directly applied on fabrics. They have good substantivity for cellulosics (substantive dyes), are easy to apply, inexpensive and offer a wide range of colours. A levelling agent or retardant (usually Na_2CO_3) is added to the water bath. It helps in producing even dyeing. At the end of the dyeing cycle, an exhaustion agent (e.g., NaCl) is added. This helps the dye to leave the liquor and get attached to the material.

Given below are some abbreviations, commonly used in describing dyeing procedures.

RFD: Ready for dyeing
MLR: Material to liquor ratio
OWF: On weight of fabric
OWM: On weight of material

Most direct dyes have good fastness to light but poor wash fastness. This can be improved by after treatments like suga fix treatment with a cationic fixing agent.

15.2.5 Disperse Dyes

These dyes are 'dispersed' in the dye bath and used for polyester, acetate, acrylic and nylon fibres. Their application may be done by either of the two approaches—high temperature high pressure dyeing (HTHP) and use of carriers like phenols.

They have an excellent fastness to washing, sunlight and dry cleaning. However, nylon and acetate may face the problem of fume fading by NO_2 in atmosphere.

15.2.6 Reactive Dyes

Invented in 1956, a century after the first synthetic dye, reactive dyes have come to occupy an important position in the industry today. The ban on azo dyes by the international leading buyers of textiles has meant a boom for the reactive dyes. As the name suggests, these dyes react chemically with the fibre resulting in excellent wash fastness and good to excellent light fastness.

The fact that they are available in almost all shades and have bright colours also goes in their favour.

15.2.7   Vat Dyes

These were initially applied from large wooden tanks known as **vats** and, thus, acquired this name. Available in a wide choice of colours, the vat dyes are insoluble in water, but dissolve in alkali, which is used to solubilise them.

15.3   STAGES OF DYEING

Application of dye can be done at the spinning, fibre, yarn, fabric or garment stage. Earlier the stage, the better is the penetration, resulting in better fastness. On the other hand, the later the stage of colour application, lower is the cost and quicker is the response to the fashion trends. It is, thus, a common practice to make use of spinning and fibre stage for obtaining 'staple' colours i.e., colours which always stay in vogue (e.g., black, navy blue). On the other hand, "fad colours", which appear in one season only to make a brief appearance and then vanish, are safer when dyed at the fabric or garment stage. There are certain traditional textile crafts which require yarn dyeing. Some of these are *Pochampallis* of Andhra Pradesh, *Patolas* and *Gharcholas* of Gujarat and *Ikats* of Orissa. Here, laborious tie-dyeing of the yarns is done to produce elaborate patterns by plain weaving in sarees, dupattas and suit pieces. It is not possible to achieve these effects by any other stage of dyeing.

A brief description of the five possible stages of dye application is as follows:

15.3.1   Solution or Dope Dyeing

Also referred to as *mass pigmentation*, it involves addition of dye or pigment to the spinning solution or dope. This can be followed for manufactured fibres only.

15.3.2   Fibre Dyeing

Fibres are packed in large closed tanks (kiers) and the dye liquor pushes through them, causing deep penetration and uniform, fast colours. The process is time consuming and also expensive. As a variation, wool fibres are processed till the combing step and only long fibres in the form of tops are dyed (top dyeing).

15.3.3   Yarn Dyeing

There are four options that exist for colouration at the yarn stage: tie dyeing of yarns according to pre-decided design, beam dyeing, package dyeing and skein dyeing.

In the construction of some traditional Indian textiles yarns for warp and/or weft are tied and dyed from lighter to darker shades. Noteworthy examples include *Patolas*, *Pochampalli* (Figure 15.1) and *Ikat* (Figure 15.2). The resulting fabric is beautiful and depicts the skill of the dyer. In contemporary times, sometimes the warp yarn is printed with a design and then woven with a plain weft to produce 'halo' effects.

Figure 15.1 Pochampalli saree.　　**Figure 15.2** Ikat saree from Orissa.

Beam dyeing refers to winding the warp yarns on a beam (warp beam) and placing such beams in a dye vessel. This has traditionally been followed for denim fabrics in which an indigo blue beam dyed warp interlaces with a white weft. The weave is a warp faced twill weave, thus looking predominantly blue on the face of the fabric and white on the reverse side.

In **skein dyeing**, yarns are prepared in skein form and hung on perforated rods which are placed in a dye vessel that pumps the liquor through the skeins.

For producing interesting designs with checks and stripes, yarn dyeing is commonly used.

15.3.4 Fabric Dyeing or Piece Dyeing

This is the cheapest and quickest way to get solid colour fabrics. For manufacturers catering to colour fashion segments, this stage of dye application offers the advantage of meeting the current trends. Fabrics can be dyed in open width using **jiggers** (Figure 15.3). For delicate fabrics such as silk and rayon (with low wet strength), dyeing is done in the rope form. This involves gathering up the fabric lengthwise and using a **winch** for dyeing it (see Figure 15.4).

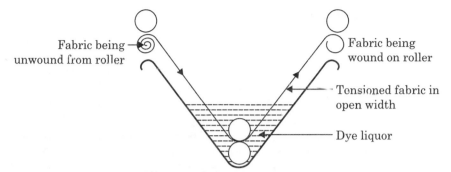

Figure 15.3 Jigger (schematic).

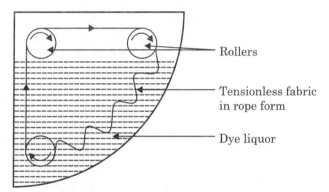

Figure 15.4 Winch (schematic).

When the fabric is a blend of two or more fibres, two dyeing options exist. The first is to produce a single, uniform colour on the fabric (**union dyeing**). Needless to say, this involves careful selection and application of dyes for each of the two components in a one-bath or two-bath operation. Alternatively, the dye selected may be such that it can dye both the components uniformly (although a rarer possibility).

The second option is **cross dyeing** which denotes that each fibre type in the blend accepts a different dye to get its own colour. This again involves careful planning and leads to interesting design possibilities.

In **jet dyeing**, (polychromatic) attractive effects are obtained by using jets of dye solution which are thrown on moving fabrics. The effects resemble printing and they work out to be economical since many colours can be introduced in a short time.

15.3.5 Product Dyeing

This is the last stage of dyeing in which a finished product is dyed. The chief advantage would be possibility of producing unique effects and exclusivity. Many designers use this stage of dyeing as it showcases their signature style and they have to cater to a limited market.

15.4 SCALES OF DYEING

Just as there are many stages at which application of dyes is possible, so also there are many scales at which dyeing can be carried out. You must have all seen dyers in markets, stationed outside dupatta shops. Most of them have a couple of steel *patilas*, no weighing or calculations are done, and a box of dyes. Yet they are able to achieve good results.

Students in this field carry out dyeing experiments in the laboratory using glass beakers and burners. The substrate to be dyed is weighed and this weight is used for subsequent calculations. Thus, if the fabric weighs 10 grams, then the MLR (material to liquor ratio) of 1 : 100 will be calculated as $10 \times 100 = 1000$ ml or 1L. Similarly, a dye concentration of 5% owf (on weight fibre or owm i.e., on weight of material) will be calculated as $5/100 \times 10$ g = 0.5 g.

Electronic balances are used to accurately weigh the required amounts.

A similar approach is followed in research and development (R & D) laboratories. A detailed swatch card is then prepared which serves as a guide in subsequent mill dyeing. Apart from glass beakers, laboratory jiggers and padding mangles are also used for dyeing. These machines are smaller replicas of the equipments used in the industry.

For large scale dyeing, many kinds of equipments are used. The choice depends on the stage at which dyes are applied. It is also decided by the investments made.

15.5 COLOUR VALUES

R & D laboratories have to conduct tests for ascertaining the precise colour values of the dyed samples. A **spectrophotometer** is used for this purpose.

K/S values are obtained after clamping the sample. A reading upto three decimal places is given.

Comparison of K/S values is a useful way of deciding the optimum conditions. For example, if sample A has been dyed at 60°C while sample B has been dyed at 90°C, then their respective K/S values can be compared to derive the best temperature for dyeing.

Apart from total colour uptake by the sample, a clear glimpse into the hue and intensity can also be obtained. The **l*a*b* values** are used for this purpose. These are also ascertained with the help of a spectrophotometer.

L*c*h* values are also used to give accurate indication of chroma and hue.

15.6 PRINTING HISTORY

Printing seems to have evolved from painting. Primitive man was familiar with the art of colour application as evidenced from the cave paintings and even adornment of his body. It is generally believed that the art of textile printing was known in the ancient civilizations of India and Egypt as early as 1600 bc. Around 600 bc and more, the Europeans became familiar with these techniques.

In the eighteenth century, Christophe Philippe Oberkamph set up a textile printing factory at Jouy (France) and began producing the famous "Toile de Jouy" known as the finest fabrics in the world.

Printing is a form of 'localised' dyeing. While the material is put in the dye bath for dyeing, printing involves the controlled application of the dye in the form of a print paste to a definite area onto a substrate. This paste acts as a concentrated dye bath.

Apart from the dye, a thickening agent is the most important constituent of a print paste. Solvents or solution assistants, fixation agents, antifoaming agents, are other auxiliaries added to printing pastes. Choice of these reagents is based on the kind of dye, substrate cost and the technology used for colour application.

There are some basic styles or principles of printing. These are carried out with the help of various methods or technologies. These will be discussed in detail a little later. Whatever be the choice of the style and method, there are certain steps which are common in printing. These are:

  (i) Preparation of fabric
 (ii) Preparation of print paste
(iii) Printing of fabric
(iv) Drying to retain good printing effect and prevent running of the paste to unwanted areas
 (v) Fixing of dyestuff by dry heat (baking), wet development, pad batch development, flash ageing or steaming
(vi) Washing off which involves a final rinsing in cold water to remove the surplus unfixed dye stuff and print paste chemicals
(vii) This is followed by a soaping treatment in which the conditions are chosen on the basis of the fabric and dyestuff.

15.7 BASIC STYLES OR PRINCIPLES OF PRINTING

There are five basic styles of printing. These are:

1. Direct printing
2. Resist printing
3. Discharge printing
4. Mordant printing
5. Transfer printing.

Of these, first four methods are sometimes termed as *conventional* while transfer printing is referred to as an *unconventional* method.

15.7.1 Direct Printing

This involves the direct application of the print paste on the surface of a fabric. Perhaps, this might have been the oldest style used by man. Blocks and rollers are two techniques which use this principle of printing.

15.7.2 Resist Printing

As the term suggests, certain portions of the fabric or yarn are resisted or held back from taking up the print paste. The resisting agent may be physical or chemical in nature. A thread may be used to tie certain portions of a yarn or fabric, followed by dyeing as in tie dye, a technique common in Gujarat and Rajasthan. Figure 15.5(a) shows a tie-dye shawl and (b) shows a batik fabric. Molten wax is used to resist white or coloured areas in the technique of batik printing. In dabu printing, a paste of mud acts as a barrier for colour uptake. Earlier used stencils made of copper and the screens used widely today are also based on the resist printing principle. Chemical resisting agents have a different approach. Thus, if a particular dye requires on alkaline pH for being taken up, the opposite condition acts as a barrier. In printing with reactive dyes, citric acid acts as a chemical resisting agent.

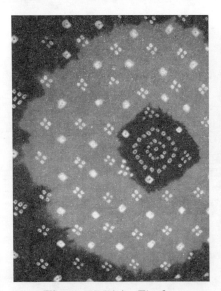

Figure 15.5(a) Tie-dye.   **Figure 15.5(b)** Batik fabric.

15.7.3 Discharge Printing

A plain dyed fabric is printed with a discharging or 'decolourising' paste which leads to the removal of colour in the printed areas. Such designs are generally characterised by a white pattern on a dark background. Sometimes these white discharged areas are then printed with a

Figure 15.6 Discharge printing.

contrasting colour (illuminating dyes). The effects produced are attractive but the strength of the fabric may get lowered. A judicious choice of the discharging agent is, thus, important, as also the complete removal of the discharge paste after completion of the process.

15.7.4 Mordant Printing

This style of printing has also been referred to as the *dyed style* or *madder printing*. Mordants are chemical substances used in dyeing and printing of natural dyes. They have the capacity of combining with both the substrate and dyestuff, thus forming a link between the two. Application of mordants can be done separately, either before or after dyestuff has been printed. Sometimes *insitu* application is also done i.e., applying the mordant along with the dyestuff. Tannic acid is a mordant commonly used for cotton while metallic salts (such as sulphates of copper and ferrous, chromium and potassium bichromate) are applied on wool. Natural dyes have a very interesting characteristic—they attain a different colour when combined with various mordants. This is depicted in Table 15.1.

Table 15.1 Characteristic of Natural Dyes

Natural dye	Mordant	Colour obtained
Alizarin	Aluminium (Al) compounds	Red
	Chromium (Cr) compounds	Brown
	Tin (Sn) compounds	Pink
Cochineal	Al	Crimson
	Cr	Purple
	Sn	Scarlet

15.7.5 Transfer Printing (Sublimation Printing)

As the name suggests, the print is 'transferred' from a special paper onto the fabric substrate. Invented in the 1960s, transfer printing finds wide application for printing of synthetic fabrics in the form of yard goods or garments, home furnishings, shower curtains, carpets and even knits. Generally, disperse dyes are used for printing paper. These dyes change into vapour phase (sublime) when heated to high temperatures (200°C). This helps in their movement from the paper to the fabric which is kept pressed in close contact. Sublimation refers to a phenomenon in which a solid compound passes directly into a gaseous state and never reverts to a solid state again upon cooling. Salient advantages of transfer printing include printing of all the colours and the entire design at the same time, sharp results, reduced cost and time as well as reduced use of natural resources. The drawbacks include slower production rates and limitation of dyes and substrates that are appropriate for this style of printing.

15.8 METHODS OF PRINTING OR PRINTING TECHNOLOGY

15.8.1 Block Printing

This is the oldest and perhaps the simplest method of printing a fabric. Still extensively used in Indian cottage industries, block printing involves the use of carved blocks for transfer of colour. Wooden pieces (about 2–3 inches high) are cut out. Block width, shapes and sizes vary considerably from a single motif to large overall patterns. The design is traced on the wood and the surrounding areas are chipped away, making the design area raised. If a design repeat is complete with five colours, then five blocks, each with a portion of the design will be required.

Block making requires skill and patience. Even the use of blocks needs expertise since the colour uptake on the fabric and matching of various blocks depend on the pressure and positioning of the blocks respectively. Figure 15.7 shows wooden blocks.

Figure 15.7 Wooden blocks.

A variation of the wooden blocks are the metallic blocks in which the raised portions have been made with copper. Such blocks have a greater resistance to wear and tear although colour uptake may be slightly less than in wooden blocks. A simple, low cost setup is required for block printing. Level surface with padding acts as the base on which a fabric is laid out. Lines and corners are made by using a thread rolled in 'neel' (ultramarine blue) or 'geru' (red powder). These are easily removed by dusting later. The print paste is transferred to a tray which is then covered with a jute cloth or sponge to ensure even spread. A block is pressed on this surface to take up the print paste. It is then positioned carefully on the fabric and pressed with the fist. Sometimes, blocks are also given 'pitch points' to guide the printer in matching. A little touching up with a brush is needed at times, especially as the blocks wear out.

Block printed fabrics are slow to produce but rank high on exclusivity.

15.8.2 Roller printing

A sheet of metal (generally copper) is prepared with an etched out design. This is then rolled to form a roller coated with chromium and used to print the fabric that comes in close contact with it. The roller picks up the colour from a trough and doctor's blade removes colour from the plain (unetched) areas. The print paste, however, continues to remain in the carved (engraved) design regions and is transferred to the fabric. The diameter of the roller depends on the repeat size of the print and the number of rollers is decided by the number of colours.

Figure 15.8 gives a schematic representation of roller printing.

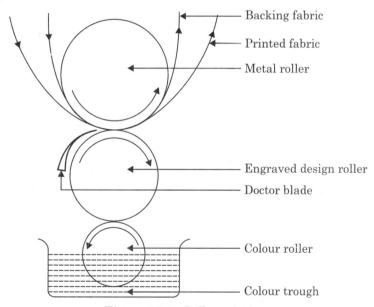

Figure 15.8 Roller printing.

This method is fast and hence quite popular. Upto sixteen rollers can be used to complete a repeat, thus enhancing design possibilities. Roller printing utilises the principle of direct printing.

Some simple analogies

In a block, the design is raised (embossed) just as in a rubber stamp. In a roller, the design is carved (engraved) just as lines in our palm. In a screen, the design area permits colour transfer while the other regions are closed just as in an alphabet stencil used on paper.

15.8.3 Tie-dye

Tie-dye is a colouration method based on the resist principle. It is done by hand and can be applied on yarns to produce *Patolas* of Gujarat, *Pochampallis* of Andhra Pradesh and *Ikats* of Orissa (discussed in yarn dyeing). *Telia Rumal* and *Mashru* are other examples. This technique also finds wide application on fabrics (Figures 15.1, 15.2).

India can boast of a rich tradition in tie-dye fabrics, with Gujarat and Rajasthan leading the way. The technique is referred to as *Bandhana* in India and is used in auspicious occasions.

Gharcholas (Figure 15.9) and *Lehria* (Figure 15.10), both are made by the tie-dye technique. Fabrics are laid out and design is transferred—often with blocks, using *geru* (burnt sienna mixture in water). This is followed by tying with cotton threads, usually taking two to four layers together. Sometimes a special thimble (metal ring with a pointed tip) is also used. Dyeing proceeds from lightest to darker shades. Washing of the fabric is done, followed by opening of the ties. Many times, the fabrics are sold in the tied form to show that it is a genuine piece.

Apart from India, some other Eastern countries have used this form of printing.

Figure 15.9 Gharchola saree.   **Figure 15.10** Lehria saree.

15.8.4 Batik

Another hand printing method, *batik* originated in Indonesia (Figure 15.11). Molten wax is applied to a fabric which is then dyed at room temperature. Wax, being hydrophobic, acts as a resisting agent in colour uptake. Today, many techniques in wax application have been evolved (e.g., coating, cracking, brushing and spraying) to attain varied and interesting effects. Sometimes application of wax is done by copper blocks (**Tjap**) or by pouring molten wax from small copper vessels (**Tjanting**).

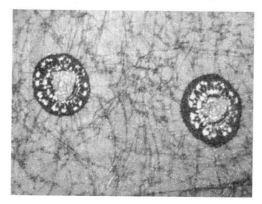

Figure 5.11 Batik.

After dyeing in one or more colours is complete, the fabric is put in boiling water. This leads to removal of the wax which on solidification can be recycled.

The process is slow and laborious, although known for its exclusivity.

15.8.5 Stencil Printing

Stencil printing originated in Japan. Sheets of paper were marked with the design which was then cut out. Colour was applied by brush, hand or spray gun. A coating of wax or varnish given to the paper ensured longer life. Slowly, these were replaced by metallic sheets. Each colour requires a separate stencil and matching has to be done very carefully. The process is slow and tedious, thus followed only in small scale setups. However, stencil printing is more widely known as a **precursor to screen printing**.

15.8.6 Screen Printing

This method employs the use of a screen of fine material. Nylon, polyester or silk have been used till the recent addition of metallic fibres. The fabric count used is such that it is possible for the print paste to pass through the interstices (spaces) between the yarns. Design areas are left uncovered while the non-design areas are coated with a waterproof emulsion. The screen is then mounted on a frame (wooden or metallic). As with other methods of colour transfer, the number of screens needed for a design will depend on the number of colours used. Width of the screen decides the repeat size of the print.

The screen is placed on the printing table on which the fabric has been spread (see Figure 5.12). Colour is poured from one end and a squeegee is used to press the colour through the screen. This is a wooden piece, as wide as the inner frame, with a blunt edge.

Figure 15.12   Hand screen printing.

One worker pushes the squeegee till the mid point from where the other worker holds it and pulls it towards him. After this, the screen frame is lifted manually and placed on the unprinted fabric. The first colour needs to be sufficiently dry before the second colour screen is placed on it. This will avoid smudging of the printed areas. Many times, the screen printing tables are equipped with a heat source beneath them. This leads to quick evaporation of moisture and hence drying of the printed areas.

A number of printing units have moved to mechanised screen printing. In such setups, the screen gets lowered onto the fabric and a colour is printed. Then the screen is lifted up and the fabric moves forward. Although initial installation costs are higher, the use of machines leads to greater speeds of production.

The above discussion deals with flat bed screen printing, done manually or mechanically. An advancement has been the rotary screen printing. A screen is prepared (in metal) for a repeat and then rolled up, as in roller printing. This method can only be done by machines and is fast catching up in the industry. Unlike roller printing, the colour source is from within the roller and so is the action of the squeegee which pushes the print paste through the screen. Once again, as for all other methods of printing, the number of rotary screens is decided by the colours used and their diameter is dependent on the repeat size.

15.8.7 Miscellaneous

Apart from the already discussed methods of printing, there are some other means of applying colour. These may have a limited commercial application but as students in this field, you need to be acquainted with these.

Photographic printing

This process is similar to developing photographs on paper. First, a coating of light reactive chemical (photosensitive dye) is applied to the fabric. Then a negative of the desired design is placed on it and light is passed. This causes the colour to develop, just as it does in a photograph. The fabric is then washed to remove the unfixed dye.

Warp printing

Perhaps inspired by the yarn tie-dye techniques, the warp yarns are printed with a screen or roller. This is followed by weaving. The final fabric has a 'hazy' design which makes it look attractive.

Flock printing

Adhesive is applied in pre-determined design areas of a fabric. Flock (small fibres of contrast colour) is then sprinkled on to the fabric. Drying follows which helps the flock to adhere to the adhesive treated areas. Brushing of the fabric removes the loose flock.

Foam printing

The dye is formed into a foamy dispersion which is then made to come into contact with a fabric. Appropriate fixation temperatures ensure that the colour enters the fabric. This method is also referred to as *bubble printing*.

　　Whatever be the method of dyeing or printing, it is important that an appropriate selection of the dye class as well as method of colour application is made. If the dyer or printer takes any shortcuts for cost cutting, it might be possible that the colour application may not be even or fast.

15.9 COLOUR FASTNESS

From a commercial point of view, it is not just important to get the desired shade. What is equally important is that these colours are long lasting. Colour fastness is the ability of a dye to retain its colour after being exposed to washing, crocking, perspiration, sunlight, fumes and other colour destroying conditions. Consumers feel that colour fastness is a very important criterion in selection and use of any product. Many a times a particular textile product has to be discarded owing to the fact that its colour has faded or bled and it is not aesthetically appealing. In other words, the product may be durable but not serviceable.

It is also important to remember that colour fastness has to be understood with respect to the factors acting on it. Thus, a fabric being purchased for use as curtains needs to be colour fast to sunlight and washing, though its colour fastness to perspiration is not so important. Similarly, for an apparel fabric that would have to face frequent launderings, it is important that the colour fastness to laundry, crocking and even perspiration is high.

Irrespective of the end use, there are certain laboratory tests that give an accurate assessment of a yarn or fabric colour fastness. These tests are conducted, using standardised equipments and treatment parameters which simulate real use conditions. This is followed by comparison with the **gray scale**. There are two gray scales in use (Figure 15.13(a) and (b)].

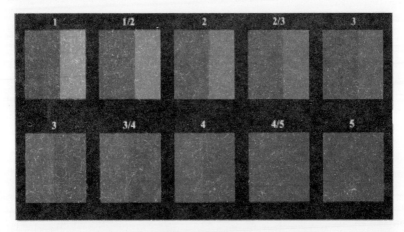

Figure 15.13(a)   Gray scale for fading.

Figure 15.13(b)   Gray scale for staining.

Each gray scale has windows which depict the grade assigned on the basis of level of fading or staining. There are also half values given. A reading of 1 indicates poor colour fastness, while a reading of 5 indicates 'no change' or excellent colour fastness. There are 10 windows in each gray scale (5 in each side).

15.9.1   Colour Fastness to Washing

Consumers expect a good fastness to washing from dyed fabrics.

Figure 15.14   Laundrometer.

A **laundrometer** (Figure 15.4) is used to obtain values of colour fastness to washing. Samples are first prepared and then immersed in the soap solution. Specifications for sample preparation and type as well as strength of soap solution are clearly laid out for various fibre types.

15.9.2   Colour Fastness to Crocking

Crocking means rubbing the fabric. Colour fastness to crocking is of greater importance in apparel (especially collars and hems) and upholstery fabrics.

A **crockmeter** (Figure 15.15) is used for this purpose. Generally, both wet and dry crocking are assessed for any sample.

Figure 15.15   Crockmeter.

15.9.3 Colour Fastness to Perspiration

Resistance to the effects of perspiration is desirable for consumers. It is important that sportswear and underwear be made from fabrics which have dyes colour fast to perspiration. A **perspiration tester** and simulated solutions are needed (Figure 15.16).

Figure 15.16 Perspiration tester.

15.9.4 Colour Fastness to Light

A **light fastness tester** is used to obtain the colour fastness to light. In this case, blue wool samples are used which are graded from 1 to 8 Figure 15.17 shows an equipment used to test light fastness.

Figure 15.17 Light fastness tester.

Specific end uses may also require dyes to be colour fast to sea water, solvents, weather, ironing and fumes.

EXERCISES

15.1 Differentiate between the following:

(i) Dyeing and printing

(ii) Natural and synthetic dyes

(iii) Direct and resist style of printing

(iv) Acid and basic dyes

· (v) Flat and rotary screen printing

15.2 Write a note on colour fastness of dyed goods to various parameters. Which fastness would be most important for everyday apparel?

15.3 Explain the discharge style of printing. Give its drawbacks.

15.4 Give stages of dyeing with a brief description of each stage.

15.5 Describe an unconventional style of printing.

15.6 Name three traditional Indian sarees and describe their method of colouration.

SUGGESTED READING

Aspland, J.R., Textile Dyeing and Colouration, American Association of Textile Chemists and Colourists, 1997.

Colourants and auxiliaries: Organic chemistry and application properties, Vol. 1, Colourants, ed. John Shore, Society of Dyers and Colourists, England, 1990.

Pellew, C., *Dyeing and Printing*: *Dyes and Dyeing*, Abhishek Publications, Chandigarh, 1998.

Scott, G., *Transfer Printing (onto man-made fibres)*, B.T. Batsford Limited, London, 1977.

Shenai, V.A., *Technology of Textile Processing*, Vol. 2, Sevak Publications, Mumbai, 1987.

PART VI
Consumer Concerns

"... in the world of fabrics, some products perform extremely well while others may disappoint you as a consumer"....quoted from introduction to Part I. Moving full circle, this new Part (VI) is being introduced in the second edition. The aim is to address common dilemmas faced by consumers. A clarity of concepts can lead to intelligent decision making resulting in enhanced consumer satisfaction.

CHAPTER

16

Choosing an Appropriate Fabric: Guidelines for Consumers

16.1 INTRODUCTION

Today, the market is flooded with a profusion of fabrics, each vying for consumer attention (and wallet!). Add to that the over persuasive attitude of some shop sellers or the complete lack of knowledge of others and what results is utter confusion in the minds of consumers. This chapter aims to equip consumers with the knowledge of a checklist that will help them select an appropriate fabric. Following points need to be considered:

- Appearance
- Comfort
- Performance
- Durability and
- Care

To create an acronym and help instant recall, let us call it the **ACP DC** list (no reference to the police though!).

Before beginning a discussion on each of these checklist points, it must be stressed that these factors must be viewed relative to each other and against the background of the intended end use. For example, while selecting a fabric for apparel use, appearance might be the most important point in the buyer's mind, while performance might supercede other factors while selecting a home textile fabric.

You would all agree that the final flavour of any dish is decided by the ingredients that are used in preparing it. Likewise, a fabric is the result of five inputs, viz., constituent fibres, yarn type, fabric construction method used, finishes imparted and colour application. One can also call these the 'green room' factors which help prepare the 'on stage' fabric! Parts II to V of this textbook have discussed various options that exist in these five input spheres. Each of the checklist points, viz., ACP DC will be discussed in the context of the five 'green room' factors.

Before venturing out into the market, a consumer should be clear about what is needed and how much money is allocated for this purchase. Such clarity will minimize falling into the trap of 'impulsive' buying which is often repented later.

A 'first glance' at a textile fabric or product puts it into one of these three categories: (a) very attractive, must buy, (b) not sure, may or may not buy and (c) not at all appealing hence no chance of buying it. If the product falls into (a) or (b) options, then the consumer should rate it against the rest of the checklist points to arrive at a wise purchase decision which would ensure satisfaction.

16.2 APPEARANCE

This is the first visual impression of any fabric that a consumer gets by merely looking at a textile product. And as is often said, 'appearances can be deceptive' so let us dwell on the impact of the five 'ingredient' factors on appearance.

Generally speaking, natural **fibres** like untreated cotton and wool lack lustre, while linen and silk have an inherent sheen. Synthetic fibres can be produced with varying lustres by regulating the amount of delustering agent used. These could be bright, semi-lustered or dull-lustered/delustered. The third option is the most prevalent one. (Refer Chapter 4, Fibre Properties).

As far as **yarn structure** is concerned, it must be understood that filaments produce a more smooth appearance as compared to spun yarns made from shorter length staple fibres which appear rough. Also, texturing will produce slightly irregular surface appearances. A cord and ply yarn will appear less regular than a simple yarn. It may be clearly noted that no type of yarn is being labelled as inferior, and attractive appearance is a subjective thing.

Fabric construction method has a direct relation with the final appearance of a fabric. As individual categories, wovens, knits, non wovens, braided fabrics, laces and nets have clearly discernible and distinguishing visual characteristics. Part IV of this textbook delves into these construction methods.

Even within one category of fabrics, many different effects are produced. For example, satin weave gives a smooth, soft and lustrous look owing to its long surface floats, while plain weave might produce a dull looking fabric. Let us take another example: a gauze weave fabric will be transparent, while a basket weave will produce a coarse and bulky structure.

Finishes applied to a fabric have a direct impact on its appearance. For example. a stiffening finish like parchmentization will produce a stiff, transluscent looking fabric like Organdy. An acid finish can produce transparent effects and hence a more delicate look.

The fifth and final 'behind-the-scene' factor, viz., **colour application** through dyeing and printing has the most dramatic impact on appearance of any textile. As has been discussed in Part V, a host of styles and methods of colour application are employed for fabrics using a wide range of dye classes. Each would impart its characteristic features to the final product.

Generally speaking, a consumer can shortlist some fabrics that appear attractive visually and then move on to grade them on the basis of subsequent checklist points.

16.3 COMFORT

Comfort has two aspects: physical and psychological. The relative importance of both these will vary depending on a host of factors. Age of the consumer is a key factor. For example, an elderly person might always opt for a soft fabric for apparel use, while a fashion conscious young teenager might decide to choose a rough jute fabric if adhering to the latest fashion trend provides more psychological comfort while scoring low on physical comfort. We would now dwell briefly on the inter relationship of the five ingredient factors that impact the comfort of a fabric. The property of comfort is in turn dependent on a host of parameters like elongation and elasticity, heat retention/conduction, moisture absorbency, water vapour transmission, air permeability/ insulation, stiffness, weight, electrostatic propensity as well as hand and skin contact (Kadolph, 2007).

Comfort of a fabric will be greatly influenced by the **fibres** it is made of. Part II carries details of fibre properties. The same would be acquired by the fabric made from these. Broadly speaking, cellulosics have a high moisture absorption, while synthetics have a very low uptake. It is for this reason that a cotton fabric proves to be the most comfortable on a hot humid day, so typical of Indian summers. The problem of static charge buildup commonly faced by synthetics can create discomfort for the wearer/user.

Yarns constructed with excessive fuzzy structure might prove to be uncomfortable. On the other hand, smooth, slippery, untextured yarns might result in clammy fabrics that cling to the skin and reduce comfort.

Fabric construction method will play a role in deciding many parameters of comfort. The rise in popularity of knits in recent years is due to the high comfort they offer to the wearer. Even within one category of fabrics, comfort properties can vary considerably. For example, among wovens, plain fabrics offer considerable comfort and are thus preferred for apparel of newborns as well as elderly persons. On the other hand, a decorative surface figure weave with long uncut floats will prove quite uncomfortable for both age categories mentioned earlier.

Finish applied to a fabric is a major contributor to its comfort properties directly or indirectly. Imparting of a water proof finish will make a fabric appropriate for use during rains but totally non-absorbent to perspiration, thus lowering the wearers comfort. In the last section of Chapter 14 on finishes (Part V), a discussion on interrelatedness of finishes is presented. Thus imparting of a soil release finish also gives the fabric an enhanced absorbency and results in greater comfort indirectly.

Application of colour can also affect comfort. For example, *Khari* printing with a thick binder can result in a harsh finish that is not comfortable for delicate skin. In other styles of printing (e.g., discharge), certain strong chemicals may be used for removal of dye in design areas. These might cause allergenic reactions in persons with sensitive skin, thus compromising on comfort.

With that we conclude our discussion on the second checklist point, i.e., comfort. You may also note that comfort will play an important role in selection of fabrics with apparel as the end use in mind. However, when consumers are selecting fabrics for use in the home (like fabric for curtains), comfort gives way to performance as a key deciding factor.

16.4   PERFORMANCE

As with the earlier checklist points that guide consumers in selecting an appropriate fabric, its performance too will depend on the five 'ingredient' factors: fibre type, yarn type, fabric construction method, finish and colour applied. It is vital that a consumer must be clear about the expected performance from that fabric. This would vary considerably with the end use. For example, a fabric for trousers must have a good body and resist wrinkle formation. On the other hand, a fabric for table cloth intended to hang on the sides must have a good drape so that it falls Gracefully and does not poke out stiffly.

16.5   DURABILITY

Durability is defined as the ability to last or endure, the power of lasting or continuing in any given state without perishing (Joseph, 1972). For each textile product, consumers will have some expectation of durability. With time, there is a shift in consumer expectations as well. Gone are the days when an item of clothing (for instance, a pair of jeans) was kept for a decade. The 'fast fashions' in vogue now have considerably shortened the life of a product. Today, many disposable non wovens have also entered the market and our homes (for example, tissues replacing cloth napkins), thus reducing the emphasis laid on durability. However, a wise buying decision will be one that considers durability of the product. It must also be kept in mind that consumers may change their wardrobes frequently, but it would not be practically possible to change their home textiles, viz., upholstery fabrics, bath towels, curtains, floor rugs, bed linen, etc. Hence the present discussion on durability is important.

Fibre type will have a direct impact on how long a fabric will last. The family of synthetics has high wear life as compared to natural fibres. Linen, a natural cellulosic, is an exception, since it is extremely durable and actually becomes better with age. One must also note that sufficient and proper care procedures followed by consumers will go a long way in preserving any textile product.

Yarns made with low twist and irregular structure may prove to be less durable than regular, high twist structures.

Fabric construction will play a major role in deciding durability of the final product. Among wovens, plain and twill weaves will last long, while satin weaves may face the problem of snagging of its long floats. Among decorative weaves, dobby and jacquard wear well but surface figure weave with long uncut floats might be more susceptible to snaggings, and thus prove to be less durable.

As far as knits are concerned, weft knit structures can 'run' and show ladder formation. Warp knits are more durable.

Non wovens have carved a greater share in recent years. They can be either disposable or non disposable type. The former will not have any durability issues though they may pose some serious threat to the environment. For the non disposable type of non wovens, durability will depend on a host of factors. Type of fibres, method of bonding and care procedures will all play a vital part in deciding how durable a structure will prove to be.

Finishes vary in their durability quotients and are classified into temporary, durable and permanent finishes (refer Chapter 14, Classification of Finishes). A consumer must be aware of the expected durability of the finish applied. Alternatively, the sellers must be equipped with correct information in this context. However, most of the times, there is a dearth of technical information in this area.

Colours applied on the fabric by dyeing and printing will have varying durability. In general, the earlier a colour is introduced in a fabric, the longer it lasts. As discussed in Chapter 15, colour application can be done at fibre, yarn, fabric or product stage. Durable colour application will also result from a judicious selection of an appropriate dye class and by following the correct and recommended application procedure.

It must also be kept in mind that colour fastness has many dimensions. Their importance will vary relatively, depending on intended end use. Thus, for example, colour fastness to perspiration may be important for an apparel fabric and fastness to crocking (rubbing) is required for cushion cover fabrics, but these will not be important for curtain fabrics. Coming back to the need of perspiration fastness for an apparel fabric, it may be recalled that as consumers we may have had the experience of an apparel item which lost its colour due to perspiration (or any other factor like washing or sunlight). We have to discontinue its usage, since the item is not 'serviceable' although it might still be durable. Such premature discard leads to consumer dissatisfaction.

16.6 · CARE

Care or maintenance of any fabric includes washing, drying, ironing, stain removal and storage. It is dependent on its constituent fibres , yarn type, its fabric construction method, finishes and colours applied to it. Part II on fibres discusses care for each fibre.

Fibre families exhibit a similar pattern in many interactions. Cellulosics can tolerate high temperatures during washing and ironing. Alkaline soaps and detergents can be used for their laundry. Cellulosics may take longer to dry. They should be absolutely dry and non-starched before storage to avoid mildew and silverfish attack.

Protein fibres are laundered using neutral detergents since alkaline pH causes harm. A lukewarm temperature is used for their washing as well as rinsing. Ironing temperatures are lower than that for cellulosics. Protein fibres exhibit lower biological resistance, being susceptible to attack by clothes moth and carpet beetles. This necessitates careful storage with the help of insect repellants.

Synthetic fibres are comparatively easy to care for. They can withstand alkaline soaps and detergents; they are also easy to dry. Most synthetics require little or no ironing. They also exhibit superior chemical and biological resistance. Thus storage does not pose any problem for synthetics.

Yarn structure that is simple and strong will be more easy to care for than complex, low strength ones. A looped yarn will have a greater risk of being snagged, if handled without caution.

Fabric construction has a major impact on care procedures. Variations exist within one category too. Wovens, for instance, will have different care requirements depending on type of weave. Basic weaves with smooth and compact structures are easy to care for. Sheer and delicate woven structures as well as pile weaves require careful handling. Knitted fabrics do not require ironing, unlike woven fabrics. This feature of easy maintenance has helped them gain wide popularity among users. Non wovens have to be given care treatments in keeping with their fibres and bonding methods used. Other fabrics like lace and nets will need careful handling, though their constituent fibres will help decide the detergent and temperature suitable for them.

Finishes given to fabrics impact their care procedures to a large extent. Many are designed to make fabrics easy to care for. Stain and soil repellant finishes, for instance, keep fabrics clean. With durable press finish, hours of ironing fabrics will be saved. An important point of consideration would be to give a care treatment that helps the finishes last longer.

Colour application by dyeing and printing is an important factor in preserving the attractive appearance of any fabric. If the colour is lost during use and care, a textile product becomes non-serviceable, even though it might still be durable. Generally speaking, washing of coloured clothes will need more care. Certain steps will have to be modified. For example, pre-soaking before laundry may be omitted. Some other steps taken to preserve colour include use of cold water and even common salt for laundry to drying in shade.

Over and above these five factors, viz., ACP DC (appearance, comfort, performance, durability and care), an important point to be kept in mind is the cost. This too has many dimensions to it. It is not only the cost of a textile product at the point of purchasing it but also the cost incurred in using, maintaining it and finally disposing it. Some products that are non-biodegradable will place a burden on the environment. As conscious consumers, it is our duty to consider these points as well.

EXERCISES

16.1 What factors should be kept in mind while selecting a suitable fabric for apparel?

16.2 "Intelligent choice of fabrics for use as home textiles is governed by seversl factors." Elaborate this statement with relevant examples.

16.3 Distinguish between the following terms with examples:
   (a) Serviceable and durable
   (b) Physical and psychological comfort

REFERENCES

Joseph, M.L., *Introductory Textile Science*, 2nd ed., Harcourt Brace Jovanovich College Publishers, 1972.

Kadolph, S.J. and Langford, A.L., *Textiles*, 10th ed., Pearson Education, NJ, 2007.

University Test Paper 1

Duration: **3** hours   Maximum Marks: **75**

Instructions for Candidates

1. Answer **Five** questions in all.
2. Q. No. **1** is compulsory.

1. Briefly explain the following (any **Five**):   **(5 × 3 = 15)**
    - (a) Crimp
    - (b) Hackling
    - (c) Spinerette
    - (d) Staple fibres
    - (e) Microscopic structure of cotton
    - (f) Polypropylene
    - (g) Terecot

2. (a) Give the production of wool fibres.   **(10)**
    (b) Explain the physical and chemical properties of
         cotton fibres.   **(5)**

3. (a) Give the chemistry and manufacturing process of
         Nylon 6, 6. Supplement your answer with suitable
         chemical reactions.   **(10)**
    (b) Write a short note on elastomeric fibres.   **(5)**

4. (a) Explain cotton spinning system in detail.   **(10)**
    (b) Explain direct yarn numbering system along with
         its units.   **(5)**

5. (a) Define textured yarn. Explain false twist and
         edge crimping methods of texturizing with diagrams.   **(10)**
    (b) Explain different stages of blending.   **(5)**

6. Differentiate between the following (any **Two**)   **(2 × 7.5 = 15)**
    - (a) Melt and Dry spinning
    - (b) Acrylic and Modacrylic
    - (c) Thread and yarn

7. Write short notes on any **Three** of the following: **(3 × 5 = 15)**
    - (a) Simple yarns
    - (b) Cashmere fibres
    - (c) Yarn defects
    - (d) Retting of flax
    - (e) Yarn twist

University Test Paper 2

Duration: **3** hours   Maximum Marks: **75**

Instructions for Candidates

1. Answer **Five** questions in all.
2. Q. No. **1** is compulsory.

1. Briefly explain the following (any **Five**):   **(5 × 3 = 15)**
    (a) Shedding
    (b) Dobby
    (c) Gauge
    (d) Acid finishes
    (e) Colour fastness against crocking
    (f) Tear strength
    (g) Float as fabric defect
    (h) Felting shrinkage

2. (a) Explain plain weave with its variations using point
         paper diagrams.   **(10)**
    (b) What are secondary motions of a loom?   **(5)**

3. (a) Discuss weft knits with respect to the stitches used.   **(10)**
    (b) Describe different types of knitting needles.   **(5)**

4. (a) Define non wovens. Explain production of needle
         punched fabrics.   **(2, 6)**
    (b) Discuss uses of non wovens.   **(7)**

5. (a) Explain various methods of imparting
         calendering finish.   **(10)**
    (b) Write a note on water repellant finish.   **(5)**

6. (a) What points are considered while selecting an
         appropriate fabric for apparel use?   **(7)**
    (b) Explain various types of technical textiles.   **(8)**

7. Write short notes on any **Three** of the following: **(3 × 5 = 15)**
    (a) Jet looms
    (b) Surface figure weaves
    (c) Comparison of weaving and knitting
    (d) Web formation in non wovens
    (e) Thread count and balance

University Test Paper 3

Duration: **3** hours   Maximum Marks: **75**

Instructions for Candidates

1. Answer **Five** questions in all.
2. Q. No. **1** is compulsory.

1. Briefly explain the following (any **Five**):   **(5 × 3 = 15)**
    (a) Drape
    (b) Dobby weave
    (c) Thread count
    (d) Herringbone twill
    (e) Colour fastness against laundry
    (f) Swivel weave
    (g) Geotextiles

2. (a) Classify basic weaves.   **(8)**
    (b) Write a note on jet looms.   **(7)**

3. (a) Differentiate between warp and weft knits.   **(9)**
    (b) Explain latch and beard needles with diagrams.   **(6)**

4. (a) Give the steps in production of non-woven fabrics.   **(12)**
    (b) Write a note on braided fabrics.   **(3)**

5. (a) Classify finishes on the basis of mode of action.   **(2)**
    (b) Write a note on mercerization.   **(4)**
    (c) Describe water repellant, anti-static and flame
         retardant finishes.   **(9)**

6. (a) Describe any three fabric defects.   **(6)**
    (b) What points should a consumer consider while
         selecting an appropriate fabric for apparel?   **(9)**

7. Write short notes on any **Three** of the following: **(3 × 5 = 15)**
    (a) Factors affected by fabric weight
    (b) Care labels
    (c) Primary motions
    (d) Weft knit stitches
    (e) Tensile strength

University Test Paper 4

Duration: **3** hours   Maximum Marks: **75**

Instructions for Candidates

1. Answer **Five** questions in all.
2. Q. No. **1** is compulsory.

1. Briefly explain the following (any **Five**):   **(5 × 3 = 15)**
   - (a) Hackling
   - (b) Microscopic structure of cotton
   - (c) Polypropylene
   - (d) Filament fibres
   - (e) Indirect yarn count
   - (f) Classification of natural protein fibres with examples
   - (g) Cashmere

2. (a) Give the chemistry and manufacturing process of Viscose rayon. Supplement your answer with suitable chemical reactions.   **(10)**
   (b) Write a short note on any 2 speciality hair fibres.   **(5)**

3. (a) With the help of a flow chart, explain cotton spinning system in detail.   **(10)**
   (b) Explain the physical and chemical properties of wool fibres.   **(5)**

4. (a) Give the production of silk fibres.   **(10)**
   (b) Explain the purpose of blending with suitable examples. **(5)**

5. (a) What are textured yarns?. Explain false twist and edge crimping methods of texturizing with diagrams.   **(10)**
   (b) Write a short note on Metallic fibres.   **(5)**

6. Differentiate between the following (any **Two**)   **(2 × 7.5 = 15)**
   - (a) Melt and dry spinning
   - (b) Acrylic and modacrylic
   - (c) Thread and yarn

7. Write short notes on any **Three** of the following: **(3 × 5 = 15)**
   - (a) Types of simple yarns
   - (b) Direction of twist
   - (c) Nylon 6, 6
   - (d) Retting of flax
   - (e) Yarn defects

University Test Paper 5

Duration: 3 hours   Maximum Marks: **75**

Instructions for Candidates

1. Answer **Five** questions in all.
2. Q. No. 1 is compulsory.

1. Briefly explain the following (any **Five**):   **(5 × 3 = 15)**
    (a) Glass fibre
    (b) Properties of textured yarns
    (c) Retting
    (d) Acetate fibre
    (e) Microscopic structure of cotton
    (f) Crimp
    (g) Tensile strength
    (h) Polymer structure of wool

2. (a) Give the chemistry and manufacturing process of
         polyester. Supplement your answer with suitable
         chemical reactions.   **(10)**
    (b) Write a short note on cashmere hair fibre.   **(5)**

3. (a) Explain in detail the cotton spinning system.
         Give suitable diagrams.   **(10)**
    (b) Classify textured yarns and briefly explain.   **(5)**

4. (a) What is yarn count? Give a detailed account of
         the yarn numbering system.   **(10)**
    (b) Give the significant differences between the physical
         properties of silk and wool fibres.   **(5)**

5. (a) Explain any four manufacturing techniques of
         texturizing yarns. Support your answer with suitable
         diagrams.   **(10)**
    (b) Give the manufacture and properties of modacrylic
         fibres.   **(5)**

6. (a) Explain the different stages of blending.   **(7.5)**
    (b) Differentiate between the wool and worsted
         systems of spinning.   **(7.5)**

7. Write short notes on any **Three** of the following: **(3 × 5 = 15)**
    (a) Effect of twist on yarn properties
    (b) Elastomeric fibres
    (c) Yarn defects
    (d) Chemical properties of polyester
    (e) Simple yarns

University Test Paper 6

Duration: **3** hours   Maximum Marks: **75**

Instructions for Candidates

1. Answer **Five** questions in all.
2. Q. No. **1** is compulsory.

1. Briefly explain the following terms (any **Five**):   **(5 × 3 = 15)**
   - (a) GSM
   - (b) Harness
   - (c) Dimensional stability
   - (d) Wool mark
   - (e) Knitting
   - (f) Singeing
   - (g) Gauge

2. (a) Give the classification of weaves.   **(5)**
   - (b) Explain the construction and characteristics of twill weave and its variations using point paper diagrams.   **(8)**
   - (c) Briefly write about any two defects found in woven or knitted fabrics.   **(2)**

3. (a) Explain the manufacturing process of needle felts.   **(7)**
   - (b) Discuss the characteristics of purl knit structures.   **(5)**
   - (c) Write a note on uses of non-woven fabrics.   **(3)**

4. (a) Give different ways of classifying finishes. Give examples.   **(5)**
   - (b) Explain the purpose and process of any **Two** of the following finishes: **(2 × 5 = 10)**
     - (a) Mercerisation
     - (b) Flame retardant finish
     - (c) Acid-basic finishes
     - (d) Water repellant finishes

5. Differentiate between any **Three** of the following: **(3 × 5 = 15)**
   - (a) Weaving and knitting
   - (b) Moiring and schreinering
   - (c) Pile and surface figure weaves
   - (d) Warp and weft knits

6. (a) Explain the factors influencing selection of factors for apparels.   **(10)**
   - (b) Write a short note on projectile loom.   **(5)**

7. Write short notes on any **Three** of the following: **(3 × 5 = 15)**

    (a)   Parts of loom

    (b)   Care labels

    (c)   Knitting needles

    (d)   Technical textiles

    (e)   Heat setting

University Test Paper 7

Duration: **3** hours   Maximum Marks: **75**

Instructions for Candidates

1. Answer **Five** questions in all.
2. Q. No. **1** is compulsory.

1. Briefly explain any **Five** of the following terms: **(5 × 3 = 15)**
   (a) Elastomeric fibres
   (b) Union dyeing
   (c) Felts
   (d) Shedding
   (e) Complex yarn
   (f) Polymerization
   (g) Water repellant finish
   (h) Cohesiveness

2. Differentiate between the following (any **Three**):   **(3 × 5 = 15)**
   (a) Woven and knit fabrics
   (b) Resist and discharge styles of printing
   (c) Dobby and jacquard weave
   (d) Wet and melt spinning
   (e) Block and screen methods of printing

3. (a) Describe the production and properties of cotton fibre. **(10)**
   (b) What are secondary properties of textile fibres? Explain any 3 in detail. **(5)**

4. (a) How yarns are manufactured using the worsted system? **(10)**
   (b) Explain the direct and indirect system of yarn count. **(5)**

5. (a) Give the classification of weaves. Discuss the characteristic and construction of twill weave and its variations using point paper diagrams. **(10)**
   (b) List the different parts of loom and explain their functions. **(5)**

6. (a) What are routine finishes? Explain any **Two** of the following in detail: **(10)**
      (a) Calendaring
      (b) Bleaching
      (c) Mercerizing

(b) Explain the basic steps in producing a non-woven
fabric   **(5)**

7. Write short notes on any **Three** of the following: **(3 × 5 = 15)**
   (a) Classification of fibres
   (b) Weft knits
   (c) Surface figure weave
   (d) Production of polyester fibre
   (e) Needle felts
   (f) Any 2 methods of yarn texturing

University Test Paper 8

Duration: **3** hours   Maximum Marks: **75**

Instructions for Candidates

1.   Answer **Five** questions in all.
2.   Q. No. **1** is compulsory.

1.   (a)   Briefly explain any **Five** of the following
          terms: **(5 × 2 = 10)**
          (a)   Ply yarn
          (b)   Crystalline regions
          (c)   Yarn count
          (d)   Resiliency
          (e)   Wales
          (f)   Shedding in weaving process
          (g)   Felts

     (b)   Give one example of any **Five** of the following: **(5 × 1 = 5)**
          (a)   Cellulosic fibres
          (b)   Pile weave fabrics
          (c)   Finishes applied on wool
          (d)   Blended fabrics
          (e)   Shutleless loom
          (f)   Knitting needles
          (g)   Complex yarns

2.   (a)   Describe the production and properties of cotton fibre. **(10)**
     (b)   List and discuss the primary properties of textile
          fibres.   **(5)**

3.   (a)   Explain the cotton spinning system in detail.   **(8)**
     (b)   Define texturization of yarn. Explain any two
          methods in detail.   **(2.5)**

4.   (a)   Enumerate the basic weaves.   **(2)**
     (b)   Explain the construction and characteristic of
          plain weave and its variations giving suitable
          point paper diagrams.   **(8)**
     (c)   Define non-woven fabrics. Explain the steps in
          production of non-woven fabric   **(5)**

5.   (a)   What are preparatory finishes? Explain any
          two in detail   **(7)**
     (b)   Describe the mechanism of dyeing.   **(4)**
     (c)   What are water repellant finishes?   **(4)**

6.   Differentiate between any **Three** of the following: **(3 × 5 = 15)**
   (a)   Weaving and knitting
   (b)   Discharge and resist styles of printing
   (c)   Melt and wet spinning.
   (d)   Block and screen methods of printing

7.   Write short notes on any **Three** of the following: **(3 × 5 = 15)**
   (a)   Parts of loom and their functions
   (b)   Classification of fibres
   (c)   Yarn count
   (d)   Surface figure weaves
   (e)   Manufacture of polyester.

University Test Paper 9

Duration: **3** hours   Maximum Marks: **75**

Instructions for Candidates

1. Answer **Five** questions in all.
2. Q. No. **1** is compulsory.

1. Explain any **Five** of the following in 3–4 lines: **(5 × 3 = 15)**
    (a) Crystalline regions
    (b) Length to width ratio
    (c) Delusterant
    (d) Longitudinal and cross-section of cotton
    (e) Tentering
    (f) Thread count of a woven fabric
    (g) Leno weave
    (h) Union dyeing.

2. (a) Describe the manufacturing process of viscose rayon.   **(10)**
    (b) Explain the chemical and biological properties of silk.   **(5)**

3. (a) Discuss the systems of yarn count.   **(7)**
    (b) Define texturing. Describe the air jet method.   **(3,5)**

4. (a) With the help of a schematic diagram, give the parts of a loom.   **(5)**
    (b) Explain satin weave with its point paper diagram.   **(5)**
    (c) Enumerate weft knitting stitches. Discuss any **one**.   **(5)**

5. (a) Discuss 'Resist methods' of printing in detail.   **(10)**
    (b) Discuss the process of yarn dyeing.   **(5)**

6. Write short notes on any **Three**:   **(3 × 5 = 15)**
    (a) Calendering finish
    (b) Weighting of silk
    (c) Surface figure weaves
    (d) Web formation in bonded fabrics
    (e) Retting.

University Test Paper 10

Duration: **3** hours   Maximum Marks: **75**

Instructions for Candidates

Question No. **1** is compulsory. Attempt any other **Four** questions. Draw diagrams wherever necessary.

1. (a) Explain any **Five** of the following in 2-3 sentences: **(5 × 2 = 10)**
    (a) Cord yarn
    (b) Tow
    (c) Spinneret
    (d) Elastic recovery
    (e) Boucle yarn
    (f) Thread count

    (b) Fill in the blanks (any **Five**):   **(5)**

    (a) _____ is an additional process for the manufacture of worsted yarns.

    (b) Silk is composed of a protein known as_____

    (c) Cross-section of cotton fibres is_____ shaped.

    (d) If a yarn 50-m long weighs 200 mg, its denier is _____.

    (e) Polyester is spun by_____ form of chemical spinning.

    (f) Longitudinal section of wool fibres is characterized by_____

2. (a) Give the classification of natural fibres with examples.   **(10)**
    (b) Enumerate the primary properties of textile fibres. Briefly explain any one of them.   **(5)**

3. (a) Describe the manufacture of viscose rayon fibre with the help of flow chart.   **(8)**
    (b) Discuss the process of ring spinning with the help of a diagram.   **(7)**

4. (a) What is the difference between thread and yarn?   **(2)**
    (b) Why are yarns textured? Explain any two methods of texturing in detail.   **(8)**
    (c) Compare the chemical properties of cotton and wool fibres.   **(5)**

5. (a) Explain the primary and secondary motions of a loom. **(10)**

   (b) Classify the basic weaves. **(5)**

6. Write short notes on: **(3 × 5 = 15)**

   (a) Retting

   (b) Open end spinning

   (c) Indirect system of yarn count

Index